EVERYDAY QUILTING

the complete beginner's guide

Jennifer Fulton

Publisher Mike Sanders
Editor Christopher Stolle
Designer Rebecca Batchelor
Art Director William Thomas
Photographer Katherine Scheele
Proofreaders Mary Anne Stolle & Jean Bissell
Indexer Beverlee Day

First American Edition, 2023
Published in the United States by DK Publishing
6081 E. 82nd St., Suite 400, Indianapolis, IN 46250

Copyright © 2023 Dorling Kindersley Limited
DK, a Division of Penguin Random House LLC
24 25 26 27   10 9 8 7 6 5 4 3 2
002-334137-JAN2023

Published in the United States
by Dorling Kindersley Limited

ISBN 978-0-7440-7604-2
Library of Congress Catalog Number: 2022941416

Reprinted and updated from *Idiot's Guides: Quilting*

All images © Dorling Kindersley Limited

Printed and bound in China

For the curious
www.dk.com

This book was made with Forest
Stewardship Council ™ certified
paper – one small step in DK's
commitment to a sustainable future.
**For more information go to
www.dk.com/our-green-pledge**

Note: This publication contains the opinions
and ideas of its author(s). It is intended to
provide helpful and informative material on
the subject matter covered. It is sold with the
understanding that the author(s) and
publisher are not engaged in rendering
professional services in the book. If the
reader requires personal assistance or
advice, a competent professional should be
consulted. The author(s) and publisher
specifically disclaim any responsibility for any
liability, loss, or risk, personal or otherwise,
which is incurred as a consequence, directly
or indirectly, of the use and application of
any of the contents of this book.

Trademarks: All terms mentioned in this
book that are known to be or are suspected
of being trademarks or service marks have
been appropriately capitalized. Alpha Books,
DK, and Penguin Random House LLC cannot
attest to the accuracy of this information. Use
of a term in this book should not be regarded
as affecting the validity of any trademark or
service mark.

To my husband, Scott, who encourages my love of quilting, and to my daughter, Katerina, who shares it.

Contents

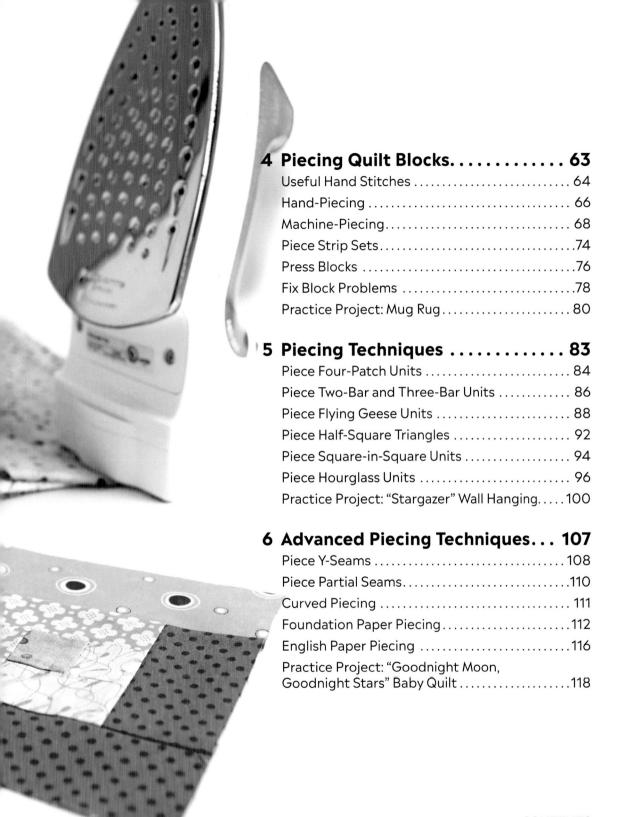

Introduction

There are so many reasons you might want to learn to quilt. Maybe you know how to sew a little and you're looking for a way to expand and challenge your skills. Maybe you don't know how to sew at all, but you dream of creating a beautiful quilt for yourself or someone you love. Or maybe you want to learn to quilt so you can spend free time with friends, playing with beautiful fabrics and creating something wonderful. Whatever your reasons or your previous sewing experience, this book will show you how to create your first quilt from start to finish.

Right now, the process might seem like an overwhelming mystery, but I can assure you that making a quilt is easier than it might seem. Because you're just beginning, I'd advise you to rein in your enthusiasm (just a little!) and start with a small project. Sure, you might have your heart set on making a bed quilt. But believe me, you'll get a lot more satisfaction and fun out of starting (and finishing!) a simple, small project, such as a mug rug (coaster), table topper, or table runner, than you would from starting and later abandoning a larger project. Once you've learned how to complete your first quilt project, moving on to more complex projects will be easier.

With color photos and simple step-by-steps, this book guides you through your quilting journey. At the end of each chapter, you'll get a chance to practice what you've learned. After learning a little about color theory, you'll start by choosing the fabrics for your first project and then use them to make a mug rug. Later chapters will test your new quilting skills with gradually more challenging projects.

One piece of quilting advice: Don't focus on perfection. Sure, you should always strive for it, but don't let mistakes ruin your quilting experience. Please don't stress over seams that don't match up perfectly or points that get cut off in the seam—because they'll happen. There's a famous quilt story (completely untrue but fun) that Amish quilters would always put a deliberate mistake (a Humility block) in their quilts in order to avoid achieving perfection, which might offend God. Every quilter knows, though, that you don't have to manufacture a mistake for one to find its way into your finished quilt. Really. Believe me, they'll just pop up on their own without any help from you. Just know that this happens to everyone, even the most experienced quilters. So the next time you find that you've sewn some blocks together wrong, just smile and say: "This quilt might not be perfect, but it sure looks like perfection to me!"

Each project in this book features an alternative version that uses different fabrics and sometimes includes other variations. My hope is that the original and alternative quilt versions will inspire you to change the quilts so they appeal to you. For example, by substituting your own fabrics, the quilt will express more about you and less about the designer. As you gain confidence, I encourage you to continue to make changes to the quilt patterns as you like. For example, you might change a quilt's size by making more or fewer blocks or change its border style from a simple straight border to a pieced or appliquéd border. Each change, no matter how small, makes a quilt truly an expression of who you are—and what could be more beautiful?

Acknowledgments

During the making of this book, my quilting friends shared not only their encouragement, but their time and talents. Without them, this book would never have become a reality. I thank them all from the bottom of my heart, especially my best friend, Alice Martina Smith. I simply can't thank her enough for her kind comments, quilting guidance, and loving support. In addition to the editors at Alpha/DK, I'd like to thank Sherry McConnell (technical editor, Benartex) for generously sharing her time and her quilting wisdom and for making my designs so much better as a result.

The following friends created the beautiful quilts (and the alternate versions) you'll find in this book: **Pieced pillowcases:** Stephanie Waters; **Mug rugs:** Terry Lichtenfelt; **"Stargazer" wall hanging:** Mary Strinka; **"Goodnight Moon, Goodnight Stars" crib quilt:** Michelle Hoel; **"Funky Flowers" wall hanging:** Elizabeth Meek; **"Peppermint Twist" twin quilt:** Susie Walden, Bonnie Borntrager, Kathy Yull (quilter); (alternate) Alice Martina Smith, Lois Vincent, Vickie Smith (quilter); **"Strawberry Preserves" lap quilt:** Suzie Wetzel, Stephanie Brokaw (quilter); **"Princess Charlotte" crib quilt:** Shari Harrison; **"Elephants on Parade" crib quilt:** Pat Wilser, Theresa Cantwell (quilter), Marsha Huber (alternate); **"Life in the Tide Pool" lap quilt:** Lynn Thomas, Ruth Middleton, Cathy Franks (quilter); **"Conga Line" lap quilt:** Ruth Rose, Lois Vincent, Vickie Smith (quilter), Connie Weiger (alternate); **"Star-Crossed" wall hanging:** Ann Petrie, Susan Street Cook (quilter); **"Swimming in the Gene Pool" wall hanging:** Maureen Weflin, Julie Edwards (quilter), Nancy Jo Clapp (alternate); **"Snake Eyes" lap quilt:** Pam Murdock, Cindi and Dan Clayton (quilters); **"Mirage" wall hanging:** Dallas Reed, Connie Lancaster (quilter), Susie Walden (alternate); **"Interwoven" twin quilt:** Bobbie Mennel, Pam Durant, Cathy Franks (quilter); Katerina Fulton (alternate); **"Fall Romance" table runner:** Barbara Hayes, Katerina Fulton, Carol Owens (quilter).

In addition, the ladies at the following quilt shops were amazingly patient and helpful during my numerous intense searches for that "just right" fabric: Always in Stitches (Noblesville, Indiana), Quilt Expressions (Fishers, Indiana), Quilts Plus (Indianapolis, Indiana), Crimson Tate (Indianapolis, Indiana), and The Back Door (Greenwood, Indiana).

Where to Find the Templates

 Several of the quilt projects in this book use foundation paper-piecing and appliqué templates that are available online. Whenever you see this icon, go to **www.dk.com/us/information/ quilting** to download and print the templates.

Need More Help?

Need more help, such as a video or an online class? Come learn quilting with me at **www.inquiringquilter.com**. If you make any of the projects in the book, I'd love to see them! Tag me on social media @inquiringquilter.

Getting Ready to Quilt

What Is a Quilt?

A quilt is a reflection of someone's artistic talent, expressed through the careful selection of fabrics and colors as well as the choice of hand or machine construction. Quilts don't have to be heirloom quality to express your artistry. They can also be made more spontaneously, using a random mix of fabrics and improvisational construction techniques. Regardless of how a quilt is made, it represents a piece of collective history and culture as well as someone's private memories. A quilt should be used and loved. And when a quilt wears out because it was loved too much, it should be treated kindly.

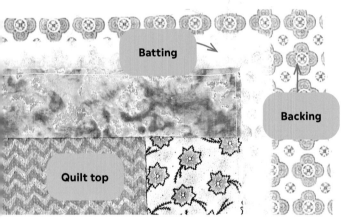

Batting

Backing

Quilt top

A quilt is made up of two layers of fabric—the quilt top and the backing—with batting in between. The quilt top, batting, and backing are then quilted (stitched) through all layers to create a finished quilt. You can quilt by hand or machine or you can send your quilt to a professional quilter, who'll quilt it on a longarm sewing machine.

A quilt top can be made from a single piece of fabric (wholecloth) to show off your quilting skills. However, a quilt is usually a series of quilt blocks sewn together to form the quilt center, which is often surrounded by borders. Blocks can be pieced by hand or machine or they can be appliquéd.

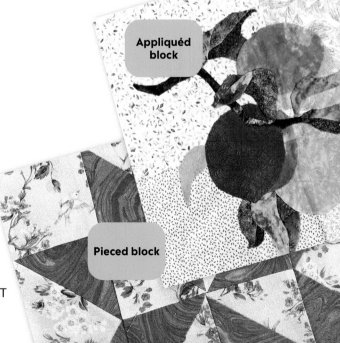

Appliquéd block

Pieced block

You can add as many borders as you like to a quilt in order to get the size and look you want (or desire). Borders can be made from a single strip of fabric or pieced. The border corners can be straight or mitered, like the corners of a picture frame.

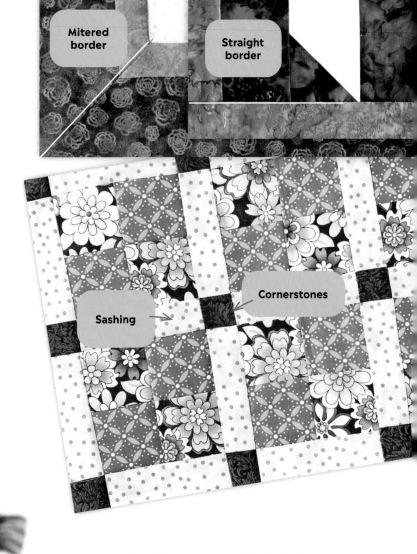

Mitered border

Straight border

Cornerstones

Sashing

Binding

Quilt blocks can be spaced apart with sashing strips. Adding sashing not only makes a quilt bigger, but it might also make it easier to piece because you don't have to match the seams of neighboring blocks. Sashing can include cornerstones at sashing intersections.

A quilt's edges are finished with a binding that's hand- or machine-stitched. If the quilt will be used as a wall hanging, a sleeve is added to the back for the hanging pole. Finally, a label with your name, date, and any other important information can be added to the back of the quilt.

A block is made up of smaller units, with names like "four-patch" and "flying geese." You make these units first and then sew them together to create blocks. Quilt blocks are sewn together in a variety of ways, such as horizontally or diagonally. If you set your blocks diagonally (on point), you use setting triangles at the end of each row to create a straight edge to the quilt top. To help you lay out your quilt blocks in your chosen setting, use a design wall.

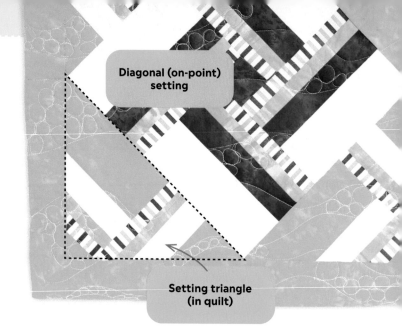

Diagonal (on-point) setting

Setting triangle (in quilt)

Common Quilt Blocks

In the early days of quilting, a quilt block's design and name came from the images that comprised a woman's daily life, such as keeping a fire going in the hearth (Log Cabin), churning butter (Churn Dash), and keeping the flies away (Shoo Fly).

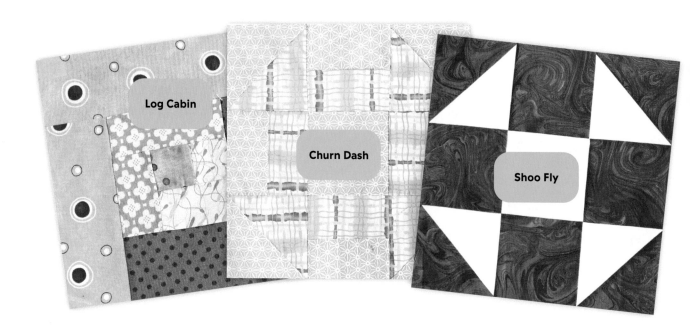

Log Cabin

Churn Dash

Shoo Fly

Women quilted to remember family and friends, with blocks like the Friendship Star and signature blocks (on which signatures are collected before a parting or to remember an anniversary or wedding).

Signature block

Friendship Star

Joanie ♡

Quilting sometimes expressed a woman's religious views, with blocks like Jacob's Ladder and Children of Israel. Blocks often have multiple names that reflect the quilter's life and culture. For example, Jacob's Ladder is also known as Underground Railroad, Road to California, Stepping Stones, and Wagon Tracks.

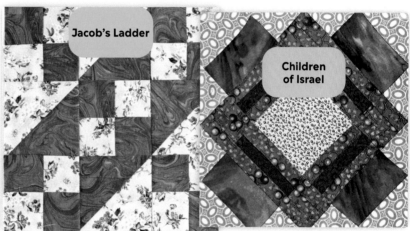

Jacob's Ladder

Children of Israel

In the days before women could vote, they expressed their political opinions through quilt blocks, such as the T Block (to favor temperance) and Clay's Choice (to support Henry Clay and his antislavery stance).

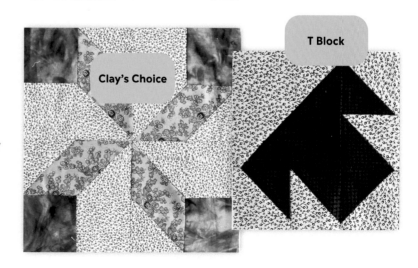

T Block

Clay's Choice

Prepare Your Sewing Machine

You're probably eager to get started on your quilting journey, but before machine-piecing, machine-appliquéing, or machine-quilting a quilt, you should take the time to properly prepare your sewing machine for the job. Repeat this process after every eight hours of sewing and any time you encounter problems while making a quilt by machine. If you need to load a stacked thread spool and your machine's spool pin can't be set vertically, use a thread stand and place it just behind your machine on the sewing table.

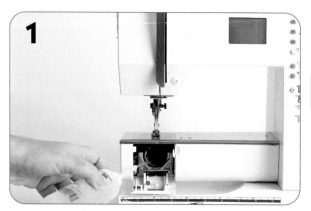

Clean and oil your machine before starting.

After every eight hours of sewing, you should unplug the machine, clean out the lint, and add a drop of sewing machine oil. Use only sewing machine oil (not other oils).

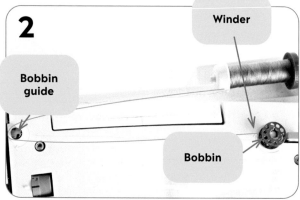

Thread your machine for bobbin winding.

Select the appropriate bobbin thread for your task (machine-piecing, machine-appliqué, or machine-quilting). Usually, you'll match the bobbin thread to the top thread to make the tension even. For specialty threads, such as metallics or monofilaments, use bobbin weight thread in the bobbin. Place a bobbin on the winder and follow the instructions in your manual for threading your machine for bobbin winding.

- -

Did you know that thread ages? If you have old thread you've inherited from your mom, display it but don't use it. Old thread will throw off the machine tension and cause problems if you try to sew with it.

- -

3

Locking lever

Lock the bobbin in place.

Wind the thread around the bobbin clockwise two or three times. Lock the winder in place by pushing it to the right or by pushing a locking lever toward the stationary winder. This turns off the needle's up/down function.

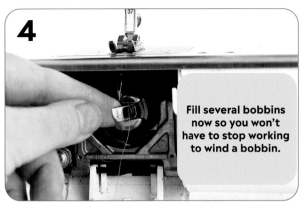

4

Fill several bobbins now so you won't have to stop working to wind a bobbin.

Wind the bobbin and then insert it.

Press the foot pedal to start winding the bobbin. The machine stops automatically when the bobbin is full. Load the bobbin using the instructions in your manual. Be sure to follow the correct thread path when loading the bobbin.

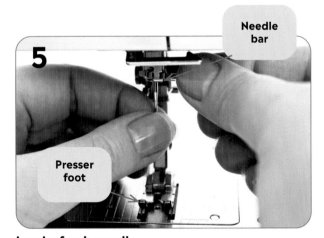

5

Needle bar

Presser foot

Load a fresh needle.

Lower the presser foot and raise the needle bar by turning the handwheel. Loosen the needle clamp and insert a needle appropriate to the task. Typically, the flat part of the needle faces the back. (However, on a Singer Featherweight machine, the flat part faces left.) Tighten the needle clamp.

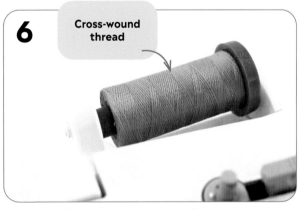

6

Cross-wound thread

Load the thread on the spool pin.

Select the appropriate thread for your task and then load the thread on the spool pin. Typically, you'll use 50 weight cotton thread for piecing a quilt. Place cross-wound threads horizontally on the spool pin and place stacked threads (straight-wound threads) vertically. Secure the spool with the spool cap.

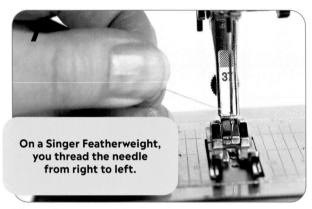

On a Singer Featherweight, you thread the needle from right to left.

Thread your machine.

Raise the presser foot. (It's important that the foot is up to ensure that the thread slides through the tension discs.) Follow the path for threading your machine as listed in your sewing machine manual. Typically, you run the thread to the first guide, down through the tension slit, up to the take-up lever, and down to the needle guide(s). Thread the needle from front to back.

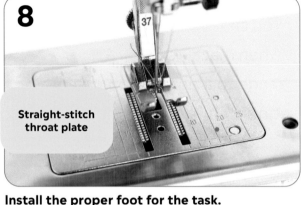

Straight-stitch throat plate

Install the proper foot for the task.

Install the appropriate machine foot for your task—whether machine-piecing, machine-appliqué, or machine-quilting. A single hole/straight stitch plate like the one shown here is best for any kind of straight stitching, especially piecing.

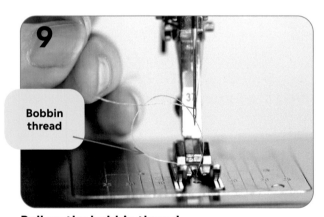

Bobbin thread

Pull up the bobbin thread.

Hold the top thread and turn the handwheel one stitch. Pull on the top thread until the bobbin thread appears. Place both thread tails under the presser foot, with the thread tails toward the back.

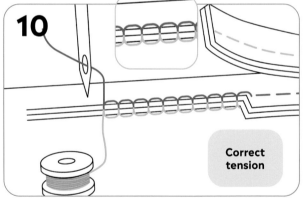

Correct tension

Sew some fabric to test the machine's tension.

Place the right sides of two fabric scraps together and sew a test seam. Remove the test scrap from the machine and examine the front and back of the seam. When the tension is even, just the top thread shows on the front and only the bobbin thread shows on the back.

If you can buy a straight-stitch throat plate for your sewing machine, using it when machine-piecing or quilting will improve your work. Just be sure to change to a zigzag throat plate when machine-appliquéing with a zigzag or satin stitch.

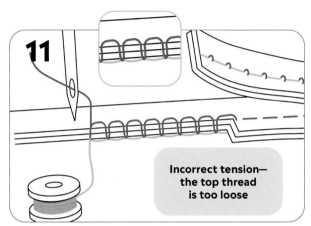

Incorrect tension—
the top thread
is too loose

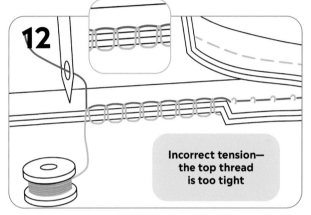

Incorrect tension—
the top thread
is too tight

If the top tension is too loose, tighten it.

When the top tension is too loose, the bobbin thread is pulled to the back. Increase the top tension by turning the tension dial or the digital tension to a higher number.

If the top tension is too tight, loosen it.

When the top tension is too tight, the bobbin thread is pulled to the top. Decrease the top tension by turning the tension dial or digital tension to a lower number.

Hand-Piecing Supplies

For hand-piecing, use a **(1)** size 7–11 Appliqué/ Sharps needle or size 11 Straw/Milliners needle. If you have arthritis or trouble seeing a small needle, choose a smaller size. (For example, a size 9 needle is longer and thicker than a size 11 needle.)

Use high-quality **(2)** 50 weight cotton thread in a neutral color, such as light or medium gray, beige, olive, or white. A **(3)** needle threader helps you thread needles quickly. A **(4)** seam ripper is used to remove stitches when needed. A domed case can keep threaded needles ready to use and tangle-free. To protect your finger, choose a comfortable **(5)** thimble.

Use **(6)** small, sharp scissors for snipping threads, **(7)** fabric shears for cutting fabric, and inexpensive paper scissors for cutting piecing templates. Make your templates using template plastic or freezer paper (greaseproof paper) and a permanent marker.

An **(8)** Add-A-Quarter ruler and **(9)** a quarter-inch seam marker are used to measure quarter-inch seam allowances, which you can mark with **(10)** fabric marking pens or pencils. A **(11)** sandpaper board holds the fabric in place while you trace around your piecing templates.

Pin fabric pieces for piecing using **(12)** fine, short appliqué or **(13)** silk pins. Tame your pins with a **(14)** pin cushion or magnetic pin catcher Press your seams with a good iron. Plan your quilt top by using a design wall.

Machine-Piecing Supplies

For machine-piecing, use a Sharp 70/10 or 80/12 or a Quilting 75/11 needle. Because of their high thread count, use a Jeans 70/10 or 80/12 needle to piece batiks. Use high-quality 50 weight cotton thread in a neutral color, such as medium gray, beige, or olive.

A **(1)** quarter-inch foot is invaluable for machine-piecing accuracy. Using a **(2)** straight-stitch throat plate also improves your accuracy.

A stiletto is useful for holding down corners as you're sewing over them. Because it's hard to sew an accurate quarter-inch seam, use an Add-A-Quarter ruler or quarter-inch seam markers to mark your sewing line.

Use small, sharp scissors for snipping threads and a seam ripper to remove stitches when needed. Pin the fabric pieces together for piecing using long, fine pins. Tame your pins with a pin cushion or a magnetic pin catcher.

A **(3)** 45mm rotary cutter, **(4)** acrylic quilting rulers, and a **(5)** self-healing cutting mat are used to cut fabric. Use a 6 × 24-inch acrylic ruler for evening up the edge of the fabric before strip cutting and squaring up a finished quilt. Use a 12½-inch or larger square acrylic ruler for squaring up finished blocks. Use a 6½-inch square acrylic ruler for squaring up block units. Place **(6)** anti-slip dots or film on the back of your quilting rulers and use a **(7)** rotary cutting glove to ensure your safety when rotary cutting. Whenever possible, purchase nonslip rulers by Quilter's Select, Creative Grids, or Omni-Grid.

Hand-Appliqué Supplies

Appliqué is a process in which you stitch small shapes (such as a leaf or a letter) to a background fabric. Appliqué can be done by hand or by machine.

For hand-appliqué, as in hand-piecing, you'll need a sandpaper board, marking pencils, appliqué/silk pins, a pin cushion or pin catcher, a thimble, small scissors, fabric shears, paper scissors, a needle threader, and a seam ripper. A domed case isn't necessary, but it's useful for keeping multiple needles threaded.

(1) Template plastic or freezer paper can be used to make your appliqué templates.

You can finger-press or use a **(2)** glue stick or spray sizing to turn under seam allowances. You can even use **(3)** appliqué glue to hold pieces in place while appliquéing.

For hand-appliqué, use a **(4)** size 10-11 Appliqué/Sharps, Betweens, or Straw needle.

Appliqué your pieces using a **(5)** high-quality 60 weight cotton or 50 weight (2-ply) thread in a color that matches the appliqué or 100 weight silk thread in neutral colors.

Machine-Appliqué Supplies

Appliqué by machine can be done in a variety of ways. Depending on the method you choose, you might not need all these supplies.

Use template plastic or **(1)** freezer paper to make your appliqué templates.

Mark appliqué fabric using a **(2)** sandpaper board and marking pencils. Cut out your appliqué shapes using sharp appliqué scissors.

You can choose to use a glue stick or spray sizing to turn under seam allowances and appliqué glue or appliqué, satin, or flowerhead pins to hold pieces in place while appliquéing.

For machine-appliqué, use a **(3)** size 70/10 or 80/12 Appliqué/Sharps needle and a high-quality **(4)** 30, 50, or 60 weight cotton thread in a color that matches the appliqué or **(5)** invisible thread. Use the same thread in the bobbin or use **(6)** bobbin fill (if using a specialty thread).

An **(7)** open-toe, **(8)** darning, or **(9)** appliqué foot allows you to see the edge of the appliqué as you zigzag or blanket stitch it. Change to a **(10)** zigzag stitch plate for machine-appliqué.

To prevent puckering, use **(11)** cutaway, tearaway, or washaway stabilizer underneath the background fabric. One method of machine-appliqué uses lightweight fusible web to fuse the pieces in place. Another method uses lightweight fusible interfacing and a chopstick, knitting needle, or similar tool for turning appliqué shapes right side out. Protect your iron from fusibles with an **(12)** appliqué sheet.

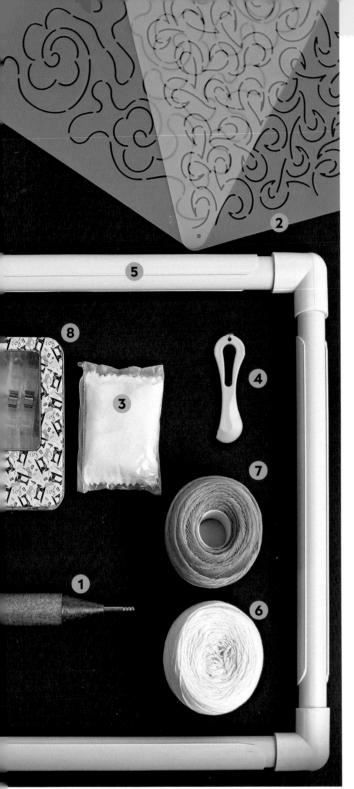

Hand-Quilting Supplies

For hand-quilting, use cotton/polyester, wool, silk, or bamboo batting.

You can thread-baste the quilt layers using a darning, upholstery, basting, or curved needle and cotton or cotton/polyester basting thread in a color that contrasts with your quilt top. You can pin-baste the quilt layers using size 1 or 2 rustproof safety pins and a **(1)** Kwik Klip.

To mark your quilting designs, you can use **(2)** quilting stencils and quarter-inch quilting tape or painter's tape plus removable marking pens, chalk or water-soluble pencils, a **(3)** chalk pounce pad, or a **(4)** hera marker.

Hand-quilt using a size 9 or 10 Quilting or Betweens needle to start—using a size 12 as you gain confidence—and good-quality hand-quilting thread, such as YLI, Gutterman, or King Tut 40 weight or Aurifil 28 weight. A needle threader and thimble are useful for hand-quilting.

A **(5)** quilting hoop or frame helps hold your quilt layers while you quilt.

Tie your quilts instead of hand-quilting them using **(6)** #8 or #10 crochet thread, **(7)** #3 or #5 pearl cotton, 4-ply yarn, or embroidery floss and an embroidery, tapestry, or curved needle with a large eye and a sharp point.

Machine-Quilting Supplies

The quickest way to finish a quilt is to quilt it by machine. Learning to free-motion quilt a quilt (quilting in any direction by lowering the feed dogs on your machine) takes some practice. However, straight-line quilting, which uses a regular sewing stitch and a walking foot to maintain an even feed, is easy to master even for a beginner.

For machine-quilting, you'll use many of the same supplies as for hand-quilting, including batting, quilting stencils, quilting tape, and a removable marking pen/pencil or chalk pounce pad. Unlike hand-quilting, you can use Golden Threads quilting paper, fusible quilt batting, or 505 Temporary Adhesive to prepare a quilt for machine-quilting.

Quilting gloves or fingertip grips help you grip your quilt as you machine-quilt it. Quilt clips keep the part you're not quilting rolled up. After quilting, you can machine-stitch the binding down or hand-stitch it with the help of **(8)** binding clips.

Choose your needle based on the thread you want to machine-quilt with. A bobbin-fill thread (such as Superior Bottom Line, Aurifil Bobbin, Sulky Bobbin, Wonderfil Decobob, and The Finishing Touch [for Baby Lock/Brother machines]) is often useful when working with certain top threads, such as metallics, monofilament (invisible), and other decorative threads.

Thread Type	Suggested Needle
Monofilament: Aurifil Monofilament, Superior MonoPoly, and YLI Wonder Invisible. Use a 50 weight cotton or bobbin fill.	Topstitch 70/10 Quilting 75/11 Jeans 70/10 Sharp/Microtex 70/10 or 60/8
60 weight thread: Superior Bottom Line, Quilter's Select Perfect Cotton Plus, or Sulky Polylite. Use a 50 weight cotton or bobbin fill.	Topstitch 70/10 Quilting 75/11 Sharp/Microtex 70/10 or 60/8
50 weight cotton thread: Aurifil, Superior SoFine, Superior Masterpiece, or Mettler Silk-Finish. Use the same thread or bobbin fill.	Topstitch 80/12 Sharp/Microtex 80/12 Quilting 75/11
40 weight thread: Aurifil, Superior King Tut, Mettler Silk-Finish, Wonderfil Master Quilter, or Fabulux. Use the same thread or bobbin fill.	Topstitch 90/14 Quilting 90/14 Sharp/Microtex 90/14
Metallic thread: Superior Metallics, WonderFil Spotlite and Dazzle, Mettler Metallic, Madeira Metallic, or Supertwist. Use bobbin fill in the bobbin.	Metallic 80/12 or 90/14 Embroidery 90/14 Topstitch 90/14
Rayon and silk thread: Madeira Classic, YLI Silk, WonderFil Dazzle, Mettler Amanda, Superior Kimono Silk, or Tiara Silk. Use the same thread in the bobbin.	Embroidery 75/11 Topstitch 70/10

PRACTICE PROJECT

Create a Design Wall

A design wall is a flat surface constructed from foam core insulation board and quilt batting. You can lean it against a wall or mount it permanently. The natural static of the batting causes your quilt blocks to cling to it, allowing you to arrange quilt blocks prior to sewing them together.

Use a design wall to test out fabrics for a future quilt or to play with the layout (setting) of your blocks until you find an arrangement you like. Although you can make a quilt without using a design wall, using one makes it much easier to plan and organize a quilt project.

- -

To make it easier to transport and store your design wall, have the store cut each board in half, making two large squares. You can then rig the boards for easy reassembly using four short PVC pipes.

- -

FINISHED SIZE

The size of your design wall will depend on the dimensions of the foam core insulation boards available to you and the type of projects you expect to make. Home improvement stores often sell insulation boards that are 48 × 96 inches. This is large enough to display the blocks for a crib or toddler quilt. For larger quilts up to Queen size, you'll need two boards this size.

MATERIALS LIST

- Two ¾- to 1-inch-thick foam core insulation boards
- Duct tape
- Low-loft quilt batting, large enough to cover the boards and overlap by 4 inches on each side
- Command hanging strips or another hanging system

OPTIONAL

- Four pieces of 2¾-inch diameter PVC pipe, each 36 inches long
- Four 1½-inch PVC couplings

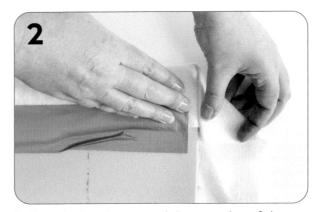

Lay a strip of batting on your floor. Place the insulation board on top of the batting print side up.

Pull up the batting around the top edge of the board and tape the entire edge with duct tape. Miter one corner and tape it down. To miter the corner, fold the corner down toward the taped edge, forming a triangle. Then fold the long edge up.

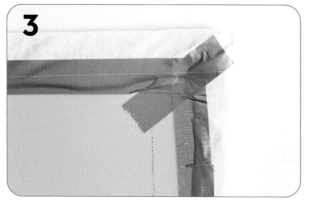

3

Pull the batting up along the neighboring long side and tape it along the entire edge. Miter the next corner and tape that down. Repeat this process all the way around the board until all the corners are mitered and all the sides are taped.

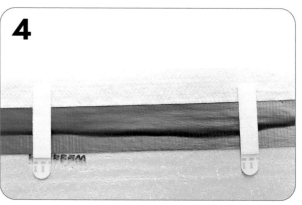

4

Repeat this process to cover all your boards with batting. To hang the board, attach Command strips (or another hanging system) along the top edge.

If you cut the boards in half for easy transport, you can reassemble them using PVC pipe. Fit two of the half pipes with a coupling and tape them to each bottom board section 1 foot from each side edge and even with the top edge. Tape across the pipe in several places. Tape two PVC pipes to each of the top sections. Tape them along the bottom edge 12 inches from the left/right edge. Overhang the pipes by ¾ inch or half the length of the coupling. To reassemble your design wall, insert the top pipes into the bottom PVC couplings.

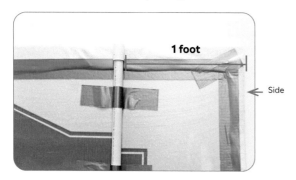

1 foot

Side

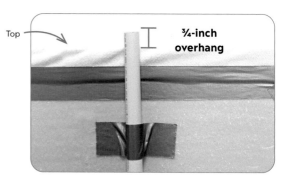

Top

¾-inch overhang

chapter 2

Selecting Fabric

Consider Color

Consider Value

Consider Saturation

Consider Scale and Style

Practice Project:
Selecting Fabrics
for a Quilt Project

Consider Color

The colors on the color wheel are arranged in groups of primary, secondary, and tertiary colors. The primary colors are red, yellow, and blue. The secondary colors—orange, green, and purple—are made by mixing the primaries. The tertiary colors—yellow-orange, red-orange, red-violet, blue-violet, blue-green, and yellow-green—are made by mixing primaries and secondaries. By studying classical color schemes, you can learn to select colors for a quilt that will go together beautifully.

When placing colors in a quilt block, remember that warm colors, such as red, yellow, and orange, come forward and attract the eye. Warm colors give you a feeling of energy and vibrancy. Cool colors, such as blue, green, and purple, recede. Cool colors are relaxing and calm. Place warm colors in the parts of a quilt you want the viewer to notice first. Place cool colors in places where you want the eye to rest.

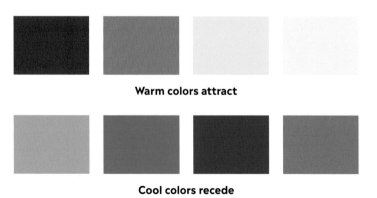

Warm colors attract

Cool colors recede

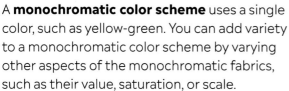

A **monochromatic color scheme** uses a single color, such as yellow-green. You can add variety to a monochromatic color scheme by varying other aspects of the monochromatic fabrics, such as their value, saturation, or scale.

An **analogous color scheme** includes three colors next to each other on the color wheel, such as green, yellow-green, and yellow. This color scheme is harmonious and restful.

A **complementary color scheme** includes a color and its opposite on the color wheel, such as blue-green and red-orange. A quilt with a complementary color scheme is vibrant and exciting. A split-complementary color scheme uses the two colors next to its opposite on the color wheel, such as blue, red-orange, and yellow-orange.

The colors in a **triadic color scheme** are evenly spaced around the color wheel, such as purple, green, and orange. A triadic color scheme is very vibrant but easily managed by selecting one color to act as the main color, with the other two acting as accent colors in your quilt.

Consider Value

There's more to selecting fabric than just choosing a nice color. To make your quilts sparkle, you also need to play with value. A fabric's value is its relative lightness or darkness. Differences in value (light, medium, or dark) create contrast and make certain parts of a quilt block stand out.

Bottom strip looks lighter

Bottom strip looks darker

To tell whether fabrics are light, medium, or dark, place them next to each other. The value of a fabric often changes in relation to the fabrics it's placed next to in a quilt, so lay them next to each other to test their values.

More than color, value is what makes a quilt sparkle. Although both of these blocks include value changes, the block on the right has higher contrast than the block on the left.

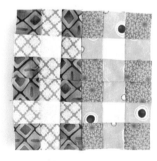
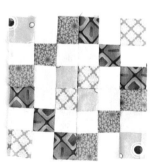

Use value contrast to create patterns in a quilt. Study the location of lights, mediums, and darks in these blocks, and notice the patterns that are created by the different placements.

Without changes of value, a quilt might lack interest. Although these blocks are similar, the one with higher contrast is more striking than the one that uses medium values throughout.

Consider Saturation

Color saturation determines the amount of a color in a fabric. Fabrics can be fully saturated with color and vibrancy or barely saturated and pale or faintly colored. By playing with the saturation of the colors in the fabrics you choose, you can create a mood in your quilt, such as vibrant, somber, or relaxing.

Fully saturated colors come forward in a quilt and catch the eye. If you select only fully saturated colors for a quilt, it will be vibrant and full of life.

A **tint** is created when you add white to a color. Tints are pale and create a relaxing mood. Because they're light in value, tints also catch the eye when placed next to colors with different saturation levels. Because tints are pale and not dominant, they provide resting places for the eyes as they move across a quilt.

A **shade** is created when you add black to a color. Shades are dark and provide high contrast and drama when placed strategically in a quilt. However, a quilt of all shades is somber in mood.

A **tone** is created by adding gray to a color. Tones create a feeling of calmness if used throughout a quilt. When used in a quilt block, the areas with tones recede and can help create dimensionality in a quilt.

Consider Scale and Style

Choose quilting fabrics with prints that vary in scale to add areas of contrast and interest in your quilts. Also think about fabric style. The style of fabric you choose for a quilt affects the overall image and mood it projects, such as historic, peaceful, rich, fun, or energetic.

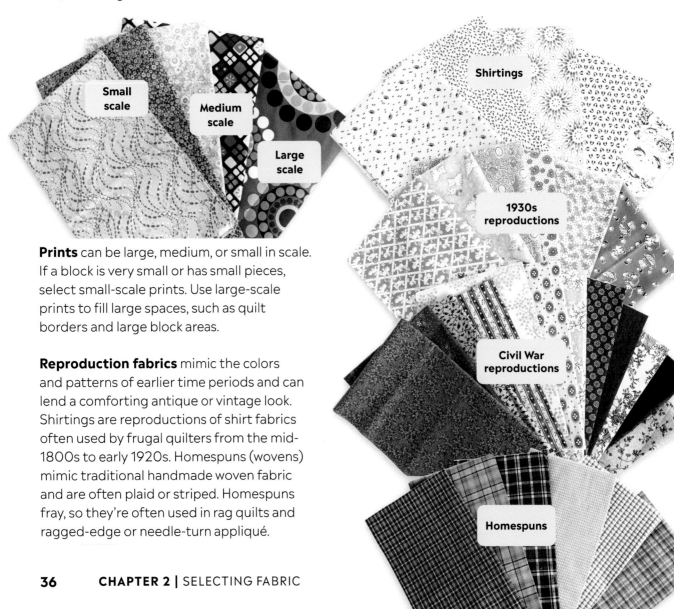

Prints can be large, medium, or small in scale. If a block is very small or has small pieces, select small-scale prints. Use large-scale prints to fill large spaces, such as quilt borders and large block areas.

Reproduction fabrics mimic the colors and patterns of earlier time periods and can lend a comforting antique or vintage look. Shirtings are reproductions of shirt fabrics often used by frugal quilters from the mid-1800s to early 1920s. Homespuns (wovens) mimic traditional handmade woven fabric and are often plaid or striped. Homespuns fray, so they're often used in rag quilts and ragged-edge or needle-turn appliqué.

A lot of modern-style quilts feature solid fabrics, but solids are also popular for use in Amish-style quilts.

Tone-on-tones are fabrics printed with the same color as the base fabric, such as white on white. Blenders are mottled or subtly printed fabrics. Use solids, tone-on-tones, and blenders for block backgrounds or to help blend colors in a quilt into a cohesive whole. They might not be exciting, but they're important because they provide a resting place for the eyes.

Geometric fabrics filled with zigzags, squares, circles or other shapes add dramatic interest, as do dots and stripes. Dots are fun and playful, while stripes can add an extra dose of excitement, especially when used diagonally.

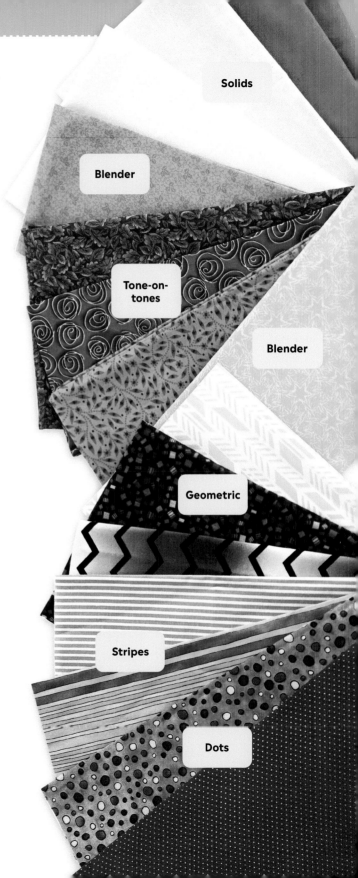

Solids

Blender

Tone-on-tones

Blender

Geometric

Stripes

Dots

Why use plain white or black in a quilt when you can use black-on-white or white-on-black prints instead? These fabrics lend an air of artistry and fun to any quilt.

Batiks are high thread count cottons that are hand-dyed using a wax-resistant technique. Batiks create an air of sophistication and drama, and they're a wonderful choice for blocks with large pieces, realistic landscapes, and appliqué.

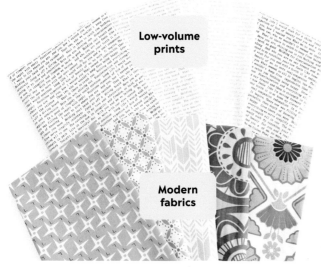

Low-volume prints

Modern fabrics

Flannel quilts are soft, warm, and cozy. Flannel is a great choice for rag quilts and quilt backs, but buy only high-quality flannels for the best results.

Modern fabrics feature large prints and geometrics. A special category of modern fabrics called low-volume prints features saturated color with lots of white. Use modern prints to create crisp, clean, modern quilts that feature large blocks with simple piecing and, of course, lots of pure white.

Flannel shrinks and stretches a bit, so always prewash it and use lots of pins and a walking foot when piecing. Flannel also frays and produces lots of lint, so be sure to clean your machine often when sewing it.

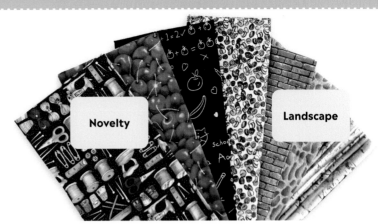

Felted wool is a terrific choice for appliqué because it doesn't fray and therefore doesn't have to have its edges turned under. You can also piece with wool or add wool appliqué to a cotton quilt top.

Novelty fabrics feature fun motifs, such as cats, dogs, dinosaurs, trucks, coffee beans, and sewing machines. Novelty fabrics are perfect for children's quilts, especially I Spy quilts. A special type of novelty fabric, known as landscapes, is perfect for depicting buildings, gardens, skies, and forests.

African fabrics and fabrics with Native American motifs allow you to celebrate your heritage or to create an exotic, adventurous mood in a quilt. African and Native American fabrics lend themselves to beaded embellishments and other fun surface treatments that are artistic and interesting.

Asian fabrics are ethnic prints that are exotic—but in a tranquil, thoughtful way. The floral motifs and touches of gold often found in these fabrics make quilts that use them look regal and opulent.

Select Fabrics for a Project

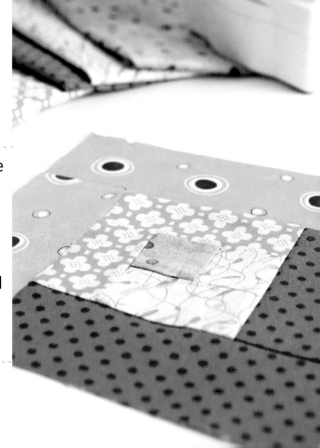

When shopping for fabrics for a quilt, you should try to buy only high-quality quilting cottons from a local or online quilt store. These high-quality cottons are easier to work with, they last longer, and their colors are less likely to run than the less expensive cotton fabrics you can find at a big-box fabric store. When shopping for your first quilt, keep in mind that some fabrics, such as flannels, minkee, T-shirts, denim, and nonquilting cottons, present special challenges for a beginning quilter.

Check out the first two projects in this book. Choose one and copy the list of fabric requirements. Use this list to work through the process of choosing fabrics for a project.

Quilt store employees are a great source of knowledge and can help you select fabrics for a project. Fabric collections, such as matched fabrics that make up a fabric line as well as precut fabrics sold in a matched set can help you choose fabrics for your quilt.

1

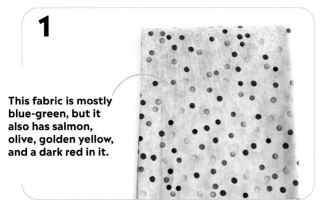

This fabric is mostly blue-green, but it also has salmon, olive, golden yellow, and a dark red in it.

Choose a fabric you like as a starting point.

To choose fabrics for a quilt, start by selecting a fabric you're attracted to. Note the specific colors in the fabric you've chosen. For example, is the blue a navy blue, blue-green, or blue-violet? Does the fabric include white or cream?

2

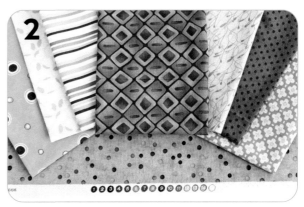

Identify the color scheme used by your starter fabric.

Use the fabric's selvage to identify the colors. Also identify the color scheme because it will help you choose the right complementary colors when you can't identify exact colors. This fabric is mostly blue-green. Adding red-orange creates a complementary color scheme. Adding green and yellow-green creates an analogous color scheme.

3

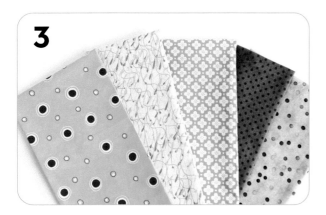

Choose fabrics for your project.

Start by pulling anything that goes with your chosen color scheme and then eliminate fabrics until you have the exact number of fabrics you need. Fabrics should vary in saturation (bright vs. grayed down), value (light vs. dark), and scale (size of prints).

4

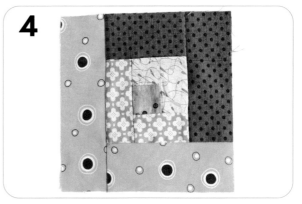

Sew a test block to see if you like your choices.

Before you cut up fabrics for a project with multiple quilt blocks, cut enough for a single block and make a test sample. You can also audition fabrics on your design wall. Live with your choices for a few days to see how you like them and make changes as needed.

chapter 3

Preparing and Cutting Fabric

Common Quilting Measurements

How to Resize a Quilt Pattern

Prepare Fabric

Rotary Cutter Safety

Rotary Cut Block Pieces and Bias Strips

Create and Use Templates

Fussy Cut a Block Piece

Practice Project:
Pieced Pillowcase

Common Quilting Measurements

In the United States, quilting fabrics are sold by the yard, in 42- and 44-inch widths. Outside of the United States, fabrics might be less than 42 inches wide. Quilt backing fabric is available in wider widths that help eliminate the need to piece your quilt back.

When you purchase fabric, you can have it cut into full yards or fractions of a yard (such as a half yard). This table shows how many inches of fabric you'll get for each fraction of a yard. For example, a half yard of fabric will yield a piece that's 18 × 42 inches or 18 × 44 inches depending on the width of the fabric (wof).

Fabric Line Precuts

Quilting fabric is sometimes packaged in convenient sizes, often in collections of coordinated fabrics called a fabric line. These precut sizes (or simply "precuts") have fun names, such as Fat Eighths and Jelly Rolls. Using precuts saves you the time and trouble of cutting fabrics yourself. However, take the time to measure a few of the precuts because they might vary slightly in size (measure from the inner points of any pinked edges). You don't need to cut the pinked edges off your precuts before using them. Don't prewash precut fabrics or they'll ravel.

Common U.S. Yardage Cuts

Yardage	Inches
⅛	4½
¼	9
⅓	12
⅜	13½
½	18
⅝	22½
⅔	24
¾	27
⅞	31½
1	36

Make your own precuts by cutting 1½-inch or 2½-inch strips or 5-inch or 10-inch squares from fabric left over after you finish a quilt project.

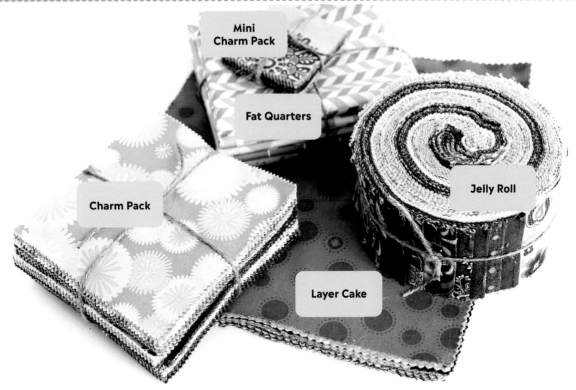

Common Quilting Fabric Precuts

Name of Precut	Width and Length
Fat Eighth	Piece of fabric 9 × 22 inches or 18 × 11 inches
Fat Quarter	Piece of fabric 18 × 22 inches
Layer Cake	Collection of fabrics, each 10 × 10 inches. A typical Layer Cake contains 42 squares, one square from each fabric in the fabric line.
Charm Pack	Collection of fabrics, each 5 × 5 inches. A typical Charm Pack contains 42 squares, one square from each fabric in the fabric line.
Mini Charm Pack	Collection of fabrics, each 2½ × 2½ inches.
Jelly Roll	Collection of fabrics, each 2½ inches by width of fabric (wof). A typical Jelly Roll contains 40 strips, one strip from each fabric in the fabric line.
Honey Bun	Collection of fabrics, each 1½ inches by width of fabric (wof)
Dessert Roll	Collection of fabrics, each 5 inches by width of fabric (wof)
Twice the Charms	Collection of fabrics, each 5½ × 21 to 22 inches
Honeycombs	Collection of fabrics, each 6-inch hexagons
Turnovers	Collection of fabrics, each 6-inch triangles

Common Quilt Sizes

Quilts are often designed to be used on beds of a particular size, but that doesn't mean your quilt needs to match these sizes exactly to look beautiful. This table shows common mattress sizes and quilt sizes in the United States. Quilt battings come in roughly these same sizes.

Common Quilt Sizes

Size	US Mattress Size	Quilt Sizes
King	76 × 80 inches	106 × 108 inches
Queen	60 × 80 inches	90 × 94 inches
Full	54 × 75 inches	82 × 88 inches
Twin	39 × 75 inches	68 × 86 inches
Twin XL	39 × 80 inches	68 × 96 inches
Lap		60 × 72 inches
Toddler		46 × 60 inches
Crib	27½ × 52 inches	36 × 48 inches

Using Precuts

With some quilt patterns, you can use precuts rather than yardage. This table provides the number of precuts you need for quilts of various sizes. Consider substituting precuts whenever a pattern calls for cutting squares, rectangles, or triangles of a common width, such as 2½ inches or 5 inches.

Approximate Number of Precuts Needed for Quilt Size

Precut	Crib Quilt	Lap Quilt	Twin Quilt	Queen Quilt	King Quilt
Fat Quarters	6 to 8	12 to 18	16 to 21	25 to 33	30 to 45
Charm Pack	2	4 to 7	6 to 10	8 to 11	11 to 13
Layer Cake	½ to 2	1 to 3	1½ to 5	2½ to 6	3 to 7
Jelly Roll	½ to 1	2	2	2½ to 3	3 to 3½

If you like a fabric line, consider buying several different precuts because patterns often use them together, such as one Charm Pack and one Layer Cake. If you didn't buy enough, you can alternate blocks with solid squares or add sashings and borders.

Using Fat Quarters

If you plan to buy fabric for your quilt in Fat Quarters, you need to calculate how many pieces you can cut from each one. The minimum number listed here assumes you're using almost the entire Fat Quarter. Look for patterns that are marked "Fat Quarter friendly," which means they use up most of the Fat Quarter in cutting the required pieces.

Squares in a Fat Quarter

Size of Square (Unfinished Size)	Number in One Fat Quarter
1½ × 1½ inches	168
2½ × 2½ inches	56
3½ × 3½ inches	30
4½ × 4½ inches	16
5 × 5 inches	12
5½ × 5½ inches	12
6½ × 6½ inches	6
7½ × 7½ inches	4
8½ × 8½ inches	4

How to Resize a Quilt Pattern

The fun of quilting comes from making a quilt your own. Whether that means choosing fabric that's different in color and style than what's shown in the pattern, adding pieced or appliqué borders, or making the quilt in a different size, you should explore your inner artist by choosing your own quilting path. Adjusting the size of a quilt pattern requires some careful calculation but greatly expands your options.

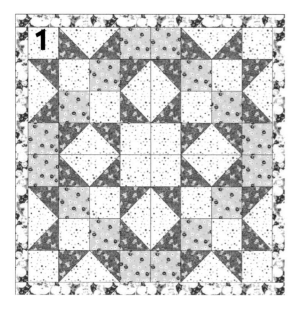

Using the finished block size in the pattern, calculate the number of blocks you need for the new quilt size.

For example, you have a pattern for a red-and-yellow wall hanging with four 10-inch blocks. You'd like to adjust this pattern to make a crib/toddler quilt. A crib/toddler quilt is usually about 42 × 54 inches. If you make your quilt three blocks wide and four blocks long, it will measure 30 × 40 inches. You can add borders to make it a little larger.

Divide the number of blocks you want by the number of blocks in the original pattern.

In this case, you want 12 blocks and the original pattern called for 4: 12 ÷ 4 = 3. You'll use this ratio (3) to help you adjust the fabric requirements in the pattern to meet your new needs.

If the pattern doesn't include the block size, subtract twice the width of the borders from the width of the finished quilt size to calculate the width of the quilt center. Divide this by the number of blocks across and round up.

Wall Hanging Fabric Color	Wall Hanging Requirement	Crib Quilt Fabric Color	Crib Quilt Requirement
Yellow	¼ yard	Blue	¾ yard
Red	¼ yard	Purple	¾ yard
White with dots	⅜ yard	White with dots	1⅛ yard

3 Multiply the original fabric requirements by the ratio to calculate the new amount of each fabric needed.

The wall hanging pattern calls for ¼ yard of yellow fabric. You want to use blue fabric in place of yellow for the crib quilt. To find the amount of blue fabric you need, multiply the fabric requirement by 3: ¼ × 3 = ¾, so you need ¾ yard of blue fabric. Add a bit more if you wish to allow for miscuts. Repeat this step for each fabric used.

5 Adjust backing and batting requirements.

Calculate your new quilt size plus borders. Add 4 inches to the width and length if you're quilting the quilt yourself; add 6 inches if you'll be using a longarmer to quilt the quilt. If this measurement is greater than 42 inches in either direction, you'll need to piece the backing. To estimate the backing yardage, calculate the number of 42-inch strips required to form a rectangle large enough for the back.

4 Adjust the border fabric requirements.

For straight borders, recalculate the border length to fit the new size of the quilt. For pieced borders, follow the instructions in steps 2 to 3 to calculate the yardage needed. To add a second border, use the size of the quilt center plus the inner border to calculate the yardage. Robert Kauffman Fabrics has a great app for your phone that makes quick work of calculating yardage for borders, binding, and backing-- all you need is the size of the quilt center (the size of the blocks when sewn together.)

If the same fabric is used for blocks and borders, subtract the amount needed for the borders before calculating the amount for the blocks.

Prepare Fabric

Before you cut and sew your fabric, decide if you need to prewash it to prevent the color from running or bleeding. Most high-quality quilting cottons won't need to be prewashed, but you might want to prewash highly saturated red, blue, and purple fabrics. Noncommercial hand-dyed fabrics and flannels (because they shrink so much) should also be prewashed.

Test for colorfastness.

Cut a square of the fabric you want to test and a square of white fabric in the same size. Soak them in soapy water for a few minutes, remove them, and place them right sides together to dry. If any color transfers onto the white fabric, you know you'll need to prewash. Out of white fabric? Iron your wet test fabric between paper towels.

Clip the corners before prewashing fabric.

Prewash your fabric if needed.

If you decide to prewash, you should prewash all the fabric you plan to use in the same quilt. If machine washing, clip the corners of the fabric to prevent raveling. Wash in cold water using a mild detergent, such as Orvis Quilt Soap or Tide Free. (I buy only quilting cottons, so I don't typically prewash. Instead, I add a few Shout Color Catchers when washing a quilt [in cold water only].)

Press and "starch" the fabric after washing if you plan to use it immediately. If not, store it without pressing.

You want the fabric to be stiff so you can cut it accurately. I don't recommend actual starch, but you should use a starch alternative, such as Best Press or Flatter. If you plan on hand-piecing or hand-quilting, don't "starch."

Rotary Cutter Safety

A rotary cutter helps you quickly cut fabric for a quilt, but it must be used with caution to ensure safety. A rotary cutter has a round, sharp blade that cuts as you roll it over the fabric. Use a rotary cutter with a self-healing cutting mat and acrylic rulers specifically made for rotary cutting.

Place your fabric on a cutting mat. Set the ruler on the fabric where you wish to cut. Spread your fingers, placing your pinkie just off the ruler, and press down firmly on the ruler to stabilize it.

Grip the rotary cutter firmly, wrapping your palm around the handle and placing your index finger on top to provide balance and stability. Keep your wrist straight to avoid repetitive motion injury. Open the rotary cutter just before using and close it immediately after each cut.

Stand at a waist-high table when cutting. Place the edge of the blade against the edge of the ruler—just off the leading edge of the fabric. Press down while moving the blade away from you. As you glide the rotary cutter up, maintain pressure on the ruler by stopping when the cutter is opposite your fingers, spider-walking your hand up the ruler, and continuing.

For more protection, wear a rotary cutting glove on your ruler hand and buy nonslip rulers from Quilter's Select, Creative Grids, or OmniGrid.

Rotary Cut Block Pieces

To cut accurate block pieces, begin by cutting fabric into strips the width of the required pieces and then subcut them into squares, rectangles, and triangles. To figure out how many strips to cut, divide the strip length (the width of your fabric, usually 42 or 44 inches by the length of the pieces needed.

Even Up the Fabric Edge

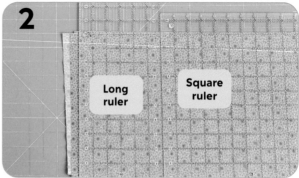

Fold the fabric in half, selvages together.

Start with fabric that's well pressed. Use a starch alternative (Best Press) as needed to remove wrinkles. Fold the fabric, selvages together, and hold it up. Offset the selvage edges slightly so the fabric hangs straight without any twists in the fabric. Lay the fabric on the mat, with the fold at the bottom (two layers of fabric). If your mat/rulers are shorter than 22 inches, lay the fabric down with the fold at the top, then bring the selvages up to the first fold at the top of the mat, creating four layers of fabric.

Line up a ruler near the left edge of the fabric.

Place a 6 × 24-inch ruler on the left edge of the fabric. Align the ruler's 2-inch line along the bottom edge of the fabric. To ensure a straight cut, butt up a large 12½-inch or greater square ruler against the long ruler, aligning its 1-inch line along the bottom edge of the fabric. Walk around to the other side of the table to even up this left edge, making sure not to bump the long ruler.

When the rotary cutter is opposite your hand, stop, spider-walk your hand and then continue cutting.

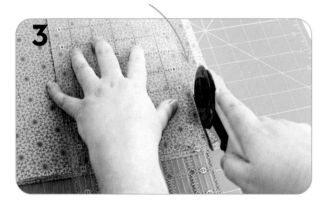

Even up the left edge of the fabric.

Press down on the rotary cutter as you glide it up along the edge of the ruler to trim the left edge of the fabric. Now that the edge is even, walk back to the other side of the table to cut fabric strips.

Cut Squares and Rectangles

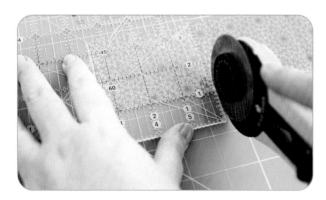

Subcut the strips into squares and rectangles as listed in the cutting directions.

Lay a strip horizontally on the cutting mat. To cut 2½-inch squares from your 2½-inch-wide strip, trim off the selvages. Align the 3½-inch mark on the ruler along the fabric's left edge and cut. Turn the cut fabric around and align the ruler's 2½-inch mark along this clean edge and trim off the selvages. Subcut the remaining squares using the 2½-inch mark on the ruler.

Use tape to mark the measuring line.

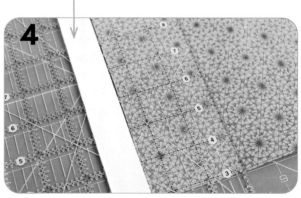

Cut fabric strips as described in the directions.

If you need to cut 2½ inch squares, cut a strip of fabric 2½ inches wide. Align the 2½-inch vertical mark on the ruler along the newly cut edge and the 2- or 3-inch horizontal mark along the fold. Cut a strip and hold it up to make sure it's straight and not forming a V. Refold and restraighten the left edge of the fabric (steps 2 and 3) at least every 3 to 4 cuts to eliminate any Vs.

These directions are for right-handers. If you're left-handed, place the ruler on the right edge of the fabric and cut with your left hand, stabilizing the ruler with your right.

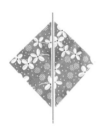

Cut Half-Square Triangles (HSTs)

Cut a square first and then cut the square in half diagonally. Cut the square ⅞ to 1 inch larger than the finished size of the HST.

Cut Quarter-Square Triangles (QSTs)

Cut a square first and then cut the square diagonally in both directions. Cut the square 1¼ to 1½ inches larger than the finished size of the QST.

Cut Corner Setting Triangles

Setting triangles are used to set quilt blocks on point (see page 152). Cut corner setting triangles like HSTs by cutting a square in half diagonally. Divide the finished size of the block you want to add the corner setting triangle to by 1.414, round up to the nearest ⅛ inch and then add ⅞ inch to calculate the size square to cut. For example, for 12-inch finished quilt blocks, cut corner setting triangles from 9⅜-inch squares to set them on point.

Fold large setting triangles in half and use a horizontal line on your ruler to cut accurately.

Cut Side Setting Triangles

Cut side setting triangles as you do QSTs by cutting a square in half diagonally in each direction. Multiply the finished size of the block to which you want to add the side setting triangle by 1.414, round up to the nearest ⅛ inch, and then add 1¼ inches to calculate the size square to cut. To set 12-inch finished quilt blocks on point, cut side setting triangles from 18¼-inch squares.

Cut 60° Triangles

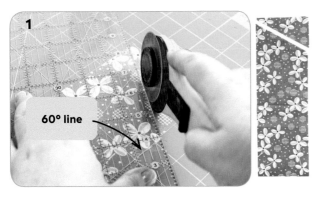

Cut a strip the finished height of the triangle plus ¾ inch. Align the 60° line on your ruler along the bottom edge of the strip, with the right edge of the ruler near the right edge of the fabric strip. Cut off the right edge of the strip at an angle.

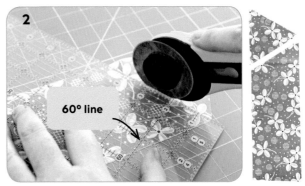

To cut the other side of the first triangle, rotate the ruler and align it along the bottom of the strip using its other 60° line and cut at a diagonal.

To cut the next triangle, rotate the ruler again and align it along the bottom of the strip using the first 60° line. Cut at a diagonal, creating another 60° triangle. Repeat to cut the strip into triangles.

Cut Diamonds

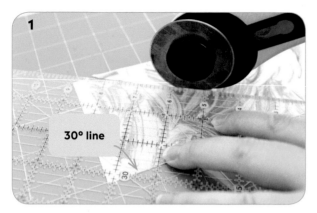

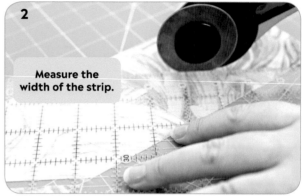

Cut a strip the finished height of the diamond plus ½ inch. Align the 30°, 45°, or 60° line on your ruler along the bottom edge of the strip. Cut off the left edge of the strip at an angle.

Using the same degree line, align the ruler along the bottom of the strip. Measure the width of the strip out from your first cut and then cut the right side of the diamond. Repeat to cut the remaining diamonds from the strip.

Rotary Cut Bias Strips

Bias is created when you cut fabric diagonally and not parallel to the selvage or cut edges. Bias edges are usually avoided in quilting because they're stretchy and hard to sew together accurately. However, if you want to create curving flower stems for appliqué or bind a quilt with a curved outer edge, you'll need bias strips that stretch and bend.

Selvage edge

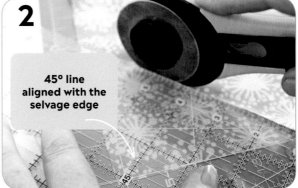

45° line aligned with the selvage edge

Place fabric in a single layer on the cutting mat.

Spray the fabric with Best Press and press before cutting. Place the fabric in a single layer on the cutting mat, with one of the selvage edges close to you.

Cut off the left corner of the fabric.

Place a ruler near the left edge of the fabric, aligning its 45° mark with the bottom selvage edge of the fabric. Cut off the lower-left corner of the fabric.

Cut the bias strips.

Measure the width of the strip you want from the newly cut edge of the fabric. For bias binding, cut strips 2 to 2¼ inches wide. For bias flower stems, cut strips ⅝ inch to 1½ inches wide.

Create and Use Templates

A template is a pattern made from freezer paper or template plastic. They're used in appliqué and hand-piecing to mark and cut appliqué shapes and block units. You can also use templates to copy patterns out of a magazine without cutting the pages or to audition a fabric for fussy cutting.

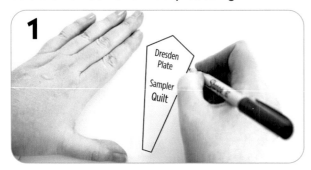

Trace and mark the template.

Lay the template over the pattern and trace the template with a fine-tipped permanent marker. For hand-piecing or appliqué templates, trace only the finished shape. Trace the unfinished/finished shape for fussy cut templates. Write the name or number of the pattern, quilt name, and grain line markings on the template. Mark the seam allowance on fussy cut templates.

Mark the fabric using the template.

Using your paper scissors, cut out the templates and store them together. If the template is made of freezer paper, iron it (shiny side down) on the fabric. Lay the fabric on a sandpaper board (right side down for hand-piecing or machine-appliqué; right side up for hand-appliqué) and use a fabric marking pencil or pen to trace the template.

Cut out the fabric piece.

For hand-piecing, mark a ¼-inch seam allowance around the traced shape and then cut it out. Cut out appliqué pieces without marking the seam allowance, leaving roughly a ³⁄₁₆-inch seam allowance as you cut.

Fussy Cut a Block Piece

Fussy cutting is the process of isolating a specific fabric motif, such as a teddy bear or flower, so it appears in a particular place in a quilt block piece. For example, if you have a fabric printed with teddy bears, you might want to cut the fabric so a teddy bear appears in the middle of each star block in a baby quilt.

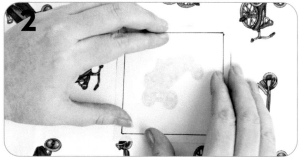

Make a fussy cut template.

Use a thin permanent marker to trace onto freezer paper or template plastic the pattern for the block unit you want to fussy cut. Trace the cut size of the shape you want and then mark a ¼-inch seam allowance on the template. Cut out your template using paper scissors.

Isolate a motif.

Lay the fabric face up on a sandpaper board. Move the template around the fabric until you find a motif that fits within the seam allowances. Motifs that almost fill the space look best rather than tiny motifs.

Add-A-Quarter ruler

Mark the fussy cut piece on the fabric.

If the template is freezer paper, iron it (shiny side down) on the fabric. Trace around the template to mark the block unit. If you're going to hand-piece your quilt block, mark seam allowances using an Add-A-Quarter ruler or quarter-inch seam marker. Cut out the motif and use it in place of the original unit in your block.

PRACTICE PROJECT
Pieced Pillowcase

Now that you know how to select fabrics for a project and how to use a rotary cutter, you're ready for your first project. Starting with a small project, like this pieced pillowcase, is a great way to hone your quilting skills. Even small projects can have fun details, like the folded accent strip, called a "flange," in this pillowcase.

FINISHED SIZE

- 20¾ × 30½ inches

MATERIALS LIST

- **Pillowcase body:** ¾ yard
- **Accent flange:** ⅛ yard
- **Border:** one Fat Eighth or ⅛ yard from each of three coordinating fabrics for a total of three Fat Eighths or ⅜ yard

CUTTING DIRECTIONS

- **Pillowcase body:** 27 × 42½ inches
- **Accent flange:** 2½ × 42½ inches
- **Border:** Four rectangles (A), 4 × 9 inches, from each Fat Eighth, for a total of 12

Making the Border

1. Arrange the 12 A rectangles in a row, with their 9-inch sides touching. Sew them together using a ¼-inch seam allowance to make Unit 1. As you sew, check your accuracy. Two A rectangles sewn together should measure 9 × 7½ inches; four strips should measure 9 × 14½ inches.

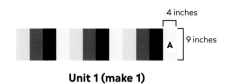

Unit 1 (make 1)

2. Press the seams in one direction. The border should measure 9 × 42½ inches.

Assembling the Pillowcase

1. Fold the pieced border in half lengthwise, wrong sides together (wst).

2. Fold the accent strip in half lengthwise (wst) and place on top of the border, aligning all four raw edges.

Unit 2 (make 1)

3. Sew the accent and border together to make Unit 2, using a scant ¼-inch seam. You want to sew with a slightly smaller seam so that later on, when you sew the accent border to the pillowcase body, this seam doesn't show. If your piecing isn't accurate, you might need to trim the edges to make them even.

4. Place the pillowcase body right side up on a table. Then place Unit 2 accent strip down on top of the pillowcase body, aligning the raw edges. (See Diagram A.) Sew together using a ¼-inch seam that's wider than the one you used to sew the accent border together.

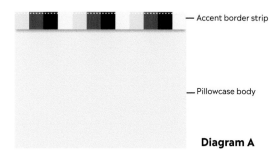

Diagram A

5. Press the seam toward the body.

6. Fold the pillowcase lengthwise, right sides together (rst), matching the raw edges. (See Diagram B.) Pin, then sew both raw edges, using a ½-inch seam, backstitching at the beginning and the end of the seam.

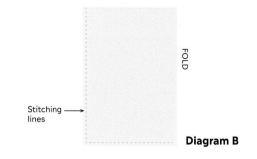

Diagram B

7. Turn the pillowcase right side out and press.

chapter **4**

Piecing
Quilt Blocks

Useful Hand Stitches

Even if you choose to machine-piece your quilt, there are times when you might work by hand, such as when you're stitching on the quilt binding, adding hanging sleeves and labels, or working with appliqué. Here are the stitches you need to know to perform such tasks by hand, along with a special knot called "the quilter's knot."

To thread the needle, pull the thread off the spool and thread that leading end through the needle eye. Cut the thread at about 18 inches. Form the knot at this end— the end closest to the spool. By maintaining the direction the thread comes off the spool, you hold the thread's natural twist and reduce its tendency to form knots as you sew.

Quilter's Knot

To form a quilter's knot, hold the needle in your left hand, and with your right hand, wrap the thread three times around the needle. Pinch the wrapped thread against the needle with your left hand. With your right hand, pull the needle up. The wrapped thread will slide down the thread as you continue to pinch it, closing into a tight knot at the end.

Running Stitches

Running stitches are used in hand-piecing. They're small and even on the front and back of the fabric. To make a running stitch, weave your needle in and out of the fabric three times at even intervals, about ⅛ inch apart. Then pull the thread to form three stitches. Straighten any ruffles in the fabric and continue.

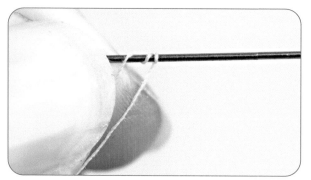

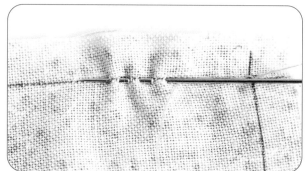

Backstitch

When hand-piecing, you often take a backstitch to hold the thread rather than using a knot. Bring the needle up from the back at point A. Bring the needle down to the right at point B. Bring the needle up a bit to the left at point C and then down again at point D.

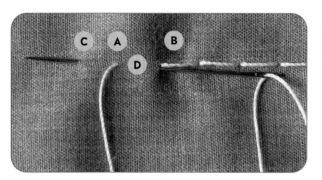

Whipstitch

Whipstitches are used to sew together blocks in English paper piecing. Bring the needle through from the back near the block edges, wrapping it around to the back again for the next stitch. Place stitches close together.

Appliqué Stitch

Appliqué stitches (also called "blind stitches") are almost hidden, making them perfect for hand-appliqué. Start by bringing the needle up at a point very near the edge of the appliqué or binding, just catching it. Come down into the background fabric, directly across from the point where you came up. Bring the needle back up again, about ⅛ inch to the left, and repeat.

Blanket Stitch

Blanket stitches are sometimes used to finish an appliqué edge. Bring the needle up through the appliqué from the back, about ¼ inch away from the appliqué edge. Wrap the thread to the back and come up again about ¼ inch to the right. As you bring the needle through, catch it within the thread loop. Pull gently to tighten the stitch and then repeat the stitch.

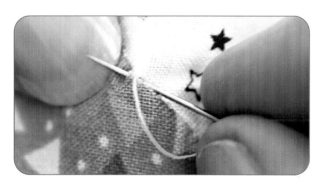

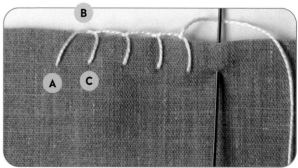

Hand-Piecing

Although time consuming, hand-piecing has some advantages over machine-piecing: It's restful, easily portable, and more easily controlled. Before hand-piecing a block, you'll need to create templates, trace around them on your fabric, and add a seam allowance. When hand-piecing, sew together block units first, then sew together each block row, and finally sew together block rows to complete a block. Use a size 7–11 Appliqué or Sharps needle or a size 11 Straw or Milliners needle threaded with hand-piecing thread in a neutral beige, gray, or white.

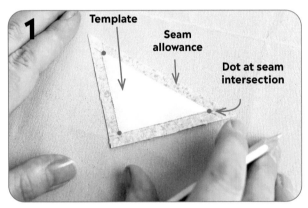

Mark each piece with a dot at each corner of the seam.

Place the fabric right side down on a sandpaper board, trace around the template, and add a seam allowance with an Add-A-Quarter ruler or quarter-inch seam marker. Mark a dot at each corner to help you align pieces for sewing and then cut the piece out.

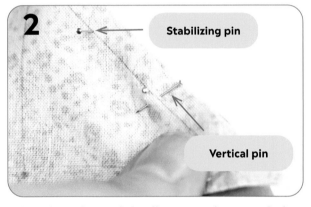

Align the edges of the first two pieces and pin.

Place the first two pieces right sides together, aligning the edges perfectly. Pin horizontally through the dots at each corner and along the seam to maintain alignment. Once the seam is aligned, remove the horizontal stabilizing pins and replace them with vertical pins.

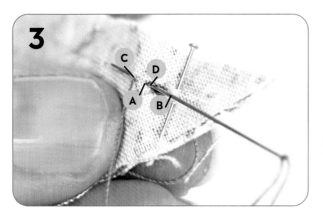

Backstitch to anchor the seam.

Don't knot your thread. Instead, use a split-backstitch. Come up through the dot at point A, down at point B, up at point C, then back down at point D—about halfway between A and B.

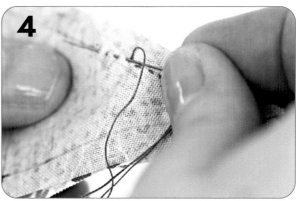

Sew the rest of the seam.

Sew the seam using a small running stitch. Take several backstitches along the seam to secure your stitches, then backstitch at the end of the seam. Remove pins as you sew. Sew together the block units and then sew together the units for each row.

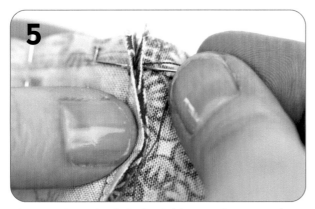

As you stitch, check the backside to make sure you're stitching on the seam line for both pieces.

Sew together rows to complete your block.

Butt (nestle) opposing seams and then pin through the dots at seam intersections to match the two seam allowances perfectly. Backstitch at the beginning and end of the row seam. When you reach an intersection between units, take a small backstitch and then poke the needle through to the other side of the seam. Take another backstitch. Take a backstitch at the end of the seam, stopping at the dot.

Machine-Piecing

Machine-piecing a quilt is faster than hand-piecing it, but both methods depend on accuracy to be successful. You can machine-piece a quilt block using any sewing machine as long as you can accurately sew a ¼-inch seam allowance. To piece a block, sew block units, such as HSTs, together first and then join them together to create block rows. Sew block rows together to complete a block. To improve piecing accuracy, you sew onto and off of small scraps of fabric folded in half. These scraps are called leaders and enders.

Piece a Simple Block Without Units

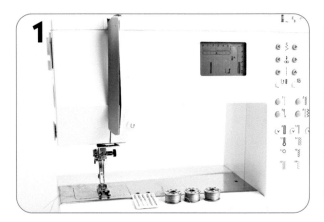

Set up your machine for piecing.

Insert a fresh Sharps, Quilting, or Jeans needle (size 70/10 or 75/11—or 80/12 if you're piecing batiks). Wind several bobbins and thread your machine with 50 weight cotton thread in medium gray, beige, or olive. Set the stitch length to 2.0 to 2.2, install your machine's ¼-inch foot, and change to a straight-stitch plate.

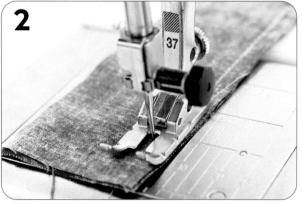

Test your seam allowance.

Place two 1½-inch fabric scraps right sides together and sew a test seam. Then press and measure the sewn unit to make sure it's 2½ inches wide. If the unit isn't 2½ inches wide, resew the seam. If needed, mark ¼ inch from the needle with tape and use that as your guide. Once you know how to sew an accurate ¼-inch seam on your machine, you're ready to sew a block!

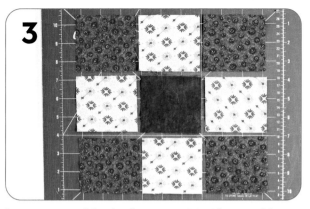

3

Lay out your block pieces next to the machine.

Blocks are usually laid out in a grid. To piece a simple block that doesn't have units, such as HSTs and flying geese, sew together adjacent pieces in each row, starting with the first two pieces.

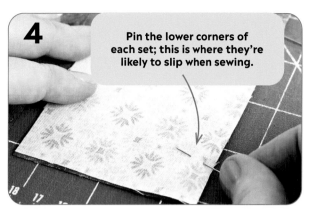

4

Pin the lower corners of each set; this is where they're likely to slip when sewing.

Pin the first two pieces in each row together.

Maintaining the way pieces are arranged in a block, flip the pieces in the second column over on top of the first pieces, right sides together. Pin the lower corners of each set. Remove each pin immediately before sewing over it.

Leader

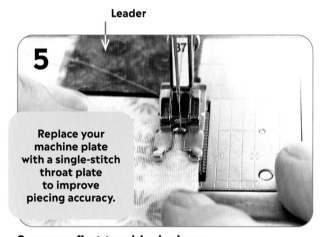

5

Replace your machine plate with a single-stitch throat plate to improve piecing accuracy.

Sew your first two block pieces.

Place a leader scrap of fabric under the presser foot and begin sewing with a ¼-inch seam. As you near the end of the leader, align the edges of the first set of block pieces, right sides together, place them under the presser foot, and continue sewing. When the first set is almost sewn, sew onto an ender. Leave the ender under the presser foot and clip to release the first set of pieces.

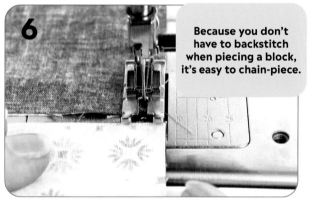

6

Because you don't have to backstitch when piecing a block, it's easy to chain-piece.

Chain pieces to save thread and time.

Alternatively, you can chain-piece your block pieces. Begin sewing with a leader, feeding the first set of pieces under the presser foot when you near the end of the leader. Continue feeding each set of block pieces under the presser foot when you near the end of the previous set. Sew onto an ender after sewing the last set.

Press the seam in each set to one side.

Cut the last set from the ender, press the connected sets, and then clip them apart. You should press toward the darker fabric to hide the seams. More importantly, you want to press so adjoining seams go in opposite directions.

Sew additional pieces to the first sets to complete each row.

Lay the pressed sets back on the mat. Flip the next piece in each row onto the last sewn piece in the row, maintaining arrangement of the pieces. Pin each set and sew as before. Press and then continue adding pieces until each row is complete.

Sew the rows together and press.

Pin seam intersections diagonally so you can sew onto the seam allowance to hold it in place before removing the pin. Alternate how you press row seams in neighboring blocks so the seams nestle when blocks are joined.

Piece a Block with Units

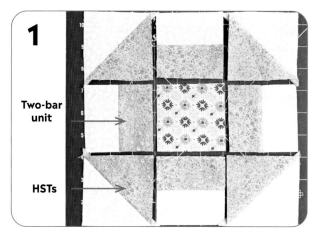

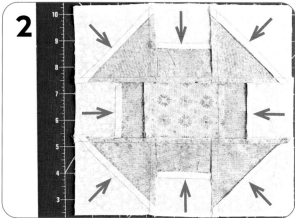

If a block has units, sew them first.

If a block contains common quilt units, such as HSTs and two-bar units, sew those units together first. Lay completed units on your mat, arranging them as they should look in the completed block. Sew units into block rows as before, then sew the rows together.

Press units, making adjustments as needed.

Press seams toward the dark unless it makes more sense to press differently because of the layout of your block. For example, pressing away from HST units helps maintain the points.

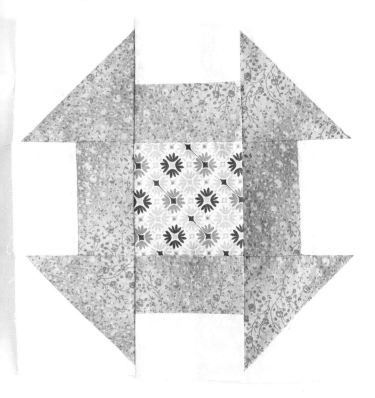

Piece a Block with Intersecting Seams

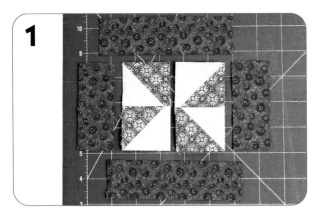

Where multiple seams intersect, you must pin carefully.

This block uses four HSTs to create a pinwheel in the center. Because of the multiple intersecting seams, you'll need to pin carefully. Start by sewing two sets of HSTs together.

Pin through the points.

Pin to match the points in the pinwheel.

Place the two sets of HSTs right sides together. Insert a pin horizontally through the points formed by the HSTs. Open the two sets to check that you've pinned through both points.

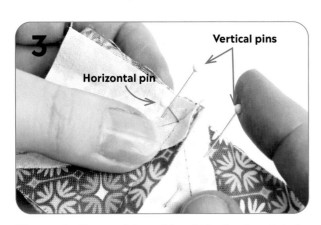

Vertical pins

Horizontal pin

Pin vertically on either side of the horizontal pin.

With the horizontal pin holding the points in place, pin vertically on either side of the seam. Remove the horizontal pin and sew the HSTs together. As you near the seam intersection, sew through the X formed by the intersecting points.

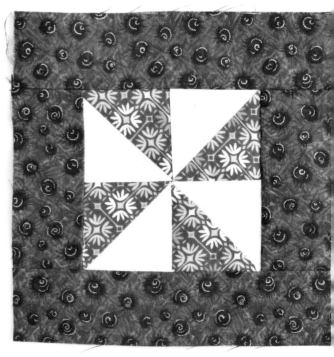

Piece a Block with Points

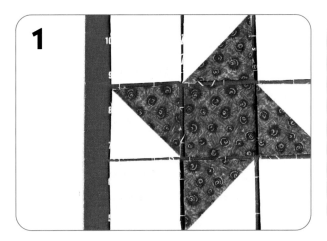

Pin carefully whenever points are involved.

If a unit has a point, such as HST or flying geese, you should pin at the point in order not to chop it off in the seam when joining it to other units (even units without points). Hopefully, the point is ¼ inch from the fabric edge, but if it's off only slightly, pinning the point to the ¼-inch seam on the other side helps fix that.

Pin at the point.

Place the HST on top of its neighboring square, right sides together. Pin horizontally through the point of the HST and then pin at the ¼-inch seam on the square. Place a vertical pin diagonally through the seam to hold the pieces in place as you sew. Remove the horizontal pin.

Piece Strip Sets

Piecing a quilt doesn't have to mean sewing lots of individual pieces together. For some quilts, you can just sew two long strips together and subcut them into the units needed for a block. Sewing long seams can be tricky, though, especially when you're trying to maintain an accurate seam allowance. When strip sets aren't sewn accurately, they tend to curve. However, there are tricks you can use to maintain accuracy when sewing strip sets.

If sewing long seams accurately is hard for you, cut the strips in half (22 inches long instead of 44 inches long).

The most important thing you can do to create accurate strip sets is to cut the strips perfectly. Press your fabric before cutting it into strips, spray it with Best Press, and press. This will stiffen the fabric, making it easier to cut and sew. You can also use precut strips for some patterns.

Press all seams in the same direction—unless doing so causes shadowing of a darker fabric through a much lighter one—and then press open the seams.

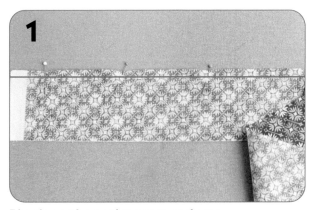

Pin along the entire seam and sew.

Place two strips right sides together. Match the ends (if cut to the exact same length; otherwise, match only the starting end) and pin. Pin along the entire seam and then sew the two strips together. Place the dark fabric on top, with the seam away from you. Press, nudging the dark fabric over with the tip of your iron.

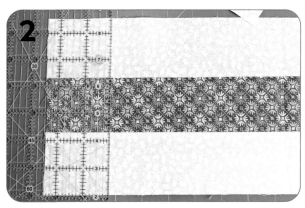

Add the next strip to the pieced strip set.

Pin the strip all along the seam as before. Start sewing at the opposite end of the strip set to prevent curving. Measure the width of the strip set and resew as needed to make it perfect. If strip sets include more than three strips, sew the strips in pairs and then join the pairs.

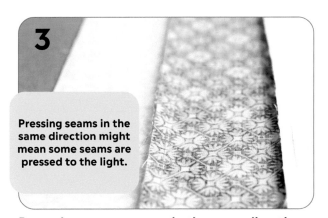

Pressing seams in the same direction might mean some seams are pressed to the light.

Press the seams open or in the same direction.

One way to ensure you don't press folds into the long seams is to place the seams vertically on the ironing board and press with the iron horizontal to the seam. Press from the center of the strip out to the edge and then from the center out to the other edge.

Subcut the completed strip.

Subcut the completed strips into the units required by your quilt blocks. For most quilt blocks, you subcut using the unfinished width of one strip; for others, you subcut using the width of the strip set.

Press Blocks

Taking the time to press fabric well before you cut it and to press block units as you piece them is important. For most quilt blocks, press seams to one side—toward darker fabric. Pressing seams to one side helps create opposing seams that nestle (butt) together when you join units to blocks. Unless your pattern includes specific pressing directions, you'll need to plan how to press the units in your block to place opposing seams next to each other. Pressing a certain way also helps some block units look better. If your block has triangular pieces, pressing away from them can help preserve their crisp points. Where many seams come together (as in a pinwheel block), press the seams open or fan them out to reduce bulk. If you're piecing flannel, making a miniature quilt with tiny pieces, or planning to quilt by hand, you might want to press open your seams. Pressing on a wool pressing mat improves your pressing and helps to make blocks more accurate.

Plan how you'll press block units.

In most cases, it makes sense to press seams to dark fabrics as long as that will result in opposing seams when a block is sewn together. Pay attention to the direction of the seams at the edges of your blocks; you'll want opposing seams to help sew the blocks together.

If you press a seam incorrectly, press it flat again to set the seam before trying to re-press.

Set the seam first and then let it cool slightly.

Press using a cotton setting; don't use steam because it might cause fabrics to stretch and distort. Spray the fabric with Best Press. Press down with the iron for a few seconds to set the seam. Don't iron back and forth across a seam because this will stretch it.

3

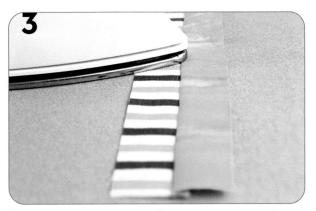

Press perpendicular to the seam to press the seam to one side.

Lay the fabric with the seam away from you. Press perpendicular to the seam, using the tip of the iron to gently nudge the seam over in a few places. Press the seam fully with the iron, pressing up and down and not across. Check the seam to make sure it's pressed flat, with no tucks or puckers.

4

A tailor's clapper is very useful for pressing seams open.

Press seams open where they come together.

When you have multiple seams coming together, press seams open to reduce bulk. Use your finger to press open the seam. Hold the seam open and press using the tip of your iron. Keep the tip right on the seam line. Press it flat by pressing up and down along the entire seam. Flip the seam over and press it again from the front.

5

Where points come together, fan out the center seam.

To fan out a seam, finger-press opposing seams to one side. The connecting seam is also pressed to one side. Hold the unit in your hands and gently twist the center seam in opposite directions. This will release a few stitches at the center of the seam so it will give, but that's okay.

6

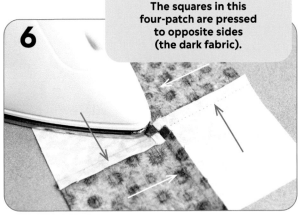

The squares in this four-patch are pressed to opposite sides (the dark fabric).

Press the fanned intersection to set it.

Gently press the center seam with the tip of your iron to set it. Turn the unit over and press the fanned-out seam again to flatten it perfectly. Use Best Press to set the seam.

Fix Block Problems

The most common problem with a block is that it ends up the wrong size. To avoid this, always measure block units, such as HSTs or flying geese, as you piece them. It might seem tedious, but it will save you a great deal of frustration. If a block unit is the wrong size, unsew the seam, check that each component of the unit is cut to the right size, and then recut if needed. If the components are cut correctly, mark the sewing line on both units and resew them.

If pieces are just a little too small, you don't need to recut. Instead, use a smaller seam allowance so the unit ends up the right size when sewn. If pieces are too large, trim them to size or resew with a slightly larger seam allowance.

Another common block problem is related to the layout. For example, you might have sewn two half-square triangles so they point the wrong way. The only way to fix this is to unsew the units and resew them. Laying out your block pieces before and during block construction can help prevent this common mistake.

Unsew any wrong pieces sewn together.

Unsew (rip out) a seam by picking out every third stitch using a sharp-tipped seam ripper.

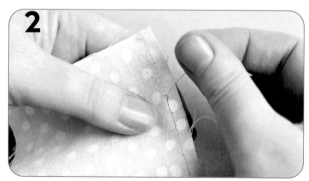

Remove the thread holding the seam.

Flip the unit over and gently pull out the bobbin thread. Don't pull on the pieces because you might stretch them out of shape. Brush off the remaining threads to clean the seam. Press both components flat.

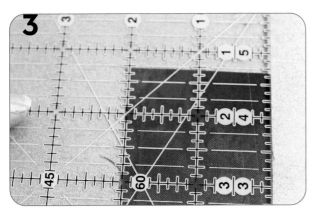

Measure the separate units before resewing.

Check each unit of the block for size before sewing them back together and trim or recut as needed. Remember that unsewn units are ½ inch larger than the finished size and units sewn on one side are ¼ inch larger than the finished size.

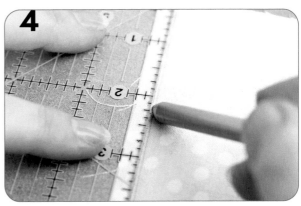

Mark units to aid in accurately reconstructing a block.

If a unit's measurements are slightly off, mark the exact seam you need to sew in order for it to end up the right size. Measure the unit from the edge opposite the seam and mark the seam line at the finished size plus ¼ inch. If the unit is sewn on one side, mark the seam line using the finished size.

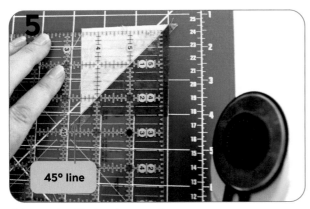

45° line

Trim units if they're too large.

If a unit is too big, you might be able to trim it to the right size. For example, if your half-square triangle is too large, trim it to size by laying the ruler's 45° mark on the HST's diagonal, measuring from one edge, and cutting the opposite side.

Remember that the end of a seam is where you often have the most trouble (inaccuracy). Pay attention as you sew a seam all the way to the very end. Sewing off onto an ender will help you maintain an accurate seam allowance all the way to the end of a seam.

PRACTICE PROJECT

Mug Rug

A mug rug is a small quilt you can use as a coaster. This uses a quilt block called a Log Cabin. One side of the block features light fabrics and the other side dark fabrics.

FINISHED SIZE

- 6 × 6 inches

MATERIALS LIST

- **Light green #1:** ⅛ yard or Fat Eighth
- **Light green #2:** ⅛ yard or Fat Eighth
- **Light green #3:** ⅛ yard or Fat Eighth
- **Dark blue #1:** ⅛ yard or Fat Eighth
- **Dark blue #2:** ⅛ yard or Fat Eighth
- **Backing:** ⅛ yard or Fat Eighth
- **Batting:** 6½ inches square

CUTTING DIRECTIONS

- **Light green #1:** 1 square (A), 1½ × 1½ inches
- **Light green #2:** 1 rectangle (C), 1½ × 3½ inches; 1 square (A), 1½ × 1½ inches
- **Light green #3:** 1 rectangle (F), 2 × 6½ inches; 1 rectangle (D), 2 × 3½ inches
- **Dark blue #1:** 2 rectangles (B), 1½ × 2½ inches
- **Dark blue #2:** 2 rectangles (E), 2 × 5 inches
- **Backing:** 1 square, 6½ × 6½ inches

Assembling the Block

Diagram A

1. With the center square on the left, join light green #1 and light green #2 A squares (Diagram A). Press the seam allowance away from the center A square.

Diagram B

2. With the center square on the left, sew one rectangle B to the bottom of the Log Cabin block (Diagram B). Pin so the A seam doesn't flip over. Press to the B rectangle.

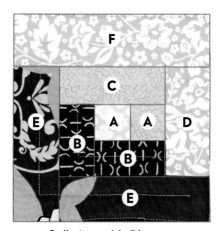

Quilt Assembly Diagram

3. In a Log Cabin block, you sew "logs" to the center square in a clockwise direction. After you sew one B to the block and press, sew the other B, then C, D, both Es, and F. (See Quilt Assembly Diagram.) Press toward each new log after sewing it to the Log Cabin block. The block should measure 6½ inches square.

Quilting and Finishing

A pillowcase finish doesn't use binding and is the simplest way to finish a quilt, like for this mug rug.

1. Trim the batting just a bit smaller than the quilt back. Place the block face up and then layer the backing (right side down) and batting on top and safety pin all the layers. (The batting is on top.)

2. Sew a ¼-inch seam all the way around, leaving a 2½-inch opening in the middle of one side. Backstitch at the beginning and end of the seam.

3. Clip the corners diagonally.

4. Turn the quilt right side out. Push the corners out with a knitting needle.

5. Tuck in the seam allowances at the opening and press. Topstitch all the way around the edge of the mug rug, sewing closed the opening. To topstitch, simply stitch near the edge.

6. Quilt as desired. The sample mug rug was quilted with straight lines running down the center of each log, spiraling out from the center.

Experiment with fabrics and quilting patterns on your mug rug.

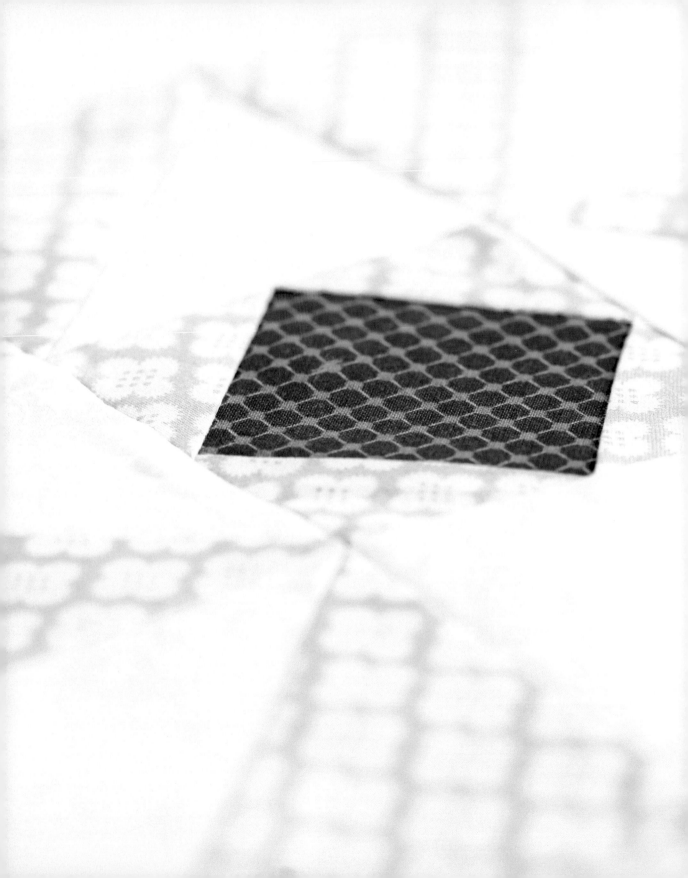

chapter **5**

Piecing Techniques

Piece Four-Patch Units

Piece Two-Bar
and Three-Bar Units

Piece Flying Geese Units

Piece Half-Square Triangles

Piece Square-in-Square
Units

Piece Hourglass Units

Practice Project:
"Stargazer" Wall Hanging

Piece Four-Patch Units

A four-patch is a unit made with four squares of equal size arranged in a 2 × 2 grid. The squares alternate light and dark, creating a small checkerboard pattern. The four-patch unit is one of the simplest block units to piece and here are two ways to make one.

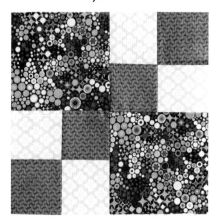

The first method shows you how to construct the unit using four separate squares. The second method uses fabric strips to construct a bunch of similarly colored four-patches. If you decide to make four-patches using a different method than prescribed in a pattern, adjust the yardage and cutting requirements accordingly.

Method 1: Makes One Four-Patch

1

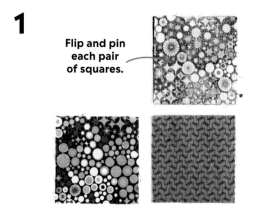

Flip and pin each pair of squares.

Arrange the four squares and then sew the pairs together.

Lay out the four squares as you like. Flip the pieces in the first column on top of the pieces in the second column, right sides together. Pin the lower corners of each square and sew together. Remove each pin right before sewing over it.

2

Press to the dark to create opposing seams.

As you press each pair, lay them back down on your ruler or mat to keep the proper arrangement.

Sew the four-patch together.

Place the two rows right sides together. Pin diagonally just past the nested seams. Sew the rows together, being careful that the seam doesn't flip over or slip.

Flatten the center seam to reduce bulk.

Press the center seam open or fan it by twisting the seams in opposite directions. Press the seam, turn it over, and press it again to flatten it. Use Best Press to set the seam.

Method 2: Makes Several Identical Four-Patches

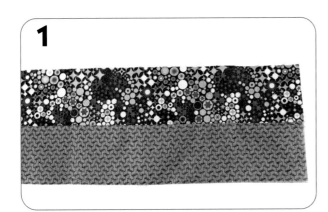

To make several identical four-patches at once, start with a strip set.

Cut a light and a dark strip the same width as the four-patch squares given in your pattern. For example, if you need 2½-inch squares, cut 2½-inch strips the length of fabric and then sew them together to create a strip set, pressing to the dark.

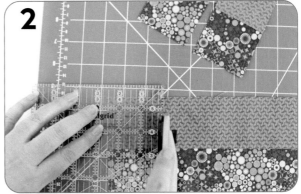

Subcut the strip set and then sew the two units together.

Subcut the strip set using the same measurement you used to cut the strips. In the example, you'd cut the strip set every 2½ inches. You now have the two rows of your four-patch. Pin the two sets so two different fabrics are facing each other and sew them together as shown in Method 1.

Piece Two-Bar and Three-Bar Units

A bar unit is made with rectangles of equal size, arranged one on top of the other. A two-bar unit consists of one light and one dark bar to provide nice contrast. A three-bar unit consists of alternating light and dark bars.

Here are two ways to make bar units. The first method shows you how to construct the unit using separate rectangles. The second method uses strip sets to construct a bunch of similarly colored bar units.

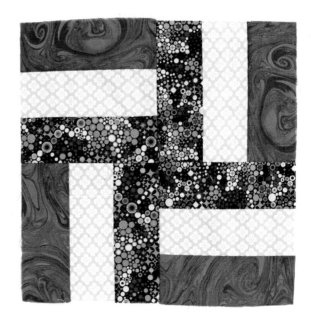

Method 1: Makes One Bar Unit

Cut pieces and sew the first two bars together.

Cut the bars to the size specified in the pattern and lay them out. Maintaining the arrangement, flip the bottom bar on top of the next bar, right sides together. Pin the lower corners of the bars. Remove each pin right before sewing over it.

Press to create opposing seams.

Consider where the bar units will appear in the finished block and press the bars to create opposing seams.

3

Add an additional bar if needed.

If you're sewing a three-bar unit, flip the last bar onto the completed two-bar unit, right sides together. Pin in the lower corner and sew the final seam. Press, creating opposing seams with adjacent blocks as needed or pressing to the dark.

If you decide to make bar units using a different method than prescribed in your quilt pattern, adjust the fabric yardage and cutting requirements.

Method 2: Makes Several Bar Units

1

Press strips to the dark fabric as you add them.

Create a strip set.

Cut a light and a dark strip the same width as the rectangles given in your pattern. For example, if you need three-bar units with 1½ × 3½-inch rectangles, cut three 1½-inch strips and sew them together to create a strip set.

2

Subcut the strip set.

Measure the width of your strip set and use that measurement to subcut the strip set into the dimensions you need. In the example, the three-bar units should finish at 3½ inches wide, so cut the strip set every 3½ inches to create the three-bar units.

Piece Flying Geese Units

Flying geese units are pieced rectangles that feature a "goose" and the "sky." The "goose" is a large triangle in the center of the rectangle surrounded by two smaller "sky" triangles. When the goose is dark and the sky is light, a directional arrow shape is dominant. There are many ways in which you can piece flying geese units: Method 1 creates one flying geese unit, while Method 2 creates several similar ones.

If you decide to make flying geese using a different method than prescribed in your quilt pattern, adjust the fabric yardage and cutting requirements.

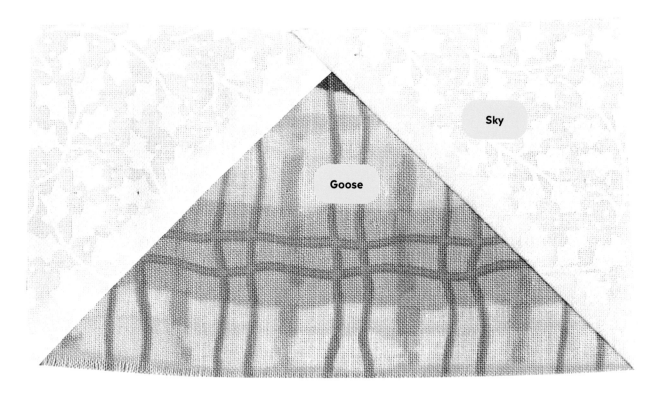

Method 1: Makes One Flying Geese Unit

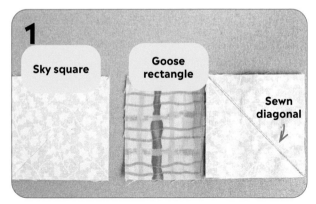

Sew one sky square to the goose rectangle.

Cut two squares the same width as the goose rectangle to create the sky. To make a 2 × 4-inch finished flying geese unit, start with a 2½ × 4½-inch rectangle and two 2½-inch squares. Draw a diagonal on the wrong side of the sky squares. Place one of those squares on top of one end of the goose rectangle, right sides together. Sew just inside the drawn line, closest to the corner.

Press the square, creating a sky triangle.

This is the "stitch-and-flip method" because after you stitch the square, you flip part of it back. Press the square toward the corner of the rectangle, forming a sky triangle. Trim the excess fabric under the sky triangle, leaving a ¼-inch seam allowance. By leaving the goose rectangle intact and not trimming it, you ensure the flying geese unit will be the correct size. You can also trim the goose and the sky fabric to reduce bulk in the corner.

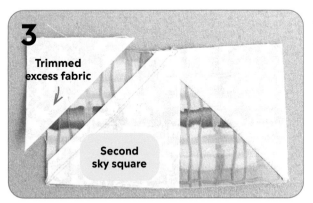

Sew the second sky square onto the goose rectangle.

Place the second sky square on top of the other end of the goose rectangle, right sides together. This square will slightly overlap the first sky triangle at the center point. Repeat the stitch-and-flip method from Step 2.

Sawtooth Star blocks use flying geese units.

Method 2: Makes Four Matching Flying Geese Units

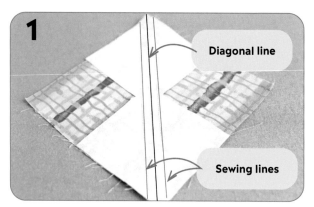

Diagonal line

Sewing lines

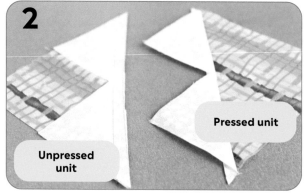

Unpressed unit

Pressed unit

Cut pieces and sew the sky squares to the goose square.

The goose square is the size of the finished unit length plus 1¼ inches. For a 2 × 4-inch finished flying geese unit, cut a 5¼-inch goose square. The sky squares are the finished width of the unit plus ⅞ inch. In this case, you need four 2⅞-inch sky squares. Draw a diagonal line from corner to corner on the wrong side of the sky squares. Draw sewing lines ¼ inch on either side of the drawn line. Place two sky squares in opposite corners of the goose square. Stitch on the sewing lines.

Cut on the diagonal and press.

Cut on the diagonal line, creating two units. Open each unit and press the goose base toward the sky triangles. You now have two heart-shaped units.

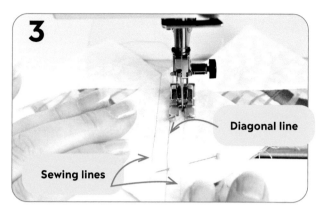

3

Diagonal line

Sewing lines

Sew a sky square to one of the heart units.

Place a sky square on the heart unit in the
unsewn corner, right sides together. Stitch
on the sewing lines.

4

Cut on the diagonal and press.

Cut on the diagonal you just drew. Press the sky
triangle away from the goose. You now have two
flying geese units. Repeat steps 3 and 4 for the
remaining heart-shaped unit to create a total of
four flying geese.

Piece Half-Square Triangles

A half-square triangle (HST), also called a "triangle square," is a square bisected diagonally; one half is usually light-colored and the other half dark. There are two ways in which you can piece HSTs: Method 1 creates two matching HSTs, while Method 2 uses triangle papers, which can be purchased at quilting stores or online, to create many HSTs.

A quarter-inch seam marker is very useful when making HSTs using Method 1.

Method 1: Makes Two Matching HSTs

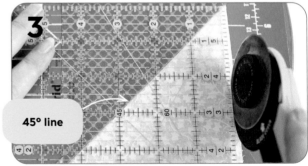

1

Diagonal line

Sewing lines

Cut squares, mark lines, and sew.

Cut squares the finished size of the HSTs you need plus 1 inch. To create two 4-inch HSTs, cut two 5 × 5-inch squares. Place the two squares right sides together and draw the diagonal and the sewing lines ¼ inch from both sides of the diagonal on the wrong side of the light square. Sew directly on the sewing lines.

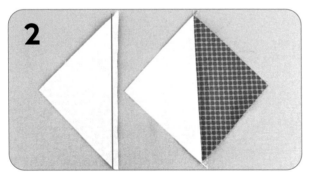

2

Cut the half-square triangles apart and press.

Cut on the diagonal. You now have two half-square triangles. Press toward the dark triangle.

3

45° line

Trim each half-square triangle to size.

Trim your half-square triangles to size by placing your ruler's 45° mark on the HST's diagonal and trimming two sides. For HSTs that finish at 4 inches, trim to 4½ inches.

Method 2: Makes Multiple Matching HSTs

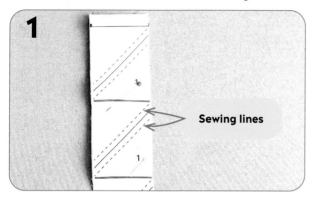

1

Sewing lines

Place the fabrics together, with triangle paper on top.

Cut the fabrics to the size indicated on the triangle papers, then layer them right sides together with the light fabric on top. Place one triangle paper on top and pin away from the sewing lines.

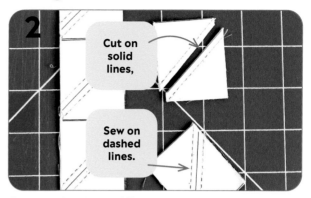

2

Cut on solid lines,

Sew on dashed lines.

Sew on the dotted lines and then cut the triangles apart.

Reduce your stitch length to about 1.2 to 1.5mm. Change to a larger needle (size 14) to help perforate the paper. Sew on the dotted sewing lines in the directions of the arrows (if any). Cut the triangles apart by cutting on the solid lines using a rotary cutter.

3

Press and remove the triangle paper.

Press the half-square triangles with the paper on, pressing to the dark fabric. Remove the triangle paper by folding the paper back over the seam and running your fingernail over the seam to score it. Hold the triangle at the seam and tug gently at the paper.

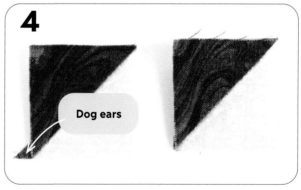

4

Dog ears

Trim the dog ears.

Trim the "dog ears"—the small triangles at one or both ends of the seam (depending on the triangle papers you use).

Piece Square-in-Square Units

A square-in-square unit (sometimes called "diamond-in-a-square") is a center square set on point with triangles surrounding it. Sewing the triangles on a square is tricky, but the methods shown here will help you be successful. Choose the one that works best for you.

Method 1: Makes One Square-in-Square Unit

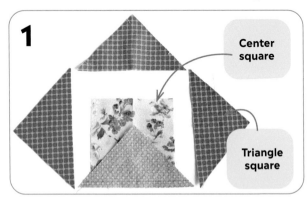

Cut the center square and triangle squares.

Divide the finished size of your block by 2, multiply by 1.414, add ½ inch, and cut a center square that size. To make a 5-inch finished unit, cut a 4-inch center square. Cut two triangle squares half the size of the finished block plus 1 inch. Cut the triangle squares in half diagonally and then mark the ¼-inch seam allowance on the cut edge of the triangle. Fold the center square and the triangles in half to mark the midpoints.

Trim the dog ears.

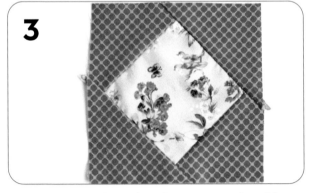

Sew the triangles and press.

Align the first triangle with its cut edge along one side of the center square, right sides together. Use the folds in the center square and the triangle to help you center the triangle. Sew the triangle to the square and press away from the square. Then repeat this process to add the other triangle. Trim the dog ears.

Sew the remaining triangles to opposite sides of the square and press.

Fold the center square in half in the other direction to mark the midpoints. Fold the triangles in half. Align a triangle along each edge, sew, and press. Trim the block to size. The points of the center square should measure exactly ¼ inch to the edge of the finished unit.

Method 2: Makes One Square-in-Square Unit

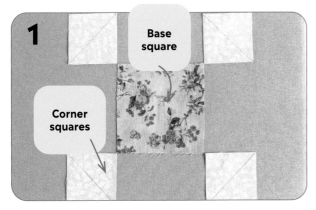

Cut the base square and corner squares.

Cut the base square the finished size you want plus ½ inch. For a 3-inch finished square-in-square unit, cut the center square 3½ inches. Cut the corner squares half the finished size plus ½ inch. In this example, cut the corner squares 2 inches. Mark the corner squares diagonally. This will be the sewing line.

Stitch and flip a corner square.

Place a corner square in a corner of the base square, right sides together, and stitch on the diagonal line. Flip the corner square over the diagonal and press to the corner. Then trim the excess corner square underneath, leaving a ¼-inch seam. Don't trim the base square.

Sew on the rest of the corners and press.

Place the next corner square on the base square and sew on the line. Press to the corner and trim. Use the stitch-and-flip method to add the remaining corner squares. Measure and trim the unit as needed. The points of the center square should measure exactly ¼ inch to the edge of the finished unit. To trim, measure out ¼ inch from two sides, trim both sides, and then rotate the block and trim the last two sides.

If you make square-in-square units using a different method than prescribed in your pattern, make adjustments to the fabric yardage and cutting directions as needed.

Piece Hourglass Units

An hourglass unit is a set of four quarter-square triangles sewn into a square to resemble an hourglass. The methods described here make two identical hourglass units. Method 2 allows you to mix up the colors in your hourglass units, while Method 1 is more structured. Choose the method that works best for you.

If you decide to make hourglass units using a different method than prescribed in your pattern, adjust the fabric yardage and cutting requirements.

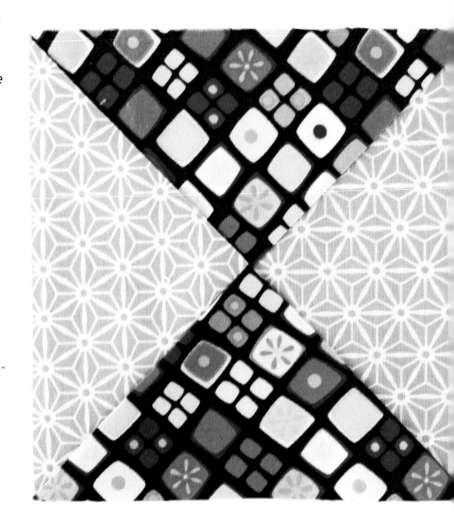

Method 1: Makes Two Matching Hourglass Units

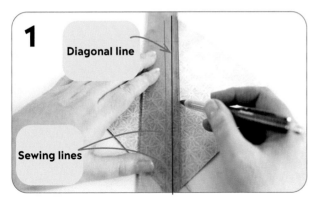

Cut two fabric squares and sew them together.

Cut two squares 1½ inches larger than the finished size hourglass units you need. On the wrong side of one square, draw a diagonal line. Draw a sewing line on either side of the diagonal, ¼ inch away. Place the marked square on top of the other, right sides together, and stitch on the sewing lines.

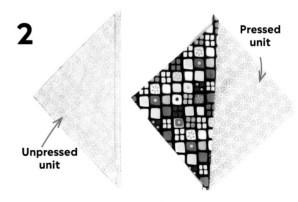

Cut the squares apart and press.

Cut on the diagonal to separate the squares. Press each half to the dark. Trim the dog ears. You now have two half-square triangle units (HSTs).

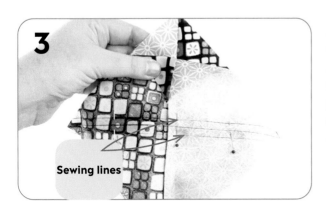

Put two half-square triangles together— light triangles on top of dark triangles.

On the wrong side of one of the HSTs, mark a diagonal perpendicular to the seam. Mark sewing lines on each side of the diagonal, ¼ inch away. Place the marked HST on top of the unmarked HST, right sides together, light fabrics touching dark. Pin and sew on the two sewing lines.

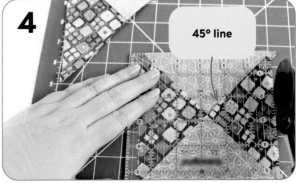

Cut on the diagonal, press, and trim to size.

Cut the units apart on the diagonal line. You now have two hourglass units. Press the center seam open and trim each unit to size. Place your ruler's 45° mark on the center seam and measure from the center out to trim the units on two sides. Rotate the units and trim the other two sides.

Method 2: Makes Two Matching Hourglass Units

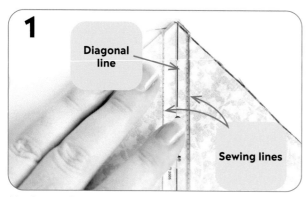

Mark two fabric squares and sew together.

Cut two squares 1½ inches larger than the finished size hourglass units you need. Draw a diagonal line on the wrong side of one square and sew lines ¼ inch away from the diagonal on either side. Place the marked square on the unmarked square, right sides together. Sew on both lines.

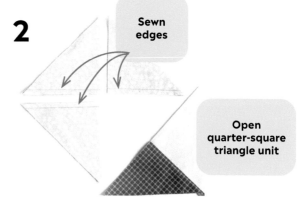

Cut the squares diagonally and press.

Cut the squares diagonally in both directions. Open the units and press to the dark. You now have four quarter-square triangle units.

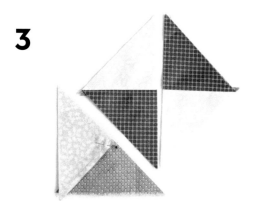

Sew pairs of quarter-square units together.

Lay out two quarter-square triangle units. Put them right sides together and nestle the seams. Pin the units along the long edge and then sew them together using a ¼-inch seam allowance to make one hourglass unit. Repeat for the other pair of quarter-square triangle units.

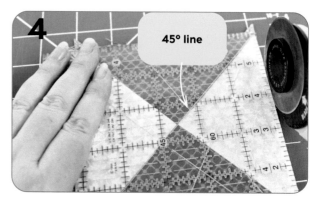

Press and trim each hourglass unit.

Press the center seam open and trim each unit to size. Place your ruler's 45° mark on the center seam and measure from center out to trim the units on two sides accurately. Rotate the units and trim the other two sides.

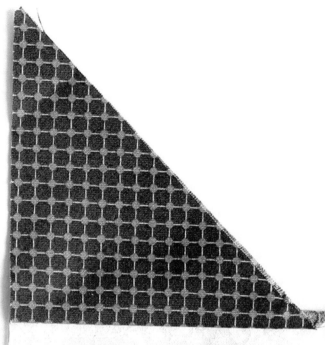

PRACTICE PROJECT
"Stargazer" Wall Hanging

The colors in this wall hanging reflect the colors of my favorite lily, the Stargazer. It's perfect for practicing four-patches, half-square triangles, and flying geese. If a pattern calls for several half-square triangles that are similarly colored, the simplest way to make them is with triangle paper. To make the flying geese, you'll use the stitch-and-flip method.

FINISHED SIZES

- **Overall:** 30 × 30 inches
- **Blocks:** 12 × 12 inches

MATERIALS LIST

- **Thangles 2-inch finished triangle paper** (7 strips)
- **Light lime green:** ⅛ yard or Fat Eighth (blocks)
- **Dark lime green print:** ¼ yard (blocks)
- **White:** ⅜ yard (blocks, Border #2)
- **Dark rose:** ¾ yard (blocks, Border #1, Border #2, binding)
- **Blue-green:** ⅜ yard (Border #2)
- **Backing:** 1 yard
- **Batting:** 36-inch square

CUTTING DIRECTIONS

Light lime green:

• 16 squares (A), 2½ × 2½ inches (blocks)

Dark lime green print:

• 16 rectangles (D), 2½ × 6½ inches (blocks)

White:

• 7 rectangles (C), 2½ × 10 inches for use with Thangles (blocks, Border #2)

• 16 rectangles (B), 2½ × 4½ inches (blocks)

• 16 squares (A), 2½ × 2½ inches (blocks)

Dark rose:

• 4 strips, 2 × 42 or 2¼ × 42 inches as you prefer (binding)

• 2 rectangles, 1½ × 24½ inches (Border #1)

• 2 rectangles, 1½ × 26½ inches (Border #1)

• 7 rectangles (C), 2½ × 10 inches for use with Thangles (blocks, Border #2)

• 32 squares (A), 2½ × 2½ inches (blocks)

Blue-green:

• 4 rectangles (E), 2½ × 24½ inches (Border #2)

Backing:

• 1 square, 36 × 36 inches

Note: Cut border strips first. Trim border strips to the right size after sewing the quilt center.

Making the Block Units

1. Using Method 1 for piecing flying geese units, make 16 flying geese. Use one white B rectangle and two dark rose A squares to make each flying geese unit (Unit 1). Measure and trim each Unit 1 to 2½ × 4½ inches, then resew as needed. Press toward the corners and away from the white "geese."

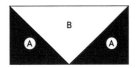

Unit 1 (make 16)

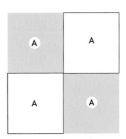

Unit 2 (make 4)

2. Using Method 1 for piecing four-patches, sew two light lime green A squares and two white A squares into a four-patch unit (Unit 2) that measures 4½ inches square. Make four Unit 2s. Measure each Unit 2 and trim as needed. Press open both seams.

3. Using Method 2 for piecing HSTs, make 40 half-square triangles (HSTs) using triangle paper. Use one white and one dark rose C rectangle and one 2-inch triangle paper strip to make six HSTs at one time. Check that each HST is 2½ inches square and then trim as needed.

Unit 3 (make 8)

4. Sew one HST to the end of a dark lime green rectangle D to create Unit 3. Lay out Unit 3 first, making sure you align the HST unit correctly, and flip it onto the rectangle without changing the alignment. Make eight Unit 3s. Measure and trim to 2½ × 8½ inches. Press to the dark lime green rectangle.

5. Sew two HSTs together to make Unit 4. Lay out the unit to ensure correct orientation of the HSTs. Make eight Unit 4s. Unit 4 should measure 2½ × 4½ inches. Press to the left HST.

Unit 4 (make 8)

6. Sew one HST to the left end of a dark lime green rectangle D and press to the rectangle. Sew Unit 4 to the other end to make Unit 5. Press Unit 4 to the dark lime green rectangle. Make eight Unit 5s. Measure and trim to 2½ × 12½ inches.

Unit 5 (make 8)

Assembling the Quilt Blocks

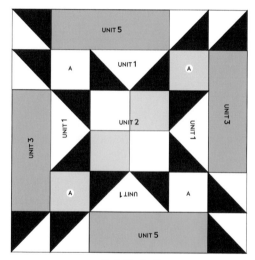

Block Z (make 4)

1. Join units, light lime green A squares, and white A squares to create Block Z. Assemble the center star first. Then add Unit 3s to either side and Unit 5s to the top and bottom.

2. When sewing each row and then finally sewing the rows together to create the center star, be sure to match up the center point of the flying geese unit to the center of the four-patch (Unit 2). Pin the flying geese carefully so you don't crop the points. If the points of your flying geese aren't exactly ¼ inch from the edge of the unit, mark your sewing line so it runs right through the point.

3. When assembling the center star, press to the A squares and in toward the four-patch center. Make sure the green squares in the corners and in the four-patch unit run in the correct direction. The center star should measure 8½ × 8½ inches.

4. Sew the Unit 3s to the sides of the center star. Pin the intersections carefully. Press toward the Unit 3s. Sew the Unit 5s to the top and bottoms of this unit, then press away from the center star. Create four Block Zs. Block Z should measure 12½ × 12½ inches.

Assembling the Quilt Center

1. Using the Quilt Assembly Diagram, join four Block Zs to form the quilt center. Lay out the blocks on your design wall, and when sewing them together, pay attention to the orientation of the lime squares running diagonally through the blocks.

2. Press seams open where the Block Zs are joined. The quilt center should measure 24½ × 24½ inches.

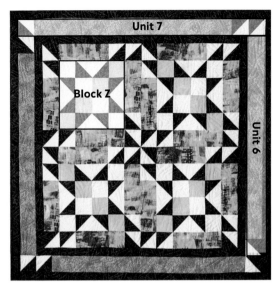

Quilt Assembly Diagram

Adding the Borders

1. Measure down the quilt center. Cut the dark rose side Border #1 rectangles that length. Sew these strips to the sides of the quilt center. Press toward the strips.

2. Measure across the quilt center. Cut the dark rose top and bottom borders that length. Sew these strips to the top and bottom of the quilt center and press toward the strips. The quilt should measure 26½ × 26½ inches.

Unit 6 (make 2)

3. Measure down the quilt center and cut two blue-green E rectangles that length minus 2 inches. Sew one HST to the right end of one blue-green E rectangle to create Unit 6. Check that the orientation of the HST is correct. Press to the blue-green strip. Make two Unit 6s.

4. Refer to the Quilt Assembly Diagram and sew a Unit 6 to each side of the quilt, making sure the HSTs are aligned correctly. Press toward Border #1.

Unit 7 (make 2)

5. Measure across the quilt center and cut two blue-green E rectangles that length minus 6 inches. Sew one HST to the left end of one blue-green E rectangle and press to the rectangle. Check the Unit 7 diagram for correct orientation of the HST. Sew two HSTs to the right end of the blue-green rectangle to make Unit 7. Press to the blue-green strip. Make two Unit 7s.

6. Refer to the Quilt Assembly Diagram and sew a Unit 7 to the top and bottom of the quilt, making sure the HSTs are aligned correctly. Press to Border #1. The quilt should measure 30½ × 30½ inches.

Quilting and Finishing

1. Remove the selvages from the backing fabric before basting the quilt. Prepare the quilt for quilting and quilt as desired. The sample quilt was quilted with spiraling triangles. If you want to quilt using a simpler straight-line pattern, quilt this piece in a grid of straight lines that run across and down the quilt, spaced every 2 inches so they run through the centers of the squares and other units.

2. Square up the quilted quilt and bind it. Add a label and a sleeve for hanging.

For an equally beautiful but less challenging project, consider making a table topper (16 × 16 inches) using a single Block Z. Follow the directions for making the inner star and HSTs for Block Z, but add the inner 1-inch border to the star unit. Cut the E rectangles and the D rectangles 2½ × 8½ inches and use them to create the second border. Add final border strips 1½ inches wide and cut to fit, approximately 1½ × 14½ inches (sides) and 1½ × 16½ inches (top/bottom).

This table topper was quilted by tracing a 4-inch circle all over. Where the circles overlap, a classic "orange peel" quilting design is created. Quilt half the peel diagonally across the quilt, then quilt the other half back to form the design. Although it looks like you're quilting circles, you're really quilting small curves from point to point.

chapter **6**

Advanced Piecing Techniques

Piece Y-Seams

Piece Partial Seams

Curved Piecing

Foundation Paper Piecing

English Paper Piecing

Practice Project:
"Goodnight Moon,
Goodnight Stars"
Baby Quilt

Piece Y-Seams

As the name suggests, a Y-seam joins three block pieces together in such a way that the intersecting seams look like a Y. The top part of the seam forms a V and the bottom forms an I. Y-seams can be challenging, but with careful pinning, they're doable, even for a beginner.

Pieces joined in a Y-seam often have some bias edges, so be careful not to stretch them as you sew. Spraying your fabric with Best Press and pressing your fabric before you cut your pieces and pinning carefully before sewing will help eliminate these problems.

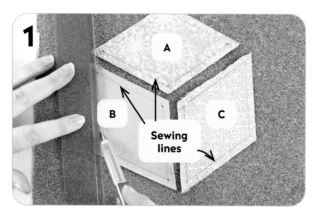

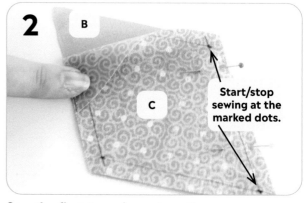

Mark the sewing lines and dot the corners.

After cutting the pieces as directed by your pattern, lay each piece right side down on a sandpaper board and mark sewing lines ¼ inch from each edge. Place a dot in each corner, at the intersection of the seams.

Sew the first two pieces together.

Arrange the pieces of the block (A, B, and C) next to your sewing machine. Place the two pieces (B and C) that form the I of the Y-seam right sides together and pin. Sew the seam, starting and stopping exactly at the marked dots. Backstitch at the beginning and end of the seam.

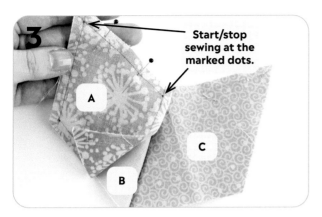

Begin sewing the inset piece.

Lay the inset piece (A) on top of the (B) piece, right sides together, matching the dots. Pin and then sew from dot to dot, backstitching at the beginning of the seam. Sew with the inset piece on the bottom, from the outside point toward the center. Stop at the dot with the needle down. Don't backstitch.

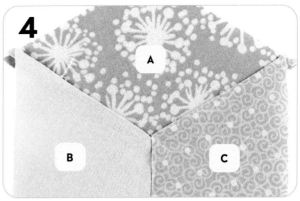

Finish sewing the inset piece.

Lift the presser foot. Align the other side of the inset piece (A) with the edge of the remaining piece (C). Match the dots and pin or hold the piece in place. Put the presser foot down and sew to the last dot on the outer corner. Backstitch at the end of the seam.

Press open the center seam.

Press open the I part of the Y-seam. Finger-press the seam first, spritz with water, then gently press with the iron. Press the two seams that form the V in the Y-seam toward this open center seam.

Alternatively, fan out the center seam.

Fanning out the center seam will reduce bulk. Finger-press the seams in the same direction first and then press with an iron.

Piece Partial Seams

Some blocks can't be constructed using straight seams, such as this Bright Hopes block. Blocks like this have a piece that's sewn using a partially sewn seam. Partial seams allow you to frame the center of a block with surrounding pieces, creating a swirl effect.

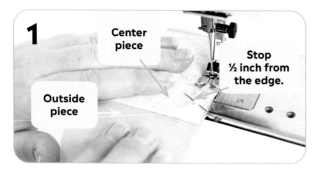

Sew the partial seam.

After cutting pieces as directed by your pattern, lay the center piece on top of the first outside piece, right sides together, and pin. Begin sewing at the edge, stopping about ½ inch from the end. Backstitch at the beginning and end of the seam, then press to the center piece.

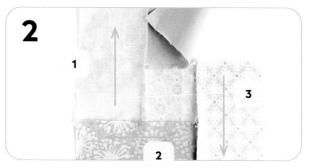

Sew the other three sides.

One by one, sew each of the other pieces to the inset piece. Rotate the block counterclockwise, adding one piece at a time. You'll be able to sew the complete seam for each of these pieces. Press each seam to the center.

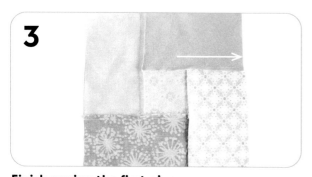

Finish sewing the first piece.

Return to the first piece, folding it back in place and aligning the edges once again. Sew the rest of the partial seam to complete it. Backstitch at the beginning and end of the seam, then press.

Curved Piecing

Curved seams add softness and motion to your quilt blocks, opening up a wide array of design possibilities. A classic quilt block that includes curved piecing is this Drunkard's Path block. To make this block and similar blocks, you need to master curved piecing. Like other piecing techniques that involve bias edges, careful pinning is the key.

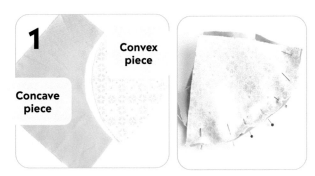

Pin the two curved pieces together.

After cutting the pieces as directed by your pattern, fold both shapes in half to find the centers. Place the convex piece on top of the concave piece, right sides together. Pin the centers, pin each end of the seam, and then pin at several places in between.

Sew the curved seam carefully.

With the concave piece on top, sew the seam slowly, being careful not to create puckers. Remove the pins right before you sew over them. Don't pull on the pieces as you sew because they might stretch. The finished seam shouldn't have any puckers.

Press the curved seam.

Press the curved seam toward the convex shape. Press using an up-and-down motion to avoid stretching the curved seam.

Foundation Paper Piecing

Foundation paper piecing allows you to piece blocks accurately by following a numbered pattern. The pattern is printed on foundation paper—a thin but stable paper you sew through and later remove after the block is pieced. Foundation paper piecing is tricky at first because you sew with the fabric on the bottom and the paper pattern on top. However, once you get the first two pieces sewn, it's easy.

To figure out the size to cut your fabric pieces, measure the width and length of that space on the foundation pattern, then add a generous ½-inch seam allowance on each side.

1

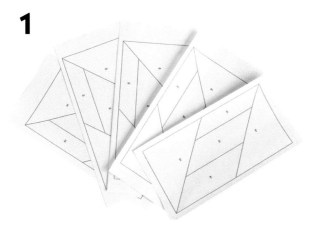

Prepare foundation papers.

Copy the pattern onto foundation paper, enlarging as needed. Copy the pattern by scanning and printing it on foundation paper or by tracing it. To enlarge a pattern, copy it on a copy machine and enter the percentage indicated on the pattern (such as 200%). Use paper marked "foundation paper" for best results.

2

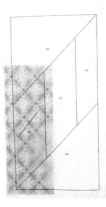

Make sure the block's outside seam allowance is also covered.

Pin fabric #1 to foundation paper.

Place fabric #1 face up on the back (unprinted side) of the foundation. Pin in place from the front (printed side) of the foundation. Hold the foundation up to the light and check that the fabric covers the #1 space, leaving a generous ¼-inch seam allowance over the line between #1 and #2. The fabric should also cover block edges by at least ¼ inch.

3

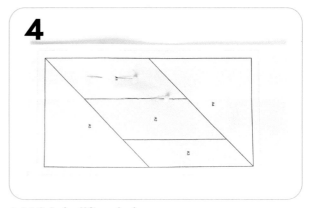

Foundation folded over cardstock

¼-inch seam allowance

Excess fabric

Trim fabric #1.

Flip to the front (printed) side of the foundation and place a small piece of cardstock on the line between spaces #1 and #2. Fold the foundation over the cardstock and use an Add-A-Quarter ruler to trim the excess fabric #1 to an exact ¼ inch.

4

Add fabric #2 and pin.

Flip to the back (unprinted) side. Place fabric #2 on top of fabric #1, right sides together, aligning #2 on the newly cut edge of #1. Flip the foundation to the front (printed side) and pin on the line between #1 and #2.

5

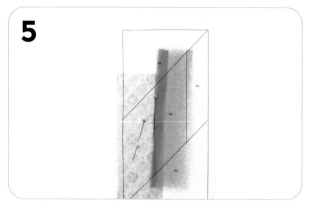

Double-check that fabric #2 is big enough to cover the space.

Flip fabric #2 over the pin and hold the foundation up to the light to check that it's large enough to cover the space for #2 plus a ¼-inch seam allowance on all sides. Adjust fabric #2 as needed.

6

Sew the seam between fabrics #1 and #2.

Turn the foundation over to the printed side and sew on the line between #1 and #2 using a short stitch length. Start and end just before or after the intersection line on the pattern. To pierce the paper more easily, use a Jeans 90/14 needle. Unpin the fabrics, flip fabric #2 over the seam, and press.

7

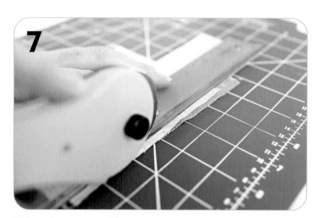

Trim the seam allowance.

On the right side of the foundation, place a small piece of cardstock on the line between spaces #2 and #3. Fold the foundation over the cardstock and use an Add-A-Quarter ruler to trim the seam allowance to an exact ¼ inch. Repeat steps 4 to 7 to add each fabric scrap in order.

8

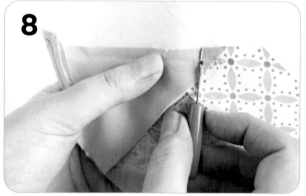

Rip out the seam if you make a mistake.

If you make a mistake, tape the seam you want to undo using Scotch brand tape. Tape the seam from the printed side and then flip the block over and rip out the seam. Resew the seam right through the tape and then remove the tape. Using the tape helps stabilize the foundation paper so it doesn't rip apart.

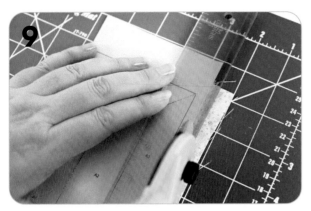

9

Trim the finished block.

When you've sewn all the pieces in order to the foundation, trim the outer edge of the finished block and include a ¼-inch seam allowance.

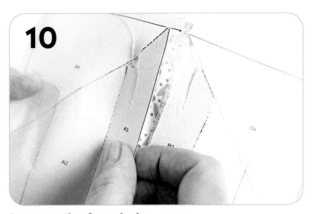

10

Remove the foundation paper.

Wait until the blocks are sewn together before removing the foundation papers. Run your thumbnail over a seam and pull gently to remove the paper. Use tweezers to remove any stubborn paper scraps.

English Paper Piecing

Like foundation paper piecing, English paper piecing ensures your finished shapes will come out perfect. With English paper piecing, you stitch fabric around a paper shape and then after the shapes are sewn together, you remove the paper. English paper piecing takes some effort, but it also allows you to sew complicated shapes, such as diamonds and hexagons, with precision.

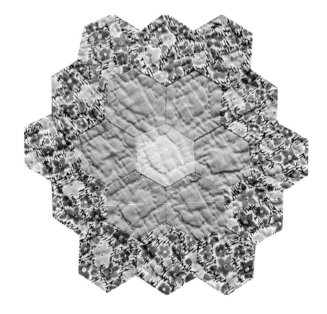

1

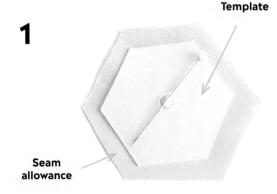

Template

Seam allowance

Pin the template to the fabric and cut around it.

You can make paper templates or purchase reusable ones. Pin the template to the back side of the fabric. Cut out the shape, leaving a rough $\frac{3}{8}$-inch seam allowance.

2

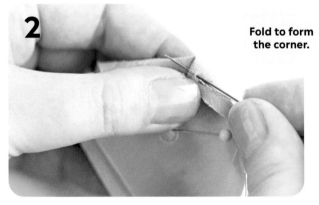

Fold to form the corner.

Baste the first corner down.

Thread a size 7 Betweens needle with hand-sewing thread. Use a contrasting color you can easily see to remove later. Make a quilter's knot. Fold one edge of the fabric over the template and then fold a neighboring edge down, forming a corner. Take two stitches in place to hold the corner down. Baste through the fabric and not the template.

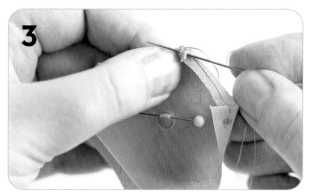

Baste the other corners.

Fold the next edge down, forming a corner. Take two more stitches at the corner to hold it down. The fabric should be taut against the template but not so tight that the template is pulled out of shape. Repeat this all the way around the shape. Knot the end to hold it. Repeat steps 1 to 3 for each shape you're using.

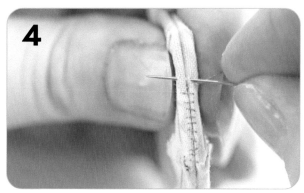

Sew the first two shapes together.

Thread an Appliqué needle with hand-sewing thread that matches your fabric. Place two shapes one on top of the other, right sides together. Make a quilter's knot and come up under the seam allowance to hide the knot. Whipstitch the top edges of the two sides together, catching only the fabric, not the template. Knot the end, then bring the needle under the seam to bury the thread.

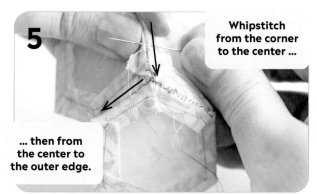

Whipstitch from the corner to the center …

… then from the center to the outer edge.

Sew the next shape to the other two.

You'll often be sewing the next shape on in a Y-seam. Knot the thread, come up under the seam, whipstitch one edge of the third piece to the edge of the first piece, and backstitch to hold it in place. Match up the other edge of the third piece with the second shape and whipstitch the two edges. Backstitch to hold the second side.

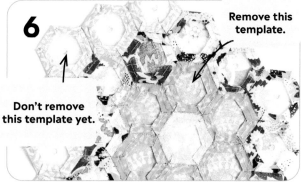

Remove this template.

Don't remove this template yet.

Remove the template.

After a shape is sewn to other shapes on all sides, you can remove that shape's template. Take out the basting stitches and gently remove the template. Some templates come with a hole in the center that helps you remove them with a knitting needle or a similar tool.

PRACTICE PROJECT

"Goodnight Moon, Goodnight Stars" Baby Quilt

This playful crib-sized quilt features a classic pinwheel block. The pinwheels are made up of half-square triangles (HSTs) that are foundation-pieced with small strips of color. Jumbo rickrack provides an unusual edge treatment.

FINISHED SIZES

- **Overall:** 40 × 40 inches
- **Foundation blocks:** 6 inches
- **Alternate blocks:** 12 inches

MATERIALS LIST

- **"Goodnight Moon, Goodnight Stars" foundation paper-piecing template and quilting motifs**
- **Foundation paper:** 20 sheets
- **White tone-on-tone:** 1½ yards (blocks, border)
- **Lime:** ½ yard (blocks)
- **Teal:** ¾ yard (blocks, binding)
- **Pink:** ⅛ yard (blocks)
- **Purple:** ¼ yard (blocks)
- **Yellow:** ½ yard (blocks)
- **Jumbo teal rickrack, 1½ inch wide:** 4¼ yards
- **Backing:** 1⅔ yards
- **Batting:** 46 inches square

CUTTING DIRECTIONS

White tone-on-tone:

• 4 squares (A), 12½ inches (alternate blocks)
• 10 squares (B), 7½ × 7½ inches, cut in half diagonally (foundation-pieced blocks)
• 4 rectangles, 2½ × 36½ inches (border)
• 4 squares (C), 2½ × 2½ inches (border)

Lime:

• 20 rectangles (A5), 2¼ × 5½ inches (blocks)
• 20 squares (A9), 2¾ × 2¾ inches (blocks)

Teal:

• 20 rectangles (A2), 2½ × 3¼ inches (blocks)
• 20 rectangles (A6), 2 × 4¾ inches (blocks)
• 5 strips, 2 × 42 or 2¼ × 42 inches or as you prefer (binding)

Pink:

• 20 rectangles (A4), 1½ × 4¾ inches (blocks)

Purple:

• 20 squares (A1), 2½ × 2½ inches (blocks)
• 20 rectangles (A7), 1¼ × 4 inches (blocks)

Yellow:

• 20 rectangles (A3), 2¼ × 4½ inches
• 20 rectangles (A8), 2½ × 3½ inches

Jumbo Rickrack:

• 4 strips, 36½ inches

Backing:

• 1 rectangle, 42 × 46 inches
• 1 rectangle, 5 × 42 inches
• 1 square, 5 × 5 inches

Note: Cut border strips before cutting anything else. Trim border strips to the right size after sewing the quilt center.

Make the Foundation Blocks

In foundation-piecing, you sew with the printed side of the foundation pattern facing up as you sew and the fabrics underneath.

1. Copy the "Goodnight Moon, Goodnight Stars" pattern onto foundation paper. Prepare 20 foundations.

2. Pin fabric A1 face up on the unprinted side of the foundation over the A1 space, leaving a ¼-inch seam allowance over the line between A1 and A2. Pin and then check that the fabric covers the A1 space with a ¼-inch seam allowance on all sides.

3. Flip to the printed side of the foundation and place a small piece of cardstock on the line between A1 and A2. Fold the foundation over the cardstock and use an Add-A-Quarter ruler to trim the excess A1 fabric to a ¼-inch seam allowance.

4. Place fabric A2 on top of A1, right sides together, aligning the edge of fabric A2 on the newly cut edge of fabric A1. Flip the foundation over to the printed side and pin on the line between A1 and A2.

5. Fold the A2 fabric over the pin and check that it's large enough to cover the space for A2 plus a ¼-inch seam allowance on all sides.

6. Turn the foundation over to the printed side and sew on the line between A1 and A2 using a shorter stitch length. Flip A2 fabric over the seam and press. Again, use cardstock to trim the unsewn edge of A2 to a ¼-inch seam allowance between A2 and A3. Align fabric A3 with the newly cut edge, check for size, and sew.

7. Continue adding fabrics in order. Trim the finished block to 6½ inches square, which includes the seam allowances. Make 20 total foundation-pieced HST blocks.

Assemble the Pinwheel Blocks

1. Sew two foundation blocks together to make Unit 1. Press open the seams. Make 10 Unit 1s. Unit 1 should measure 6½ × 12½ inches.

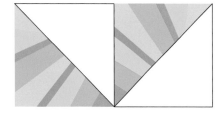

Unit 1 (make 10)

2. Sew two Unit 1s together to create a Block Z. Press open the seams. Make five Block Zs. Block Z should measure 12½ inches square.

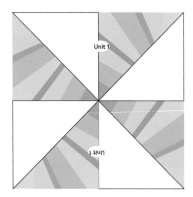

Block Z (make 5)

Assemble the Quilt Center

Quilt Assembly Diagram

1. Join white A squares and Block Zs into rows as shown in the Quilt Assembly Diagram.

2. Remove the foundation papers. Press to the white squares.

3. Join the rows together. Press the row seams in the same direction. The quilt center should measure 36½ × 36½ inches.

Add the Borders

1. Measure down the quilt center. Cut two side border strips and two strips of rickrack that same length.

2. Pin the rickrack so the middle of the rickrack is ¼ inch from one edge of the border strip. Baste the rickrack to the border strip using a scant ¼-inch seam. Repeat with the other side border strip.

3. Sew the side borders to the quilt center, catching the rickrack in the seam. To prevent the rickrack from shadowing (showing behind the white used in the blocks), trim the excess rickrack beyond the seam allowance. Press toward the quilt center.

4. Measure across the quilt center. Cut two border strips and two more strips of rickrack that same length. Baste the rickrack to the border strips. Use a scant ¼-inch seam allowance to baste.

5. Sew the white C squares to either side of the top and bottom borders, catching the ends of the rickrack in the seams. Trim the excess rickrack beyond the seam allowances so it won't shadow through. Press toward the C squares.

6. Pin the borders to the top and bottom of the quilt center, matching the seams at the C squares and the side borders. Sew borders to the top and bottom of the quilt center, catching the rickrack in the seam allowance. Trim the excess rickrack beyond the seam allowance. Press toward the quilt center. The quilt should now measure 40½ inches square.

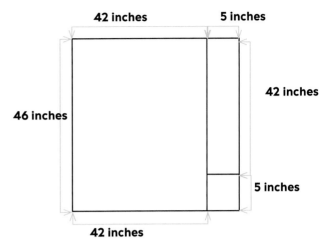

Pieced Back Assembly Diagram
Diagram shows cut sizes

42 inches · 5 inches · 42 inches · 46 inches · 5 inches · 42 inches

Quilting and Finishing

Because of the size of this quilt, you'll need to piece your backing.

1. Remove the selvages from the fabric and then piece the back as shown in the Pieced Back Assembly Diagram. Start by sewing the 5 × 42-inch rectangle to the 5 × 5-inch square along the 5-inch edge. Sew with a ½-inch seam allowance and lock your stitches at the beginning and end of the seam by backstitching. Press the seam to one side.

2. Sew the just-stitched 5 × 46-inch rectangle to the 42 × 46-inch rectangle you cut earlier. Use a ½-inch seam allowance and lock your stitches at the beginning and end of the seam by backstitching. Press the seam to one side.

3. Prepare the quilt for quilting and quilt as desired. The quilt shown uses a continuous line star pattern in the white alternate blocks. The foundation parts of Block Z were quilted using straight lines just inside the seam allowances. The white triangles in Block Z were quilted with a moon and a star.

4. Square up the quilt and bind it. Add a label and a sleeve for a wall hanging if desired.

Yardage for Alternative Sizes

	Lap	**Twin**	**Queen**
Size	64 × 76 inches	62 × 88 inches	88 × 88 inches
Block setting	5 × 6	5 × 7	7 × 7
Foundations	60	72	100
Z Blocks	15	18	25
Plain Blocks	15	17	24
White	3⅝ yards	4⅛ yards	5½ yards
Lime	⅞ yard	1⅛ yards	1½ yards
Teal	1⅜ yards	1⅔ yards	1⅞ yards
Pink	½ yard	½ yard	⅝ yard
Purple	⅝ yard	⅔ yard	⅞ yard
Yellow	1 yard	1 yard	1⅜ yards
Jumbo Rickrack	7⅞ yards	8⅜ yards	9⅞ yards
Backing	4 yards	5⅜ yards	8⅛ yards
Batting	70 × 82 inches	68 × 94 inches	94 × 94 inches

By varying the colors, you can make this quilt suitable for an adult. To make an Amish-style quilt, consider black in the background and solid colors in the half-square triangles.

chapter **7**

Appliqué

Needle-Turn Hand-Appliqué

Raw-Edge Fusible Appliqué

Turned-Edge
Machine-Appliqué

Turned-Edge Fusible
Machine-Appliqué

Practice Project:
"Funky Flowers"
Wall Hanging

Needle-Turn Hand-Appliqué

In appliqué, a fabric shape (such as a flower or a large circle) is sewn or fused to a background fabric. Appliqué can be done by hand or by machine. In needle-turn hand-appliqué, you turn under the edge of the fabric with the needle as you sew. You can turn under the edge with a bit of glue or liquid starch and a good pressing to hold the edge in place until you sew it down.

Make a template and trace the shape on your fabric.

Trace the shape onto the nonshiny side of freezer paper or template plastic and cut it out. Your template shouldn't be reversed and should look exactly like the finished shape. Lay your fabric right side up on a sandpaper board and place the template on top. Trace around the template using a marking pen or pencil. If you created a freezer paper template, iron it onto the right side of fabric shiny side down and then trace it.

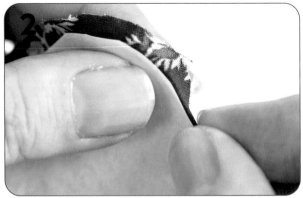

Cut out the appliqué shape and finger-press the edges.

With small, sharp appliqué scissors, cut out the shape you've traced, leaving a ³⁄₁₆-inch seam allowance. Leave a larger seam allowance along any edges that aren't turned under. Finger-press under the edges of the appliqué. Fold so the line you drew doesn't show. Don't fold under edges that go under other appliqué pieces.

Place your template on the fabric bias whenever possible. Having bias edges on your appliqué pieces will help you turn under the edges more easily.

Pin the appliqué to the background.

Cut out a background square that's slightly larger than the finished size. Pin the appliqué to the background using Appliqué/Silk pins or hold it in place using a dab of appliqué glue.

Needle

Begin appliquéing the piece.

Select a 50 or 60 weight cotton thread in a color that matches your appliqué. Select an Appliqué/Sharps, Betweens, or Straw needle in size 10 or 11. Knot your thread with a quilter's knot. Bring the needle up through the appliqué, right at the edge.

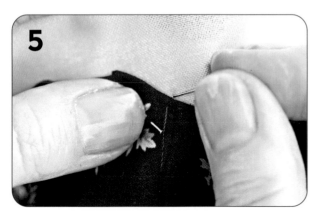

Turn under the edge and take a stitch.

Using the tip of your needle, turn under a bit of the appliqué edge and hold it under your thumb. Take a stitch into the background, directly across from where you came up in the appliqué.

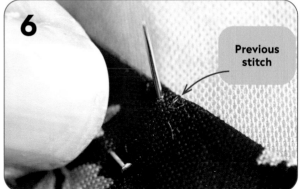

Previous stitch

Bring the needle back up into the appliqué.

Come up into the appliqué, about ⅛ inch to the left of the previous stitch, close to the edge. Pull up the needle to tighten the stitch (just barely) and then repeat steps 5 and 6 again in one motion. Turn under the edge as needed—just ahead of where you're stitching. End your stitching by running the thread under some previous stitches on the back of the piece.

Clip the dog ear.

Fold the seam allowance flat with the leading edge.

Appliqué outer points when you reach them.

Appliqué close to the outer point and begin shortening the stitch length. Take two stitches at the end of the sewing line (the point). Now you're ready to turn the other edge under. Clip off the dog ear on the seam allowance you're about to turn under and then (with the appliqué pointing up) fold the seam allowance so it's flat across.

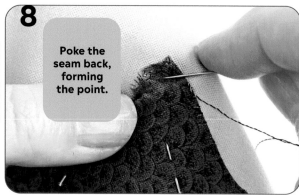

Poke the seam back, forming the point.

Stitch down the outer point.

Turn the appliqué in your hand. Use the needle to poke the tip of the seam allowance back to the left and under, then sweep the rest of the seam allowance under. Tug the thread to pull out the point if it got tucked under and then come down into the background across from the point and continue stitching.

Appliqué inner points when you reach them.

Appliqué almost to the inner point. Clip the seam allowance at the inner point straight in to the seam line. Turn under the seam allowance on the other side of the point. Then fold down the edge you're sewing to the inner point and sew to the inner point. As you sew into the inner point, catch a bit more of the appliqué rather than sew close to the edge.

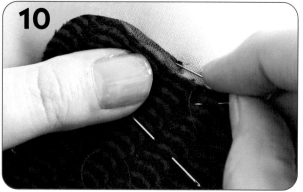

Appliqué curves.

Clip the seam allowance on the inner curves to help you turn under the edge smoothly. Don't clip outer curves. Sweep under the edge and then appliqué. For inner curves, as you near the curve, take smaller stitches and then make them farther apart as you appliqué away from the inner curve. When you're done appliquéing, trim the background to the correct size.

If you want to press your finished appliqué piece, iron it from the back on a towel to prevent crushing the appliqué. To speed up hand-appliqué, thread multiple needles at one time.

Raw-Edge Fusible Appliqué

Raw-edge fusible appliqué is one of the easiest machine-appliqué methods. With this method, lightweight fusible web is used to fuse the appliqué piece to the background. Because this method leaves a raw, unturned edge, it's a method best used for projects that are handled infrequently, such as wall hangings, table runners, and decorative items. You can finish raw-edge machine-appliqué with a straight stitch, blanket stitch, or a zigzag stitch (as shown here).

Trace the shape.

Trace your pattern's appliqué shape onto the paper side of lightweight fusible web. The shape should be the reverse of the finished shape as it will appear on your quilt. Roughly cut out the fusible. You can reduce its stiffness by cutting out the center of the fusible shape, leaving about ¼ inch around the drawn line.

Fuse the appliqué shape and cut it out.

Place the appliqué shape paper side up on the back side of your fabric and press, following the manufacturer's directions. Cover the shape with a pressing sheet before fusing to protect your iron. Roughly cut out the fused shape and then cut it again precisely on the line.

For complicated appliqué patterns with lots of pieces, consider using an appliqué pressing sheet. These silicone sheets allow you to assemble the overlapping pieces of an appliqué shape and fuse them together before fusing the assembled piece to the background fabric.

Fuse the appliqué pieces to the background.

Repeat steps 1 and 2 to prepare all appliqué pieces. Peel the paper off the back of a fused appliqué shape and fuse it to the appliqué background following the manufacturer's directions. Use a pressing sheet to protect your iron. Repeat to fuse other shapes.

Pin or fuse the stabilizer to the back.

To prevent the appliqué from puckering from your stitching, fuse the back side of the appliqué block with a cutaway, tearaway, or washaway stabilizer, following the manufacturer's directions.

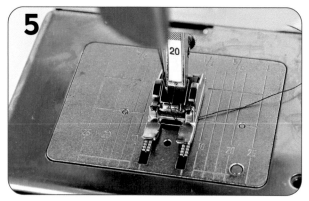

Prepare your machine to appliqué with a zigzag stitch.

Insert an Appliqué/Sharps 80/12 needle, then thread your machine with 50 or 60 weight cotton thread that matches your appliqué. Use this same thread in the bobbin. Insert a zigzag stitch plate and an open toe or zigzag foot.

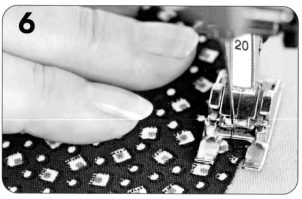

Lock the first stitches.

Pull up the bobbin thread, select a straight stitch, reduce its stitch length, and take a few stitches at the edge of the appliqué to lock your stitching. Change to a zigzag stitch and set the stitch length to 1.0 to 1.5mm. Adjust the stitch width to about 1.0mm.

Appliqué the shape with a zigzag stitch.

Align the stitch so when it zags to the outside, it just hits the edge of the background fabric. The majority of your zigzag stitch should fall onto the appliqué piece.

On outside curves, pivot when you zag.

Whenever you need to pivot, stop with the needle down. On an outside curve, pivot when the needle zags to the right, into the background. Raise the presser foot, pivot the fabric, lower the presser foot, and continue. Pivot more often on sharp curves than on gentle ones.

You can also finish your appliqué with a straight stitch or a blanket stitch.

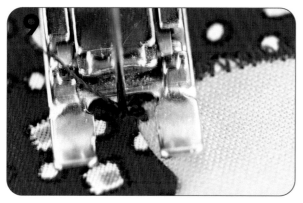

On inside curves, pivot when you zig.

Stop with the needle down to pivot. On an inside curve, pivot when the needle zigs to the left, toward the appliqué. Pivot more often on sharp curves than on gentle ones. Raise the presser foot, pivot the fabric, lower the presser foot, and continue.

At sharp outside points, pivot when you zag.

Stop with the needle down to pivot. On a sharp corner, pivot when the needle zags to the right, into the background. Raise the presser foot, pivot the fabric around the corner, lower the presser foot, and continue.

At sharp inside points, pivot when you zig.

With a sharp inside point, you want to pivot when the needle zigs to the left into the appliqué. Stop with the needle down at a point that extends from the opposite edge. Raise the presser foot, pivot the fabric, lower the presser foot, and continue.

Lock the last stitches.

As you near where you started, make sure you've clipped your starting threads. Stop with the needle on the right, in the background fabric. Change to a straight stitch with a reduced stitch length. Take a few short stitches at the edge of the appliqué to lock your stitching. Remove the stabilizer from the back of the block behind the appliqué by following the manufacturer's directions and trim the appliqué.

Turned-Edge Machine-Appliqué

When appliquéing by machine, there are several methods from which you can choose. Turned-edge appliqué is sturdier than raw-edge appliqué and is suitable for all purposes, including quilts, clothing, wall hangings, mug rugs, table runners, and decorative items.

Cut out the template and press it to fabric.

Trace the shape onto the nonshiny side of freezer paper and cut it out with paper scissors. The shape should be the reverse of the finished shape as it will appear on your quilt. Press the template shiny side down onto the back of your fabric.

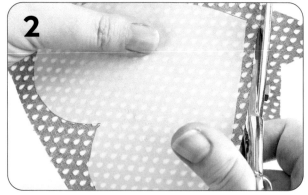

Cut out the appliqué shape.

Cut out the shape, leaving a $\frac{3}{16}$-inch seam allowance. Leave a larger seam allowance on edges that aren't turned under. (These are the edges that fit under other appliqué pieces.)

Finish a machine-appliqué edge with a zigzag, blanket, or straight stitch.

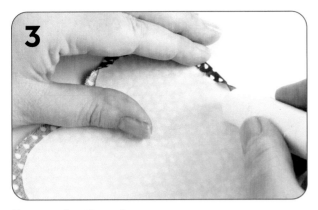

Turn under the edges.

Dab the underside of the appliqué edge with a glue stick or sizing. Fold the appliqué edges under, clipping inner curves and points. Use a cuticle stick to nudge the seam allowance and remove any folds or pleats that appear on the front of the appliqué. Don't fold the edges that go under other pieces.

Press the edges to fix them and then remove the template.

To keep the turned edges in place, press with a hot iron. Let the piece cool and then gently slip out the template. Spray with Best Press and re-press the edges as needed. Repeat steps 1 to 4 to prepare all appliqué pieces in your pattern.

Pin or glue appliqué pieces in place.

Use appliqué or silk pins to pin appliqué pieces to a background that's cut larger than needed, fitting edges underneath other pieces as needed. You can also fix appliqué pieces in place with a dab of appliqué glue.

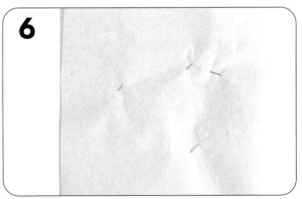

Pin or fuse the stabilizer to the back.

To prevent the appliqué from puckering while stitching, prepare the fabric behind the appliqué with a cutaway, tearaway, or washaway stabilizer, following the manufacturer's instructions.

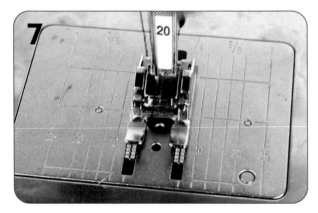

Prepare your machine to appliqué with a straight stitch.

Insert a size 80/12 Appliqué/Sharps needle. Thread your machine with 50 or 60 weight cotton thread that matches your appliqué; use the same thread in the bobbin. Prepare your machine with a straight-stitch plate and an open-toe foot.

Lock the first stitches.

Select a straight stitch and reduce its stitch length. Pull up the bobbin thread and take a few locking stitches at the edge of the appliqué.

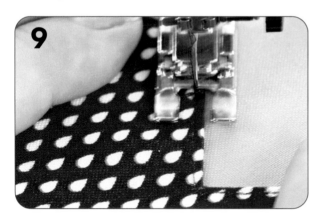

Appliqué the shape with a straight stitch.

Stitch around the shape, staying close to the edge of the appliqué. Pivot on curves and corners with the needle down. Raise the presser foot, pivot the fabric, lower the presser foot, and continue.

Lock the last stitches.

As you near where you started, make sure you've clipped your starting threads. Reduce the stitch length and take a few short stitches at the edge of the appliqué to lock your stitching. Remove the stabilizer from the back of the background fabric behind the appliqué by following the manufacturer's directions and trim the appliqué background to the correct size.

If you want to use invisible thread to stitch your machine-appliqué, use a 70/10 Appliqué/Sharps needle and a 60 weight cotton or bobbin fill in the bobbin.

Turned-Edge Fusible Machine-Appliqué

Turned-edge fusible machine-appliqué uses lightweight fusible interfacing to help create the turned edge. Turning the edges of your appliqué prevents them from unraveling when washed, making it a good technique for all types of projects. Using a fusible simplifies the process of placing appliqué pieces, but you still need to stitch down the edges of the appliqué.

Trace the appliqué shape.

Trace the shape onto the nonshiny (nonfusible) side of lightweight fusible interfacing. The shape should be the reverse of the finished shape as it will appear on your quilt. Using your paper scissors, roughly cut out the fusible interfacing.

Pin fusible interfacing to fabric and cut it out.

Place the interfacing on fabric, with the shiny fusible side against the right side of the fabric. Pin the interfacing in place, but don't iron. Using fabric scissors, cut out the interfacing and the fabric roughly, leaving a wide margin outside the drawn line.

Sew the interfacing to the appliqué shape.

Use a slightly shorter stitch length and regular 50 weight cotton thread to sew on the drawn line all the way around the shape.

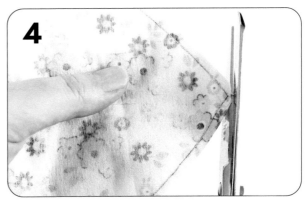

Cut out the appliqué shape.

Cut the shape out precisely using small, sharp appliqué scissors. Leave a scant ¼-inch seam allowance. Clip inner curves, trim the tip off outer points, and clip straight in to any inner points.

Turn appliqué shape right side out.

Pull the interfacing away from the fabric and cut a slit in the center of the interfacing. Use the slit to turn the shape right side out. Poke out points and curved edges using a knitting needle or similar tool. Finger press the edges, but don't iron. Repeat steps 1 to 5 to prepare all the appliqué pieces in your pattern.

Fuse appliqué pieces in place.

Cut a background square slightly larger than needed. Fuse the appliqué pieces to the background, following the manufacturer's directions. Cover the appliqué with a pressing sheet to protect your iron.

7

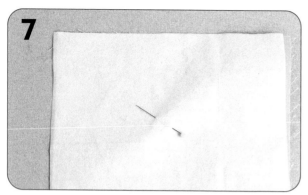

Pin or fuse the stabilizer to the back of the background fabric behind the appliqué.

To prevent the appliqué from puckering when you stitch, back the appliqué with a cutaway, tearaway, or washaway stabilizer, following the manufacturer's directions.

8

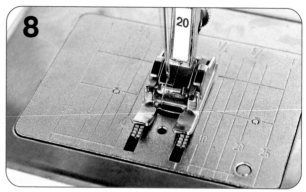

Prepare your machine to appliqué with a blanket stitch.

Insert an Appliqué/Sharps 80/12 needle, then thread your machine with 50 or 60 weight cotton thread that matches your appliqué. Use this same thread in the bobbin. Prepare your machine with a zigzag stitch plate and open-toe foot.

9

Lock the first stitches.

Pull up the bobbin thread, select a straight stitch, reduce its stitch length, and take a few locking stitches. Change to a blanket stitch and adjust its width and length to about 2.0 to 2.5mm.

10

Appliqué the shape with a blanket stitch.

Align the stitch so the straight part runs along the outer edge of the appliqué, on the background, while the perpendicular "nibbles" land on the appliqué itself. Using an open-toe foot will help you see the edge clearly.

Instead of a blanket stitch, you can also use a straight stitch, zigzag stitch, blind hem, or another decorative stitch to sew the appliqué.

On outside curves, pivot on a straight stitch.

Pivot when the needle is down in the background during a straight stitch, not when it's on the left taking a "nibble." After pivoting the fabric, make sure the appliqué is positioned so the stitch to the left is perpendicular to the appliqué edge.

On inside curves, pivot when the needle is on the right.

Try not to pivot too much on curves in order to avoid creating a V with the "nibble" part of the stitch. To do that, keep the "nibble" part of the stitch (the left part of the stitch) perpendicular to the appliqué edge as much as possible.

Adjust the stitch length at sharp points to place the nibble on the point.

You can hold back a bit to lengthen a stitch or even back up slightly in order to have the nibble part of the stitch hit the point exactly. Pivot only when the needle is on the right, in the background.

Lock the last stitches.

As you near where you started, make sure you've clipped your starting threads. Stop at a point with the needle on the right, in the background fabric. Change to a straight stitch with a reduced stitch length. Take a few short stitches at the edge of the appliqué to lock your stitching. Remove the stabilizer from the back of the background fabric behind the appliqué, following the manufacturer's directions. Trim the background to the size indicated on your pattern.

"Funky Flowers" Wall Hanging

Practice your new appliqué skills by making this funky flower wall hanging. It combines turned-edge fusible appliqué with hourglass blocks to create a distinctive look.

FINISHED SIZES

- **Overall:** 30 × 25 inches
- **Blocks:** 5-inch hourglass units

MATERIALS LIST

- **"Funky Flowers" appliqué templates**
- **Lightweight fusible interfacing:** ⅔ yard
- **Stabilizer:** 25 × 25 inches
- **Black-on-white geometric fabric:** ¾ yard (appliqué background)
- **White-on-black geometric fabric #1:** ¼ yard (appliqué, blocks)
- **White-on-black geometric fabric #2:** ¼ yard (appliqué, blocks)
- **White-on-black geometric fabric #3:** ¼ yard (appliqué, blocks)
- **White-on-black geometric fabric #4:** ¼ yard (appliqué, blocks)
- **White-on-black geometric fabric #5:** ¼ yard (appliqué, binding)
- **White-on-black geometric fabric #6:** Scrap, 5 × 7 inches (appliqué)
- **Rose batik:** Scrap, 5 × 5 inches (appliqué)
- **Orange batik:** Scrap, 3 × 1 inches (appliqué)

MATERIALS LIST (CONTINUED)

- **Blue batik:** Scrap, 5 × 4 inches (appliqué)
- **Lime green batik:** Scrap, 5 × 3 inches (appliqué)
- **Backing:** 1 yard
- **Batting:** 36 × 31 inches

CUTTING DIRECTIONS

Black-on-white geometric:
- 1 square (A), 27 × 27 inches (appliqué background)

White-on-black geometric #1:
- 1 pattern L (vase)
- 1 pattern J (flower)
- 2 squares (B), 6½ × 6½ inches (blocks)

White-on-black geometric #2:
- 1 pattern M (flower)
- 1 pattern I (flower center)
- 2 squares (B), 6½ × 6½ inches (blocks)

White-on-black geometric #3:
- 1 pattern S, T, U, V, W (flower)
- 2 squares (B), 6½ × 6½ inches (blocks)

White-on-black geometric #4:
- 1 pattern A, B, C, D, E (flower)
- 1 pattern Y, Y1 (leaf)
- 2 squares (B), 6½ × 6½ inches (blocks)

White-on-black geometric #5:
- 1 pattern M, O (flower)
- 3 strips, 2 or 2¼ inches or as wide as you prefer (binding)

White-on-black geometric #6:
- 1 pattern G (flower)
- 2 patterns X (leaf)

CUTTING DIRECTIONS (CONTINUED)

Rose batik:
- 2 patterns F (flower)
- 4 patterns Q (flower)
- 1 pattern H (flower)

Orange batik:
- 3 patterns F (flower)

Blue batik:
- 1 pattern K, N, R (flower)
- 2 patterns F (flower)

Lime batik:
- 1 pattern N, P (flower)
- 2 patterns F (flower)

Backing:
- 1 rectangle, 36 × 31 inches

Block Z

Unit 2

Quilt Assembly Diagram

Making the Hourglass Units

Although you only need five hourglass units for this project, this method makes eight. The extra units can be pieced into the backing or used to make a label on the back of the quilt.

1. Use Method 1 to make eight hourglass units. Use one white-on-black geometric #1 B square and one white-on-black geometric #3 B square to make two half-square triangles (HSTs). Press to the dark. Repeat to make four HSTs total.

2. Use one geometric #2 B square and one geometric #4 B square to make two HSTs. Repeat to make four HSTs total.

3. Place one geometric #1/#3 HST on top of one geometric #2/#4 HST, butting the seams against each other. Mark the diagonal and sewing lines, then sew to create two hourglass blocks (Unit 1). Repeat with the remaining half-square triangles to create eight hourglass units total. Trim these hourglass units to 5½ inches square. Press open the seams.

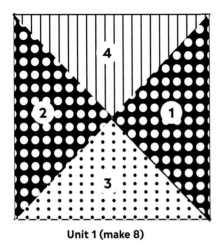

Unit 1 (make 8)

Appliquéing the Quilt Center

You'll appliqué the vase of flowers using the turned-edge fusible appliqué method.

1. Fold appliqué background A square in half both ways to find the center.

2. Trace the appliqué shapes onto the nonfusible side of lightweight fusible interfacing. Cut out each shape, leaving a rough ¼-inch seam allowance. Place a shape fusible side down, on the right side of the appliqué fabric, pin, and sew on the drawn line. Cut a slit in the interfacing and turn the shape right side out. Finger-press the edges.

Block Z—Appliqué Layout Diagram

3. After preparing all the appliqué shapes, lay them out on the background square A as shown in the Appliqué Layout Diagram and fuse the shapes in place.

4. Pin or fuse the stabilizer behind the appliqué. Stitch around each shape with thread that matches the appliqué. Use a straight stitch, loose zigzag, or blanket stitch as you prefer. The sample quilt was stitched using a loose zigzag.

5. Press the appliqué from the back and trim the background to 25½ × 25½ inches.

Adding the Hourglass Units

1. Arrange five hourglass units in a column. Use an arrangement that pleases you. Here, the hourglass units are rotated so the almost-black triangles touch the almost-white triangles.

Unit 2 (make 1)

2. Sew hourglass units to make Unit 2. Press open the seams. Unit 2 should measure 5½ × 25½ inches.

3. Sew Unit 2 to the appliqué square as shown in the Quilt Assembly Diagram. Press to the appliqué square. The quilt should measure 30½ × 25½ inches.

Quilting and Finishing

1. Remove selvages from the backing fabric before basting the quilt. Prepare the quilt for quilting and quilt as desired. The sample quilt was quilted with a mixture of geometric shapes and curved lines that follow the appliqué flowers. The hourglass units were quilted in an orange peel pattern using half-circles.

2. Square up the quilted quilt and bind it. Add a label and a sleeve for hanging.

Assembling a Quilt Top

Choose a Block Setting

You can arrange quilt blocks in a variety of layouts or settings, such as horizontal or diagonal. In addition, you can separate quilt blocks with sashing (small borders around each block), rotate the orientation of blocks, and even alternate two different blocks to create interesting patterns.

Sashing

Horizontal or straight set Blocks are arranged in horizontal rows. This is the most commonly used block setting. Often, setting two different blocks next to each other creates an interesting secondary pattern.

Horizontal set with sashing Blocks are arranged in horizontal rows, but they're set apart by sashing (pieced or not) that frames each block.

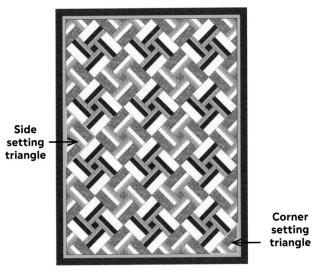

Side setting triangle

Corner setting triangle

Diagonal or on-point set Blocks are arranged in diagonal rows, with or without sashing. To make a quilt top rectangular, setting triangles (pieced or not) are added to the sides and corners.

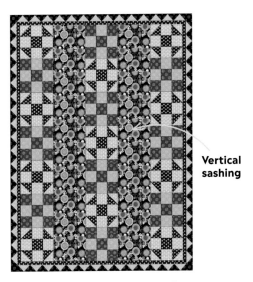

Vertical sashing

Vertical or stripy set Blocks are set in vertical columns and can be arranged on point or straight. Blocks in the vertical columns are often separated by sashing.

Half-drop

Vertical on-point half-drop If the blocks in a vertical are set on point and offset by a half-drop (the first block in a column is shifted down by half a block), the blocks create a zigzag pattern where the block columns meet.

Medallion setting Borders are arranged around a central block that serves as a focal point. The central block can be on point or straight. The borders can be plain, pieced or appliquéd, or comprised of separate blocks arranged as a border.

Sew Quilt Blocks Together

Before sewing blocks together, arrange them on a design wall so you can achieve the most pleasing arrangement of colors. You'll sew quilt blocks together in the same way you sewed the individual units of a quilt block: by sewing the blocks into rows and then sewing the rows together. For quilts in which the blocks are arranged in a vertical (stripy) set, you'll sew together the blocks in each column first and then sew the columns together. In a medallion setting, blocks are arranged and added like borders around the center block. If you're using sashing, it's added before you assemble the rows.

1

Number every block.

Lay out your blocks on a design wall.

Even if the quilt pattern suggests a certain layout, you might be happier with a different block setting, so try out several. Number blocks in the upper-left corner of every block to help you maintain their orientation and arrangement. Use a row number (1) and column letter (A) to mark blocks.

2

Sew blocks into logical groups.

For a standard or on-point (diagonal) set, sew blocks into rows. For a vertical set, sew blocks into columns. Press block seams in even rows/columns in the opposite direction of odd rows/columns. For a medallion quilt, sew adjacent blocks together to form borders and then sew them to the central block as you might sew borders on a quilt.

3

Sew rows (groups) together.

Sew rows or columns together by pinning diagonally just past each connecting seam and then sewing the long seam. If the seams in each row are pressed in opposite directions, they'll nestle. If not, it's okay to flip seams in a different direction in order to make them nestle. The twist that happens halfway down the seam in such a case will disappear when you add batting and finish the quilt.

4

Give your quilt a final press.

As you add each row, press row seams in the same direction. If you're sewing together columns, press column seams in the same direction. After you've sewn the quilt center together, re-press all the seams so they're crisp and flat. Use Best Press as needed. Your quilt is now ready for borders if you choose to add any.

Add Setting Triangles

Setting triangles are used with on-point (diagonal) settings, in which you sew blocks together in diagonal rows. Adding corner and setting triangles gives your quilt square corners and straight edges.

1 Cut side setting triangles.

To calculate the size of the square from which to cut side setting triangles, multiply the finished size of your blocks (plus any sashing) by 1.414, add 1¼ inch, and round to the nearest ⅛ inch. Cut the square in half diagonally in each direction to get four side setting triangles. Make as many side setting triangles as needed for your pattern.

2 Cut corner setting triangles.

To calculate the square from which to cut corner setting triangles, divide the finished size of your blocks by 1.414, add ⅞ inch, and round to the nearest ⅛ inch. Cut this square in half diagonally to get two corner setting triangles. Make four corner setting triangles.

3

Corner setting triangle

Side setting triangle

Block

Lay out your blocks and setting triangles on a design wall.

Laying out your quilt will make it easier to sew it together correctly. Be careful when handling the bias edges on setting triangles.

4

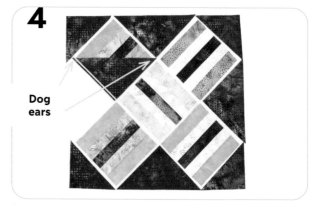

Dog ears

Sew side setting triangles onto either side of the first block.

Align the right angle of the triangle with the bottom edge of the block. A small triangle point, or dog ear, will appear beyond the top and side edges of the block. Pin and then sew. Repeat to add the setting triangle to the other side of the first block. Press toward the setting triangles.

5

Dog ears

Sew the corner setting triangle onto this unit.

Fold the corner setting triangle and the first block in half. Use the fold to align the triangle on top of the block, matching the centers of the two sides. The tips (dog ears) of the corner triangle will appear on either end of the block when properly aligned. Pin and sew, then press to the corner setting triangle.

6

Add setting triangles to the rest of the rows.

Sew rows together, adding side and corner setting triangles to each row as needed. Press toward the setting triangles. Plan the other pressing so the block seams in each row go in opposite directions and will nestle (butt) together when the rows are joined.

7

Sew the diagonal rows together.

Pin diagonally at the seam intersections and then sew the first two rows together. Notice the dog ears that appear when the setting triangles meet. Sew and press toward the second row. Repeat to sew the rest of the rows, pressing the row seams in the same direction.

8

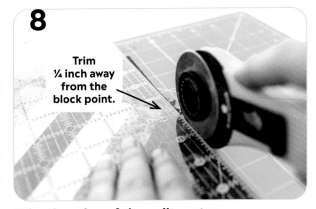

Trim ¼ inch away from the block point.

Trim the edge of the quilt center.

Align the ¼-inch line on the ruler with the corners of the blocks on one side of the quilt center, then trim. To trim the next side, align a horizontal line on the ruler with the newly cut edge. Align the ¼-inch line as before, then trim. Repeat to trim all four sides of the quilt center. You can add borders now if desired.

Add Sashing

If you choose, you can surround quilt blocks with sashing, or small borders. The sashing separates the blocks so they can shine on their own while also allowing you to make a larger quilt using fewer blocks. Sashing can be plain or pieced. It can also include cornerstones, or squares at the intersections of sashing strips. In a vertical setting, a sashing is often used to separate columns of blocks.

1

Cut pieces for sashing.

Cut sashing strips in a width that's proportional to the size of your blocks. Audition sashing by laying blocks on your fabric and playing with the spacing between blocks. Cut the sashing strips the desired width plus ½ inch. If you're using cornerstones, cut each square the width of the sashing strips.

2

Sew sashing to the right side of every block.

Cut side sashing from the sashing strips—the unfinished height of your blocks. Sew with the block on top and the sashing on the bottom to better prevent block seams from flipping. Press to the sashing.

3

Sew sashing to the left side of the first block in every row.

Sew with the block on top so you can keep the block seams from flipping. Press to the sashing.

4

Sew sashing to the bottom of every block or row.

If you're using cornerstones, cut the bottom sashing from the sashing strips—the unfinished width of your blocks. Sew cornerstones to the right of the bottom sashings first (and to the left end of the sashing strip for the first block in each row). Press to the dark and then sew sashing to the bottom of every block. If you're not using cornerstones, sew blocks in each row together. Measure the unfinished length of your rows, then cut bottom and top sashing to this length. Add a bottom sashing strip to each row.

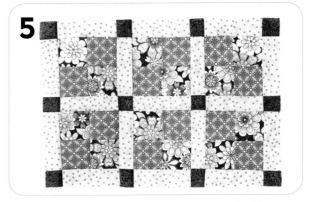

5

Sew sashing to the top of the blocks in the first row.

If you're using cornerstones, sew them to the right end of the strips first (and to the left end of the sashing strip for the first block in the top row). Then sew the sashing to the top of the blocks in the first row. Sew the blocks in each row together and sew the rows together. Press to the sashing throughout. If you're not using cornerstones, cut and sew a long sashing strip to the top of the first row and then sew the rows together.

Add Straight Borders

Adding a quilt border is a great way to frame your blocks and enhance the quilt's overall design. You can add as many borders to a quilt as you like. The simplest borders to add are straight (butted) borders that aren't pieced. To cut fabric for straight borders, fold the raw edges of fabric together (so the selvages are on the left and right). This is called "cutting from the lengthwise grain" and it reduces stretching. However, if you fold fabric with the selvages together, you can cut from the crosswise grain and use less fabric to create your borders (although you'll have to sew the smaller pieces together).

Borders with widths that are proportional to the blocks are the most attractive. For example, a 10-inch block might have a border that's 1, 1¼, 2, 2½, or 5 inches wide. You can easily add cornerstones to a straight border if desired.

Measure and fix blocks as you sew so they're the same size. Even then, your quilt center might not be perfectly square. You can fix minor problems by adding borders cut from lengthwise grain and measured to fit.

1

Cut the side borders.

Cut two side borders the desired width. Lay the quilt center flat, measure down its center, and trim the side borders to this length.

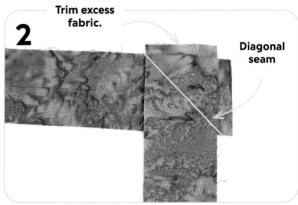

2

Trim excess fabric.

Diagonal seam

Join side border strips together as needed.

If a single border strip isn't long enough, join the strips in a diagonal seam. Lay one strip horizontally, then place the second strip on top at the right end. Mark the diagonal, then backstitch at the start and end of the seam. Trim and then press the seam to the side. Join wide strips straight across to reduce the visibility of the seam.

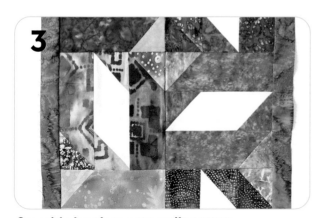

3

Sew side borders onto quilt center.

Sew borders to each side, backstitching at the beginning and end of the seam. If one side of the quilt is bigger than its border by a little bit, match the center of the border and the side, pin, and then sew with the quilt on the bottom to ease it in. Press to the borders.

4

Cut, trim, and sew borders to the quilt center.

Cut the top and bottom borders the desired width. Join border strips if needed and then measure the quilt across the quilt's center and trim the borders to this length. If the borders have cornerstones, sew them to either end of the top and bottom borders before adding them to the quilt. Sew borders to the top and bottom of the quilt and press to the borders.

Add Mitered Borders

A miter is a diagonal seam. When you miter quilt borders, the result looks like a picture frame. Like all borders, mitered borders look best when their width is proportional to the width of the quilt block. For example, if your quilt has 12-inch blocks, a border that measures 1, 2, 3, 4, or 6 inches wide will be attractive because those are factors of 12.

If you have more than one border, sew the border strips together first and then cut the border set to the right length.

1

Measure and cut the borders.

Measure across and down the quilt's center. To that measurement, add twice the width of the border plus 4 inches. For example, for 3-inch side borders, you'd add 10 inches to the quilt's length measurement.

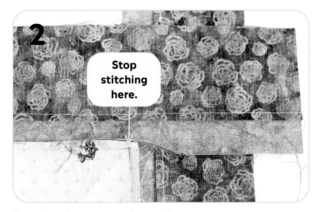

2

Stop stitching here.

Sew borders onto the quilt center.

Match the centers of one side of the quilt and its border, then pin. Sew the border, beginning and ending ¼ inch from the edges of the quilt. Backstitch at the beginning and end of the seam. Repeat for the other side as well as the top and bottom borders, beginning and ending the seams ¼ inch from the quilt edge.

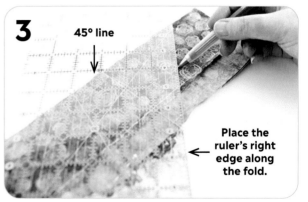

3 45° line

Place the ruler's right edge along the fold.

Mark the miters.

Mark dots at the spots where you stopped stitching each border. Fold the quilt diagonally, aligning and pinning the edges and the seams of all borders. Place a ruler's 45° line on the outer edge of the border and its right edge along the fold. Mark the diagonal miter from the dot where the border seams end out to the corner. Repeat for the other three corners.

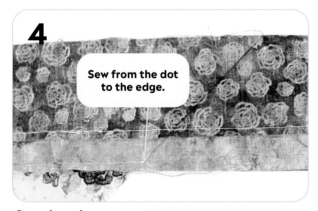

4

Sew from the dot to the edge.

Sew the miter seams.

Sew on the diagonal line you marked, starting at the marked dot and backstitching at the beginning and end of the seam. Repeat to sew the miter for each border corner.

5

Trim and press.

After checking that the miter lies flat and there are no puckers or tucks, trim the excess borders and press open the seam allowances.

Add Special Borders

Let the design of your blocks be your inspiration for a special border. You can often improve a quilt's design by adding pieced borders, appliqué borders, or other special treatments. Even for a beginner, it's easy to sew together a scrappy collection of squares or rectangles to create a simple pieced border. The type and number of borders you add to a quilt can greatly affect how it looks.

Pieced Borders

Pieced borders can be made up of squares, rectangles, or pieced units. Consider using one of the same units that appears in your quilt top for a pieced border, such as four-patches, half-square triangles, or flying geese.

The border units should fit perfectly along the width and length of the quilt center. To figure out the best fit, measure down the quilt's center, subtract ½ inch, and divide by the finished width of the units you want to use in your border. Measure across the quilt's center and repeat the process by dividing by the finished width of your units.

You might need to make adjustments to get your pieced border to fit. Add a spacer (inner border) to change the length and width of the quilt center so it's easily divisible by the width of the units you want to use to piece your border.

Borders that use squares and rectangles are the easiest to adjust. Don't let their simplicity fool you—pieced borders that use only squares and rectangles can be quite striking.

The top and bottom borders don't need to be exactly the same width as the side borders. If it works better to use 2 × 3-inch rectangles on the top and bottom and 2½ × 3-inch rectangles along the sides, do that. It will be hard to notice the difference in size.

Pieced border with half-square triangles

Spacer

Appliqué Borders

Add appliqué to a border before sewing it to the quilt center. Start with a larger background than needed for the border because the appliqué process will cause it to shrink. Trim the border to the right size after appliquéing.

You might want to appliqué a few motifs after attaching your border to place them over a seam or around a corner.

Appliqué border

Flange

A flange is a bit of folded fabric that accents an edge, like the flange that accents the pillowcase pattern in this book. To create a ½-inch flange, cut a 1½-inch strip and press it in half. Align the raw edges of the flange with the raw edge of the quilt center and sandwich it between the quilt center and the border. Sew, then press toward the border.

Piping

Piping is created by wrapping a cotton cord in fabric and sewing it close to the cording using a zipper foot. Piping adds a touch of color and texture to a border.

Foundation Paper Pieced Borders

With foundation paper piecing, you can be very creative with your borders, like with these curved flying geese.

Prairie Point Borders

A prairie point is a square of fabric folded into a triangle. You can sew prairie points around the edge of your quilt or into a border, as shown here.

Foundation paper pieced border

"Peppermint Twist" Twin Quilt

Once your quilt blocks are pieced, you can arrange them in a variety of settings. This quilt uses an on-point (diagonal) setting, which requires setting triangles to make the sides of the quilt straight. The quilt is quick to make because you construct the blocks using strip sets. If you use the red and white fabrics as shown, prewash to prevent the colors from bleeding.

FINISHED SIZES

- **Overall:** 67½ × 87¼ inches
- **Blocks:** 14 inches

MATERIALS LIST

- **Cherry red batik:** 1¼ yards (blocks)
- **Dark red batik:** 3½ yards (blocks, setting triangles, Border #2)
- **White:** 1⅔ yards (blocks)
- **Red-and-white diagonal stripe:** 1⅝ yards (blocks, Border #1, straight binding)
- **Backing:** 4⅞ yards
- **Batting:** Twin or full size, 74 × 94 inches

CUTTING DIRECTIONS

Cherry red batik:
• 12 strips, 3½ × 42 inches (strip sets)
• 12 squares (A), 2½ × 2½ inches (blocks)

Dark red batik: (See "Cutting the Fabric")
• 6 strips, 3½ × 42 inches (strip sets)
• 4 strips, 3½ × 105 inches (Border #2)
• 3 squares, 21⅛ inches (side setting triangles)
• 2 squares, 10⅞ inches (corner setting triangles)
• 6 squares (A), 2½ × 2½ inches (blocks)

White:
• 18 strips, 1¼ × 42 inches (strip sets)
• 18 strips, 2 × 42 inches (strip sets)

Red-and-white diagonal stripe:
• 18 strips, 1¼ × 42 inches (strip sets)
• 8 strips, 1 × 42 inches (Border #1)
• 8 strips, 2 × 42 or 2½ × 42 inches or as you prefer (binding)

Note: If you can't find a diagonal striped fabric, cut bias binding from a 30-inch square of regular striped fabric to create the same look.

Backing:
• 2 strips, 74 × 42 inches
• 1 strip, 12 × 42 inches
• 1 rectangle, 12 × 3 inches

Note: Cut border strips before cutting anything else. Trim the border strips to the right size after sewing the quilt center.

Cutting the Fabric

In order to get the required pieces from your dark red batik fabric, follow these instructions.

1. Cut six 3½ × 42-inch strips.

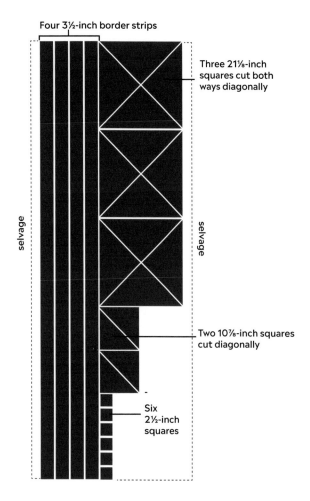

Four 3½-inch border strips

Three 21⅛-inch squares cut both ways diagonally

selvage

selvage

Two 10⅞-inch squares cut diagonally

Six 2½-inch squares

2. Refold the fabric, with the selvages on the sides. Cut four 3½ × 105-inch border strips from the lengthwise grain.

3. Cut three 21⅛-inch squares. Cut each square diagonally in both directions. Set aside two triangles for another project.

4. Cut two 10⅞-inch squares cut once diagonally, for corner setting triangles.

5. Cut six 2½-inch squares.

Assembling the Block Units

1. Piece the strip sets for the cherry red blocks by sewing one cherry red 3½-inch strip to one white 2-inch strip, then press to the dark. Sew one 1¼-inch red-and-white striped strip to one white 1¼-inch strip, then press to the dark. Sew the two sets together, placing the striped strip between the two white strips, and press to the dark. The strip set should measure 6½ inches wide. Repeat to make 12 cherry red strip sets.

2. Subcut each strip set into four 6½ × 8½-inch rectangles (Unit 1), for a total of 48 Unit 1s.

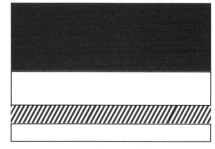

Unit 1 (make 48)

3. Piece the strip sets for the dark red blocks by sewing one dark red 3½-inch strip to one white 2-inch strip, then press to the dark. Sew one 1¼-inch red-and-white striped strip to one white 1¼-inch strip, then press to the dark. Sew the two sets together, placing the striped strip between the two white strips, and press to the dark. The strip set should measure 6½ inches wide. Repeat to make six dark red strip sets.

4. Subcut each strip set into four 6½ × 8½-inch rectangles (Unit 2), for a total of 24 Unit 2s.

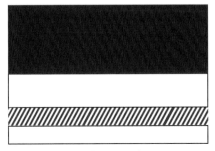

Unit 2 (make 24)

Assembling the Quilt Blocks

1. Using partial seams, join Unit 1s and cherry red A squares to create Block Z. Press to the red center square. Make 12 Block Zs. Blocks should measure 14½ × 14½ inches.

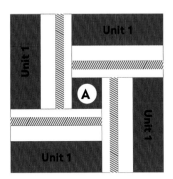

Block Z (make 12)

2. Using partial seams, join Unit 2s and dark red A squares to create Block Y. Press to the red center square. Make six Block Ys. Blocks should measure 14½ × 14½ inches.

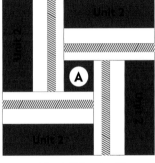

Block Y (make 6)

Assembling the Quilt Center

Quilt Assembly Diagram

1. Using the Quilt Assembly Diagram, arrange blocks in diagonal rows on your design wall. Focus on the placement of Block Zs and Block Ys. Add corner and setting triangles.

2. Sew the blocks together to make each diagonal row. Press toward the Block Ys. Add the side and/or corner setting triangles after joining the blocks, then press toward the setting triangles. The center should measure 59½ × 79¼ inches.

3. Sew the rows together. Press the seams in one direction.

Adding the Borders

1. Sew two 1 × 42-inch red-and-white striped Border #1 strips together to create a 1 × 83½-inch strip. Repeat to create four Border #1 strips.

2. Measure down the quilt center and cut two Border #1 strips that length. Sew these strips to the sides of the quilt center. Press toward the strips.

3. Measure across the quilt center and cut the other two Border #1 strips that length. Sew these strips to the top and bottom of the quilt center. Press toward the strips. The quilt should measure 61½ × 81¼ inches.

4. Measure down the quilt center and cut two dark red Border #2 strips that length. Sew these strips to the sides of the quilt center. Press toward the dark.

5. Measure across the quilt center and cut the other two Border #2 strips that length. Sew these strips to the top and bottom of the quilt center and press toward the dark. The quilt should measure 67½ × 87¼ inches.

Quilting and Finishing

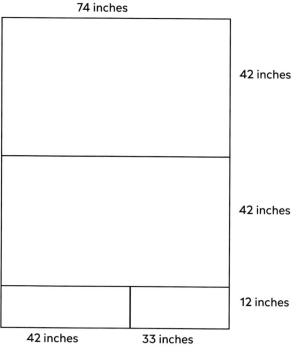

Pieced Back Diagram
(shows cut sizes)

1. Make sure you've removed the selvages from the backing and then sew the two 74 × 42-inch strips together along the 74-inch side with a wide ½-inch seam. Sew the 12 × 42-inch strip and the 12 × 33-inch strip together along the 12-inch side with a wide seam. Backstitch at the beginning and end of all seams. Sew this strip to the other two strips to create a quilt back that's roughly 74 × 94 inches. Press open the seams.

2. Quilt as desired. The sample quilt was quilted with swirling feathers radiating from the center of each block.

3. Square up the quilted quilt and bind it. Add a label.

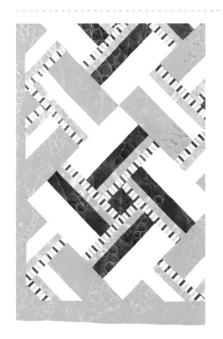

"Water Vortex" features two blocks with alternate color placement and uses pieced setting triangles, resulting in a dramatically different look. To make the setting triangles, partially piece 14 more Block Ys. For the corner setting triangles, add two Unit 2s to one A square; for the side setting triangles, add three Unit 2s instead. Sew the partially pieced blocks to the regular blocks to make the diagonal rows. Mark the four sides of the quilt center by measuring ¼ inch from the corners of the Block Zs, then trim.

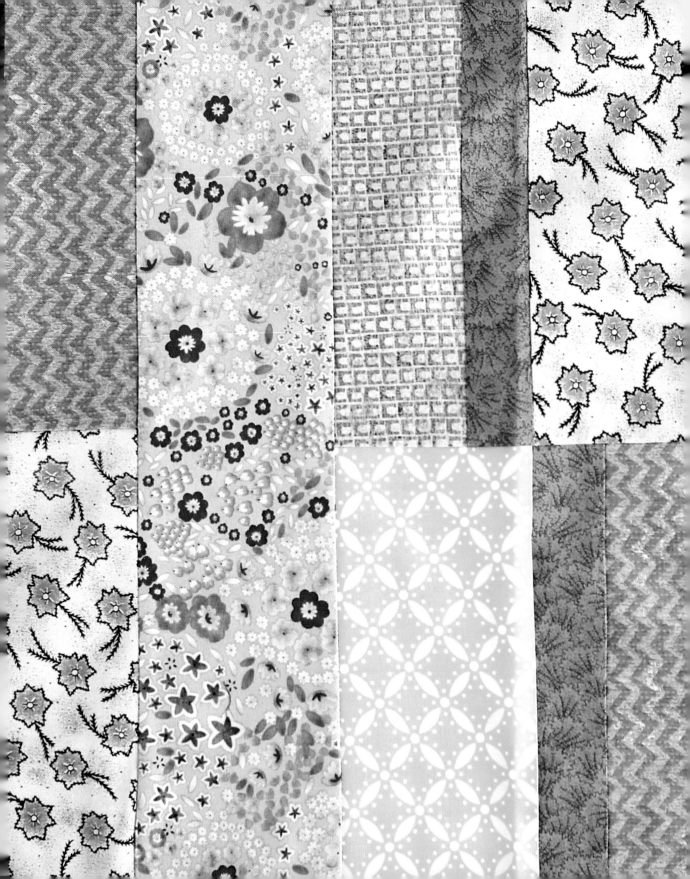

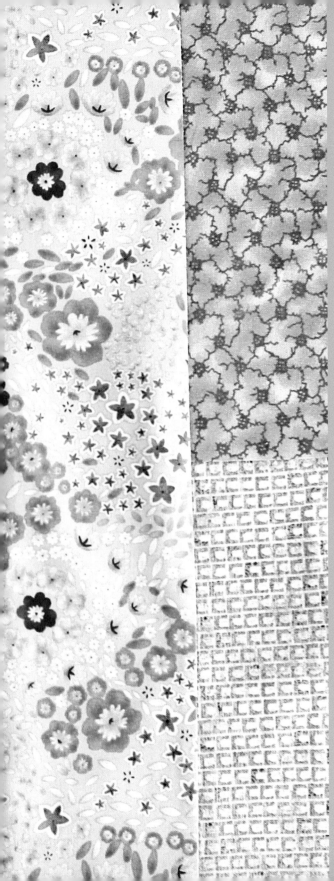

chapter **9**

Preparing a Quilt for Quilting

Piece a Quilt Back

When a quilt is too large to cut the backing from a single width of fabric, you'll need to piece the backing together. You can piece a quilt back using strips of a single fabric or a mixture of the fabrics and leftover blocks used in making the top. Backing fabric with a busy print will help hide quilting mistakes, while a plain fabric will show off your quilting. You can also use the backing print as your guide for quilting the top if you quilt from the back and follow the patterns in the fabric.

1

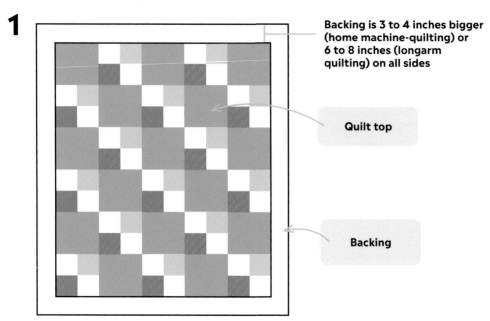

Backing is 3 to 4 inches bigger (home machine-quilting) or 6 to 8 inches (longarm quilting) on all sides

Quilt top

Backing

Measure the quilt and consider piecing options.

The backing should be 3 to 4 inches larger (if you are quilting your quilt) or 6 to 8 inches larger (if you are having a longarmer quilt it) than your quilt top on all sides. Horizontal seams reduce the amount of fabric you need and are favored by longarmers. Vertical seams are better for wall hangings because they don't have to support the weight of the quilt as it hangs. Avoid placing a seam in the middle of your backing.

Prewash backing fabric if it's different from the quilt top.

2

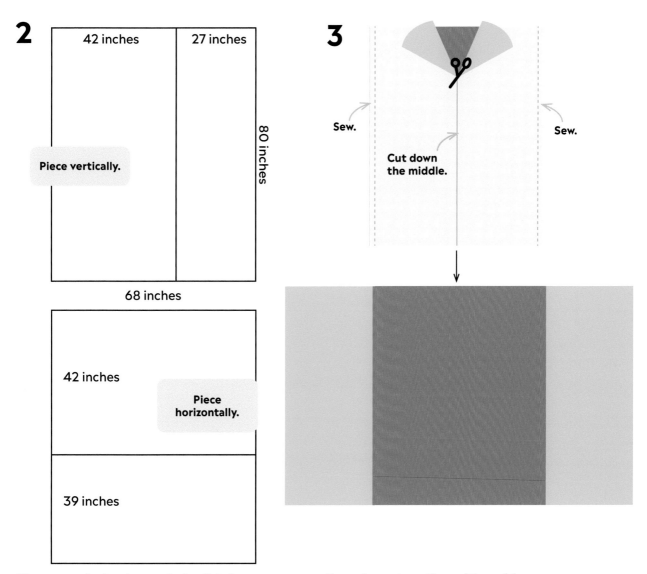

42 inches | 27 inches

80 inches

Piece vertically.

68 inches

42 inches

Piece horizontally.

39 inches

3

Sew. Sew.

Cut down the middle.

Plan your piecing to maximize fabric.

Assume your quilt is 60 × 72 inches and you're quilting it yourself. Allowing for 4 inches extra on all sides, your backing should measure 68 × 80 inches. If you piece vertically using a ½-inch seam allowance, you'll need two strips 78 to 80 inches long, or 4½ yards of fabric. Piecing horizontally, you'll need two strips 68 inches long, or 3⅞ yards.

Sew pieces together with a wide seam.

Trim selvages and sew the backing strips right sides together with a wide ½-inch seam, backstitching at the beginning and end of the seam. To avoid placing a seam in the center of a quilt, you can sew seams on both sides of the two pieces of backing fabric and cut it down the middle. Press your quilt back with Best Press before layering it with your top and batting.

Select and Prepare Batting

Batting (or "batt") is available by the yard and in precut packages. It comes in different fibers—some more suitable for hand- or machine-quilting than others. The batting you choose dictates how close together your quilting stitches must be: Some require close quilting, while others allow you to quilt farther apart. Some battings might beard, or come through the quilt top like feathers from a pillow, so always choose a quality batt, such as Quilter's Dream, Warm & Natural, or Hobbs. If your quilt top is dark, select a black batt rather than a white one. When choosing a batting, consider your quilting ability as well as how the quilt will be used.

Cotton batts are good for experienced hand-quilters who can use its low loft to quilt densely, but it might be difficult to hand-quilt for beginners. Cotton batts grab the fabric, so they're easier to machine-quilt than polyester batts, which are more slippery. They shrink a bit after washing, resulting in a slightly puckered appearance reminiscent of antique quilts. Cotton batts resist bearding and are a good choice for wall hangings because they don't stretch.

Cotton/polyester batts are a great choice for beginning hand-quilters because they're easy to stitch through. Cotton/polyester batts are often the choice of longarmers. They resist bearding, are less expensive than natural fibers, and don't shrink very much.

Polyester batts are also a wonderful choice for hand-quilters, especially beginners. Mid- to high-loft poly batts are good for tying quilts, but they're difficult to machine-quilt because polyester shifts unless basted very heavily. Polyester batts are lightweight, inexpensive, resistant to moths and mildew, and great for quilts that are frequently washed because they don't shrink. However, they're prone to bearding and they don't breathe like natural fibers.

A high-loft batt is fluffy and perfect for tying a quilt or quilting by machine where you want the quilting to be the star. Mid-loft batts show the quilting a bit less than high lofts, but they're perfect for most uses. Low-loft batts produce thin quilts and are a good choice for crib/toddler quilts, utilitarian quilts, and quilted wearables.

Wool batts are a great choice for hand- and machine-quilting, and they really show off patterns. Wool batts are warmer than cotton or polyester but lighter in weight. Wool batts are more expensive, but worth it for that special quilt. They're typically preshrunk, but some can only be hand washed or air dried. Because some people are allergic to wool, be sure to check with the recipient before using a wool batt in a gift quilt.

Silk batts are wonderful to hand- or machine-quilt. They're lightweight, don't shrink, and drape well, so they're a good choice for quilted jackets. However, silk batts are expensive and can be damaged by exposure to sunlight.

Bamboo batts are great for hand- or machine-quilting. They're very lightweight, breathable, soft, and drapable. Bamboo batts are naturally antibacterial, so they make a good choice for quilts for children. However, bamboo batts might beard.

Fusible batts allow you to skip the basting step in quilt preparation. You layer the backing, batt, and quilt top; fuse them together on both sides; let it cool; and you're ready to quilt. Fusible batts aren't suitable for hand-quilting, but they're great for small quilt projects that are machine-quilted. Quilts with fusible batts are stiff until washed.

Batting alternatives For a lighter quilt, you can use Minkee, flannel, or fleece on the back of your quilt and no batting at all.

Relax batting before using it.

Take the batting out of the bag and unfold it the night before you want to use it to allow the folds to relax. With most batts, you can also relax the folds by fluffing in a dryer on very low heat for 10 minutes.

Small pieces of batting can be joined to create the size you need.

Overlap the batting pieces and then trim both edges cleanly. Butt edges together and whipstitch by hand or by machine with an elongated zigzag stitch. You can also seam batting together with HeatnBond or Heat Press tape.

Mark the Quilting Pattern

Quilting stitches together the layers of a quilt (top, batting, and back) and adds a design element. Unless a quilting design is very simple, you typically mark the quilting lines (quilting pattern) on your quilt top prior to basting the layers. After marking the quilting pattern, you quilt the top on your machine or by hand by simply following the lines. There are a variety of methods you can use to mark your quilt pattern. (Don't mark your top if you're hiring a longarmer to quilt it.)

You can try out different quilting patterns by tracing them on cellophane with a dry-erase marker and placing the cellophane on your quilt to see how the pattern looks.

Use a Stencil

A stencil allows you to trace a quilting pattern onto your top using a pounce pad, stencil marking spray, or removable marking pencil/pen. Purchase quilting stencils at any quilt shop. You can also trace a quilting design you've found in a magazine or on the internet onto tulle using a permanent marker and then transfer it to your quilt top by pinning the tulle to your quilt and tracing the lines with a removable marking pencil/pen.

Mark a quilt using any removable method, including chalk, tape, or air- or water-soluble pens. Always test your marking method on scrap fabric from your quilt top to make sure it will come off.

Use Tape or a Hera Marker

Mark simple straight quilting lines with painter's tape or a hera marker after basting the top. To use tape, place it on the quilt top and quilt along one or both sides of the tape. For hand-quilting, mark straight lines with a hera marker by dragging it over the top. The tautness of the top in the quilting hoop allows the marker to leave a temporary crease you can quilt along.

Create a Reusable Shape to Quilt Around

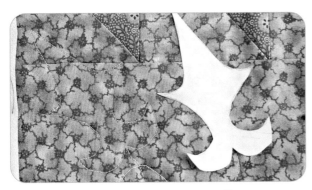

To use a repeated shape for your quilt pattern, trace the shape onto the nonshiny side of freezer paper or the nonadhesive side of Press'n Seal or Con-Tact paper. Press or iron (in the case of freezer paper) the shape onto the basted quilt top and quilt around it. Press or iron the shape in another spot and use a simple curving or curling stitch to connect the shapes.

Copy Quilting Designs onto Quilting Paper

Print or trace designs onto Golden Threads or Quilt & Tear quilting paper, vellum tracing paper, or tissue paper. Pin paper to the quilt, then quilt on the lines, stitching through the paper and the quilt. Remove the paper by running your fingernail over the quilting and gently pulling.

Follow the Backing Pattern

If the fabric you use for your backing has an interesting pattern, such as curlicues, paisleys, leaves, or flowers, you can use that pattern to quilt your top. Instead of quilting from the front, quilt from the back by following the design of the backing fabric with your stitches. This way, the pattern on the backing is replicated in the quilting on the top.

Baste Quilt Layers

If you plan to do your own quilting, you must first baste the layers of your quilt together. Basting temporarily holds the backing, batting, and quilt top in place and prevents them from shifting during quilting. You can baste using thread, safety pins, or straight pins (with foam caps that cover the tips).

Thread-basting uses long, loose stitches to keep the layers together and is a good choice for hand-quilting or intricate machine-quilting because it keeps pins out of the way. You remove the basting stitches after quilting, so use a thread that contrasts with your top for better visibility.

Pin-basting uses safety pins or straight pins with foam caps to hold the quilt layers in place and works well for machine-quilting.

If you're machine-quilting, you can also baste layers together using a fusible batt. After layering, iron the top and then the back to fuse the three layers together.

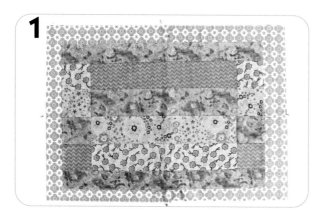

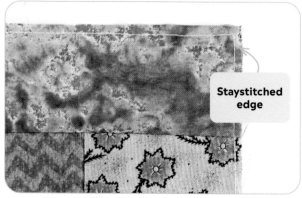

Staystitched edge

Prepare the top and backing.

Cut the selvages off the backing (if you didn't before). Press the backing and top with Best Press. Staystitch around the perimeter of the quilt top a scant ¼ inch from the edges to prevent the outer seams from separating and to keep the edges of your quilt top from stretching as it's quilted. Fold the backing and quilt top into quarters and mark the center of each side with a safety pin.

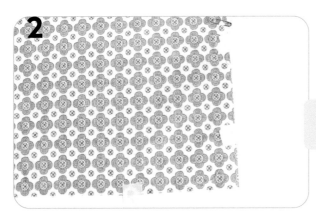

2

Tape or clip the backing to your floor or table.

Lay the backing right side down, flatten and stretch it taut, and then secure it in place by taping or clipping it to the work surface every 8 inches or so.

If your quilt is bigger than your table or floor space, work in quadrants. Pin the top-left quadrant first. Then shift the quilt sandwich carefully, tape or clip the back again, and pin the next quadrant.

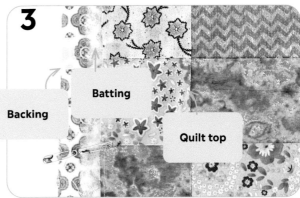

3

Backing

Batting

Quilt top

Layer the batting and quilt top.

Fold the batting into quarters. Lay it flat on the backing, matching the folds in the batting with the safety pins on the backing along each edge. Smooth any folds. Then place the quilt top gently on top, right side up. Match the safety pins on the sides of the top and back and smooth any wrinkles.

The backing will extend beyond the quilt top by 3 to 4 inches on all sides. The batting should be slightly smaller than the backing, about 2 to 3 inches larger than the quilt top on all sides.

Pin or thread the baste in a grid 4 inches apart.

To thread-baste: Thread a darning, upholstery, basting, or curved needle with cotton or cotton/polyester thread. Don't knot the thread. Start at the center of the top edge and take long, loose stitches through all layers to the bottom edge, being careful not to let the layers shift. Baste across the center horizontally from edge to edge and then continue basting horizontally, vertically, and diagonally 4 inches apart.

If closing a safety pin is painful for your fingers, use a Kwik Klip, the back of a spoon, or the edge of a knife to guide the pin tip into the closure.

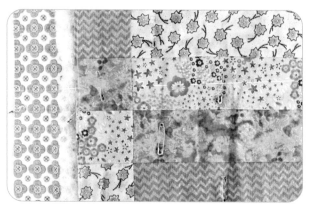

To pin-baste: Pin using 1¼-inch or 2-inch safety pins or straight pins through all layers in a grid about 4 inches apart, being careful not to let the layers shift. Pin in places where you won't be quilting if possible. Close the safety pins or cover the tips of the straight pins with foam caps as you go.

Baste the edges to stabilize them.

Trim the batting and backing, leaving 2 inches around the perimeter of the top. After removing the pins used to center the layers, roll the backing back up over the batting and the edge of the top to protect the raw edges. Baste the rolled edge down with large hand stitches. This stabilizes the edge, which will be handled frequently as you quilt.

Prepare a Quilt for Longarm Quilting

Longarm quilters use sewing machines with a long arm (head) to quilt large sections at a time. In longarm quilting, the quilt top, batting, and backing aren't basted together but are loaded onto separate rollers and stretched taut. The longarm machine sits on rollers and is moved back and forth across the quilt top to quilt it. In contrast, you'd move a quilt back and forth under your stationary home machine to quilt it.

If quilting on your home machine seems daunting, you might want to have your quilt professionally quilted. However, you might need to reserve a spot in advance with the longarmer you choose. Each longarmer is an artist, so look for one who suits your style. The cost of longarm quilting depends on the size of the quilt and the type of quilting design(s) you choose. Pantographs (all-over patterns) are the least expensive option. Custom quilting is more expensive, but it allows you to select different designs for the blocks, borders, and sashing of your quilt. Prices vary, but in the United States you should expect to pay 3 to 7 cents per square inch plus the cost of batting and thread.

1

Staystitched edge

Press the top.

Press the quilt top using Best Press, checking for loose threads and removing them. Check your top for squareness and trim as needed. Staystitch a scant ¼ inch from the edge of your top to stabilize those edges and keep them from stretching or splitting open during quilting.

2

Piece and prepare the quilt back.

Cut the selvages from the backing fabric before piecing, then press it well with Best Press. If you piece the back, avoid creating a design that must be centered perfectly.

To check whether a quilt is square, take three measurements at different points across the quilt. If the measurements are within ⅜ inch, the quilt top is square.

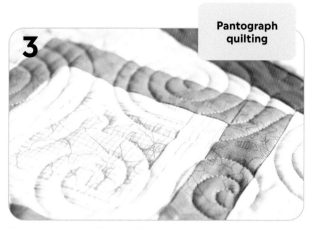

Pantograph quilting

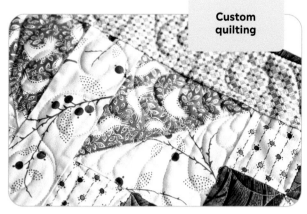

Custom quilting

Decide on a quilting design.

Pantograph quilting (also known as all-over quilting) is the perfect choice for quilts that will get a lot of use and must stand up to frequent washings. With all-over quilting, the design fills the entire quilt, extending from the blocks into the sashing and borders without stopping. Custom quilting is suitable for heirloom quilts or quilts with large unpieced areas or areas with plain fabrics. With custom quilting, complementary but different patterns fill the blocks and borders.

Package the top and backing for transport.

Mark the top edge of your quilt top and back so the longarmer will know how to load it onto the frame. Fold the top and backing carefully, then place on a hanger inside a large plastic bag. If you're shipping your quilt to a longarmer, wrap the top and back separately in plastic bags.

Plan Your Quilting

If you plan to do your own quilting, take time to choose a quilt pattern that complements your quilt project and suits your skill level. Quilting patterns can be found in quilting books and magazines as well as through online sources. As you consider quilting designs, keep two things in mind: First, the batting you choose dictates how close your quilting must be. If your batting requires quilting that's 4 inches apart, don't select a quilting pattern with quilting lines 6 inches apart. Second, remember that the quilting must be evenly distributed over the quilt top in order for your quilt to lay flat.

Consider Your Quilt

The quilting pattern you choose should complement the design of your quilt and fabric choices. Curvy quilting complements quilts with lots of straight lines. Traditional fabrics are complemented by traditional quilting designs. Decide whether you want to use an overall pattern, which covers the whole quilt, or different designs for different areas, such as the blocks, sashing, and borders. An overall pattern is best if your quilt is visually complex (lots of piecing or busy fabrics), while custom quilting is the perfect choice for areas with simple piecing and solid or tone-on-tone fabrics.

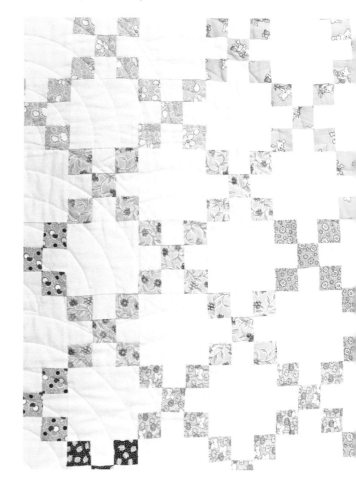

Consider Straight-Line Quilting

Straight-line quilting is the easiest type of quilting to master because straight lines are easy to follow. You can quilt straight lines up and down, diagonally, or in a grid across your quilt. Mark the lines using painter's tape and quilt on one or both sides of the tape. You can skip the marking process and eyeball a straight line or soft curve from one point of a block to another. You can also outline-quilt ¼ inch away from the seams in a block without marking by using the edge of the presser foot as a guide. Although it might seem easy to quilt in a seam ("stitch in the ditch"), it's actually somewhat difficult and not recommended for beginners.

Consider Free-Motion Quilting

Free-motion quilting allows you to quilt in any direction, creating interesting shapes and designs. Free-motion quilting can be challenging because it requires you to manually move the quilt under the needle in tempo with the speed of the machine. "Stippling" and "meandering" are good designs for a first-time free-motion project because there's no pattern you have to try to follow and you can move the quilt in whatever direction you like. "Echo quilting" repeats the curves of appliqué shapes and is also easy because you can use the edge of the presser foot as a guide as you stitch around each appliqué.

Test Quilting Designs

For more complex free-motion designs, you'll need to follow a pattern. Try out different designs by marking them on upholstery vinyl or cellophane using a dry-erase marker. Look at the quilts in this book, in magazines, and in local quilt stores for quilting ideas. When you've found one you like, copy it to Golden Threads quilting paper, Quilt & Tear, vellum tracing paper, or tissue paper. Pin the paper to your quilt and then quilt by simply following the lines. The paper should remove easily after quilting.

chapter 10

Quilting
a Quilt

Hand-Quilting

Hand-quilting a quilt ties you to the past, when people made quilts entirely by hand. Although hand-quilting can be used to achieve an heirloom look, modern quilters often hand-quilt to provide additional embellishment with colorful, thick threads. Hand-quilting is done with a rocking motion that creates stitches that are the same size on the front and back of your quilt.

Thread-baste the quilt and place the center of the quilt in the hoop.

Tighten the hoop—but not too taut. You want some "give" to help you make your stitches. You'll quilt from the center of the quilt out to the edges, quilting toward yourself or to the side.

Take a shallow stitch.

Thread a size 9 or 10 Quilting or Betweens needle with about 18 inches of hand-quilting thread. Form a quilter's knot at the end of the thread. Poke the needle through the quilt top about 1 inch from where you want to start quilting. Don't go through the backing; instead, take a shallow stitch, coming back up at the point where you want to start.

Pop the knot into the batting.

Pull up gently until the knot rests on top of the quilt. Hold the thread right near the surface and give it a gentle tug to pop the knot through the quilt top and into the batting.

Poke the needle straight down until you feel it underneath.

Rest your middle (thimble) finger on the eye of the needle and grasp the needle with your ring finger and thumb. Push the needle through the quilt (all layers) at a vertical angle to the quilt top. Feel for the needle tip with your under finger (forefinger or index finger of your nondominant hand). This finger will guide the needle point back up through the quilt to take your stitch.

Place a thimble on the middle finger of your dominant hand and use this finger to poke the needle through the quilt from the top. Leave your under finger bare at first so you can feel the needle and gain control. Later, you might want to use a self-adhesive thimble pad on that finger to protect it.

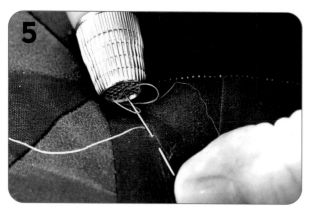

Rock back with the needle and pinch to load the stitch.

Using your thimble finger, rock the needle gently back to a horizontal position. Use your thumb to push the fabric down in front of the needle and your under finger to push up toward the middle of the needle to form a hill. Push the tip of the needle through this hill, taking a stitch that goes through all three layers.

Pull the needle through.

Gently pull the needle all the way through, creating just enough slack in the thread so you can take your next stitch. You don't need to pull the thread through all the way with each stitch—just every three stitches or so.

Repeat to take another stitch.

Poke the needle straight down a stitch away and then rock the needle back and pinch to take another stitch. Pull the needle through.

Concentrate on making even stitches on the front and back of your quilt. When you feel comfortable, you can repeat the rocking motion a few times, loading two to three stitches on the needle before pulling it through.

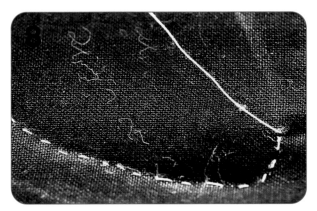

At the end of a line of stitching, knot the thread.

Make a quilter's knot and slip it down the thread, stopping about ¼ inch away from the surface of the quilt top. Push the needle down into the quilt a stitch length away, but don't go through the backing. Bring the needle back up through the quilt top some distance from the line of quilting you're making.

Pop the knot into the batting.

Pull gently on the thread to pop the knot into the batting.

Clip the thread.

Clip the thread close to the quilt top, being careful not to accidentally cut the quilt. After you cut, the end of the thread should fall back into the quilt, out of sight.

11 Reposition the hoop as needed.

You can quilt up to about 2 inches away from the edge of the hoop before you have to reposition it. Before doing that, you might want to thread more needles and quilt from the center of the hoop out in other directions. After repositioning a hoop, take up an old needle and continue that line of stitching. Remove basting stitches when you've finished the project.

Tie a Quilt

There are times when you might not wish to invest a great deal of time or money in quilting a quilt. To complete these types of quilts quickly, use a pillowcase finish to enclose the edges without a binding and "tie" the layers together using pearl cotton, crochet thread, embroidery floss, or yarn.

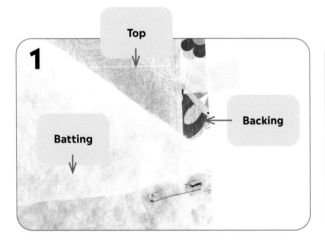

Layer quilt top, backing, and batting.

Press the quilt top and backing, then staystitch the top to a scant ¼ inch from the edge to prevent the quilt from stretching or the seams from popping open during quilting. Layer the backing (right side up), top (right side down), and batting. Safety pin along the edges every 6 to 8 inches.

Sew around the edges of the quilt.

Sew around all the edges of the quilt sandwich, using a ½-inch seam allowance. Backstitch at the beginning and end of the seam, leaving an 8-inch gap in the middle of one side for turning.

Turn the quilt right side out and sew.

Clip the corners and turn the quilt right side out by pulling it gently through the gap you left in step 2. Fold under the seam allowance along the opening and press. Stitch around the perimeter of the quilt ¼-inch from the edge to close the opening and keep the edge from rolling.

Pin-baste the quilt top.

Pin using safety pins or straight pins through all layers in a grid about 4 inches apart. Pin in places where you won't be tying. Close the safety pins or cover the tips of the straight pins with foam caps.

Tie the quilt top.

Thread an embroidery, tapestry, or curved needle with crochet thread, pearl cotton, yarn, or embroidery floss about 24 to 30 inches long. Don't knot the thread. Take a short stitch through all layers, leaving a 3-inch tail. Repeat the stitch to reinforce it. Continue to stitch in a grid 4 inches apart, leaving a tail at the end of the last stitch.

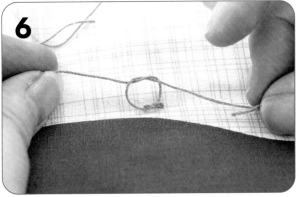

Cut and tie threads.

When you reach the end of that thread, it's time to tie. Cut the threads midway between each stitch, then tie them in a double knot. Wrap the right thread over the left and pull tight. Then wrap the left thread over the right to make a double knot. Trim the threads to ¾ to 1 inch.

Machine-Quilting

You can machine-quilt with straight lines or soft curves using a walking foot or you can free-motion quilt in any direction by dropping the feed dogs. Beginners should select a single thread color that works well on the front and the back to hide tension problems. Clean and oil your machine before starting, load a fresh needle appropriate for the thread type, and fill several bobbins. Change to a straight-stitch throat plate. Before beginning, practice stitches on a scrap quilt sandwich (batting layered between fabric).

Straight-Line Quilting with a Walking Foot

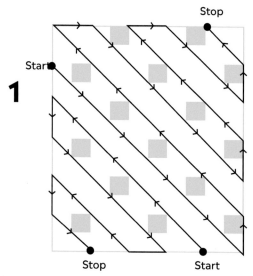

Plan your stitching.

Avoid stopping and starting as much as possible by stitching across or down the entire quilt or section and then back in the other direction. Rather than stopping when you reach an edge, stitch in the seam along the edge (to hide your path) and then quilt in the other direction.

Quilter's gloves might help you maintain your grip on the quilt.

Mark stitching if necessary and then insert a walking foot.

Mark the line of stitching with tape or select a seam or another design element to follow. If you use a bar guide with the walking foot, adjust it so you can use it to follow a seam, a design element, or a previous line of quilting.

3

Begin quilting in the center of the quilt and then hide your threads.

After stitching a short way from the needle, stop with the needle down and knot your threads. Thread the tails into a self-threading needle, insert it into the spot where you stopped, and pull it out 1 inch away to bury the knot in the quilt batting. Trim the ends, which will then fall back into the quilt layers. Check the back of the quilt for tension problems and fix them before continuing.

4

To turn corners, pivot with the needle down.

Quilt as far as you can. If you have to stop, stop with the needle down to keep the quilt from shifting. To turn a corner, stop and then pivot by lifting the foot, turning the quilt, lowering the foot again, and then continuing. When you need to finish a line of stitching, stop and then hide your threads again.

To avoid crossing back and forth across the seam when stitching in the ditch, stitch with your needle on the side of the seam that doesn't have the seam allowance.

Free-Motion Quilting

1

Start/stop

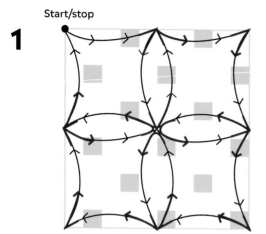

Plan your quilting to avoid starts and stops.

Use continuous line designs to avoid stops and starts. Instead of quilting each block separately, you'll quilt the blocks in one continuous line.

2

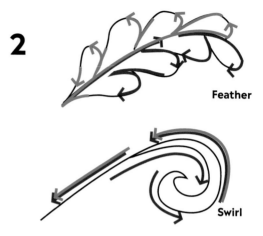

Feather

Swirl

Don't be afraid to quilt over some lines.

With such designs as feathers or swirls, you'll quilt most of the design and stitch over a previous line to complete the design using a continuous line.

3

Start

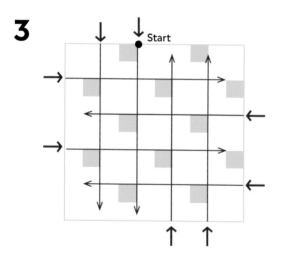

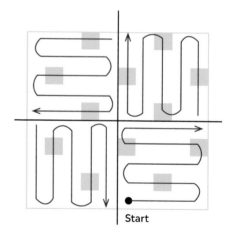

Start

Decide where to begin quilting.

To quilt block by block, stabilize the layers first by quilting the long vertical and horizontal lines between blocks. To quilt an all-over pattern, divide a quilt into four sections. Start in the lower-left corner of a section, quilt right and left, and eventually end in the upper-right corner of the section. Turn the quilt and repeat in the next section, keeping the bulk of the quilt behind and to your left.

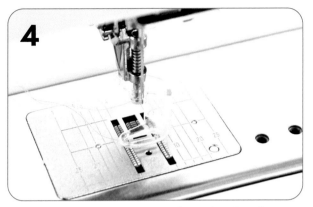

Insert an open-toe, appliqué, or darning foot.

Lower the feed dogs or cover them with an index card. Set the stitch length to 0 to save wear and tear on your machine. In free-motion quilting, the stitch length is determined by how fast you sew and how fast you move the quilt under the needle. Hold on to the top thread and bring the bobbin thread up.

Position your hands correctly.

Place your hands on either side of the needle and use them to flatten the area you want to quilt. As you quilt, you'll also use your hands to move the quilt top under the needle with light pressure and a gliding motion.

Begin quilting, hide the threads, and continue.

To achieve even stitches, balance the speed of the machine with the speed you move the quilt. Slow down slightly before changing directions to avoid piling up stitches.

If you must stop, stop with the needle down. Reposition your hands if needed and fluff the quilt to redistribute its weight to the left and behind the machine. Rest the quilt on your chest if needed rather than your lap so its weight won't pull against the needle. Keep the area you're quilting flattened with your hands.

Square Up Your Quilt

After a quilt is quilted, you need to trim the excess batting and backing. As you trim the batting and backing, you can also trim the quilt by a tiny amount if needed to ensure your quilt finishes square. Squaring up a quilt after quilting helps it hang straight and lie flat. You'll need a large square ruler, a long ruler, and a 60mm rotary cutter.

Baste the edge to stabilize all the layers.

To ensure the edge of your quilt doesn't shift when trimming, baste it by hand or machine with large stitches about ⅛ inch from the edge.

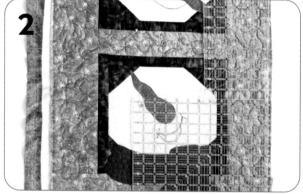

Use two rulers to create a 90° corner.

Place at least the lower-right section of your quilt on a cutting mat, making sure the whole quilt is supported. Position a large square ruler in the corner of the quilt, as close as possible to the edges. Align a horizontal line on the ruler with a strong horizontal line in your quilt, such as a border or a block edge. Align a vertical line on the ruler with a vertical line in your quilt. Place a long ruler on top of the square ruler to create a long vertical edge for cutting or marking.

3

Cut or mark the edge.

Mark this edge with a fabric marker and cut it later or cut it now with a rotary cutter. Cut along the edge of the square ruler and then shift your hand to the long ruler and continue cutting. Cut only as far as you're comfortable, then shift the long ruler up, aligning it with the already-cut edge.

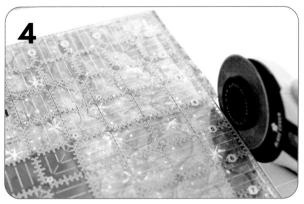

4

Cut or mark the remaining corners and edges.

As you near the upper-right corner, reposition your square ruler. Align the vertical edge against the newly cut edge, using a horizontal mark on the ruler to ensure the corner is square and 90°. Mark or cut the corner and continue around the quilt, trimming as you go.

Trim as little of the quilt top as possible while maintaining straight edges and square corners. Make sure the edge you're trimming is at least ¼ inch from any pieced blocks.

Bind a Quilt

Binding finishes the edge of a quilt, covering it in fabric. Typically, binding is cut from the crosswise grain, which provides stability and helps keep your quilt square. If your quilt has a curved edge, cut bias binding instead. You might also want to cut bias binding from striped or plaid fabric to give a quilt with a straight edge a special look.

If you want to add a hanging sleeve to your quilt, sew the top edge of it to the quilt before binding. Use a scant ¼-inch seam allowance. Hand-sew the bottom edge of the sleeve after your quilt is bound.

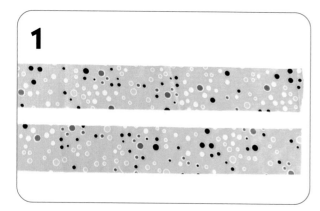

Cut the binding strips.

Binding strips can be 2 to 2½ inches wide and as long as you prefer. (I use 2¼-inch-wide binding.) The length and number of strips depend on the size of your quilt. Cut enough strips to equal the perimeter of your quilt plus 10 to 12 inches for joining the ends plus an additional ½ inch for every strip of binding you cut (to allow for the seam allowances when you sew them together).

Lay one strip on another and mark and sew a diagonal seam.

Place one strip horizontally, face up. Place a second strip on top of the first strip, face down, so the ends form a right angle. Where the strips overlap, mark and sew a diagonal from the upper-left corner to the lower-right corner. Trim the seam allowance to ¼ inch.

Trim excess fabric.

3

Join the rest of the strips.

Add a third strip to the first two using the same method. Continue joining strips until you have one long strip that's equal to the perimeter of the quilt plus 12 inches for joining the ends. After trimming, press the seams open where they're joined.

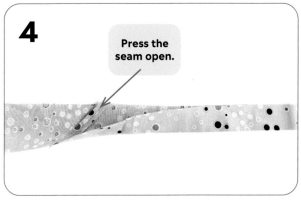

4

Press the seam open.

Press the binding in half.

Fold the binding in half, being careful to match the raw edges exactly. Press the fold, checking that seams are pressed open as you come to them.

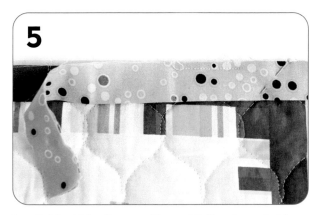

5

Lay folded binding on the quilt front, matching the raw edges.

Leave 6 inches hanging free and then pin the binding along one side of the quilt, starting about 10 inches from a corner. Use a ¼-inch seam allowance for a 2- or 2¼-inch binding or a ⅜-inch seam allowance for a 2½-inch binding. Backstitch at the beginning of the seam.

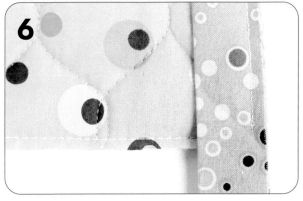

6

Sew almost to the corner and then backstitch.

Sew along the edge, stopping a distance equal to the seam allowance (¼ or ⅜ inch) from the corner. Backstitch, then remove the quilt from the machine.

7

Fold the corner up at a 45° angle.

Rotate the quilt, placing the sewn binding horizontally. Fold the binding up at a 45° diagonal.

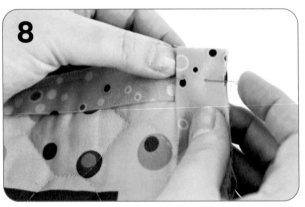

8

Fold the binding back down straight.

Hold the diagonal fold in place and then fold the binding back down, making sure to align the raw edges again. The top of the folded binding should align with the top edge of the quilt. Pin the binding in place.

9

Sew, beginning the same distance from the edge as your seam allowance.

Backstitch and then continue sewing the binding to the quilt, repeating steps 6 to 9 at each corner. Stop sewing about 10 inches from where you started. Backstitch and remove the quilt from the machine.

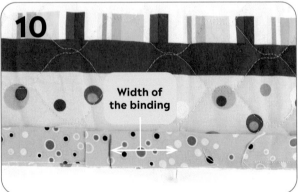

10

Width of the binding

Trim the binding ends where the strips meet.

Lay down the binding on the left and put a pin in the quilt to mark where it ends. Lay the right binding on top. Measure the width of the binding from the pin and mark the top binding at this spot. Trim the top binding at the mark.

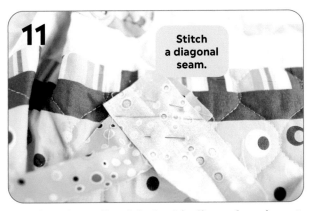

11 Stitch a diagonal seam.

Position the quilt with the binding edge closest to you.

Open up the binding on the left, right side up. Open up the binding on the right, right side down. Place the right binding on top and perpendicular to the left binding, matching edges. Pin the ends together. Mark the sewing line. On the right (top) binding, mark a sewing line diagonally from the upper left down to the lower right.

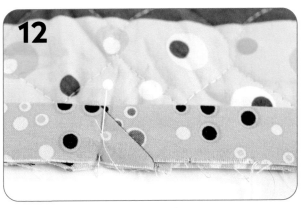

12

Sew the binding ends together.

Sew on the marked line. Check to make sure the binding fits the edge of the quilt and resew if needed. Trim the seam allowance, pressing it open. Lay the binding on the quilt and sew the remaining seam. Backstitch at the beginning and the end of the seam.

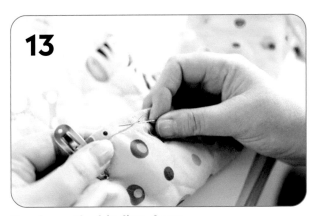

13

Hand-sew the binding down.

Roll the binding to the back of the quilt and then hand-sew it down with matching thread using a blind stitch. Binding clips will help hold the binding in place as you sew.

14

Miter the corners of the binding.

When you reach a corner, fold the corner into a miter and stitch it down. Sew the mitered corner closed up to the point. Sneak the needle out of the corner and then continue sewing the binding.

Add a Label

Adding a label to a quilt helps future generations identify who made it and how to care for it. You can piece a label into the back before layering a quilt or add it after the quilt has been quilted. Include your name, date of completion, the title of the quilt, and the name of the quilter (if it wasn't you). A label can also include other information, such as the city and state where you live, the name of the quilt pattern you used, or the reason the quilt was made. You can make a simple label as described here or print one using fabric prepared for photo printing. You can also use a leftover block as a label. Preprinted labels are also sold by the yard.

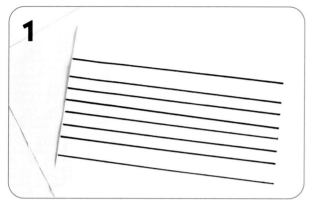

Cut a label and mark lines on freezer paper.

Cut a label from light fabric, adding ¼-inch seam allowances. Cut a piece of freezer paper the same size as the label. Mark the nonshiny side of the freezer paper with straight lines for writing. Press the shiny side of the freezer paper onto the back of the label fabric.

Write information on the label.

The lines on the freezer paper will be visible through the fabric. Use them to guide your writing. Write with a fabric pen, not a Sharpie or permanent marker. Let the ink dry for 24 to 48 hours and then set it by pressing with a hot iron (without steam).

Remove the freezer paper and add fabric borders to the label.

Use scraps left over from your quilt to make the borders. Press under a ¼-inch seam allowance around the outside of the label and then pin the label to the lower-right corner of the quilt back.

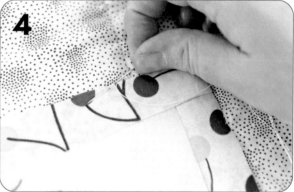

Stitch the label to the back using a blind stitch.

Be sure to sew through the label and backing only; don't let the stitches go all the way through to the front of the quilt.

Add a Hanging Sleeve

If you plan to hang your quilt for display, you need to add a sleeve on the back, along the top edge. Quilt shows require a 4-inch sleeve; for home display, you can use a width that works with your hanging system (such as a dowel or curtain rod). A perfect sleeve has enough give to accommodate the roundness of the hanging rod while allowing your quilt to hang straight and not fall forward on the rod.

Cut fabric for the hanging sleeve.

To make a 4-inch-wide hanging sleeve, cut the fabric 9 inches wide and 1 to 2 inches shorter than the width of your quilt. Sew a small hem on the short ends of the strip.

Fold to form the edges of the sleeve.

Fold the sleeve in half lengthwise and press to mark the center. Open up the sleeve, fold each edge to the center line you just pressed, and press the newly folded edges. These will form the top and bottom edges of the finished sleeve.

3

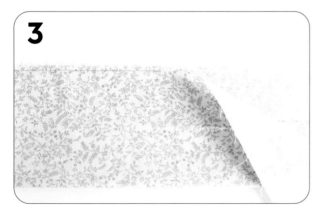

Fold the sleeve wrong sides together and sew.

Open the folded edges, fold the sleeve wrong sides together, and sew the raw edges using a ¼-inch seam allowance. Press the seam to one side, being careful not to disturb the previously pressed edges.

4

Position the sleeve on the quilt back and sew.

Center the sleeve on the back of the quilt, 1 inch from the top edge, and pin. Place the seam on the back of the sleeve so it's hidden. Sew the edges pressed in step 2 and the short edges with a blind stitch. The sleeve will poof out a bit when you sew it on, but it will fit perfectly when a rod is slipped through it.

Wash and Store Quilts

Quilts should be washed only when needed. Even a quilt that's used daily should be washed just once a year (unless children or pets are involved). Assuming you used quality quilting cottons and didn't embellish your quilt, you can safely wash your quilt in a home washing machine. To freshen a quilt without washing it, use a hand vacuum and secure the end of a piece of hosiery to the vacuum nozzle.

1. **Wash in cold water on the gentle cycle with a mild detergent.**

   Use an unscented detergent or a quilt soap, such as Orvis. An extra cold rinse cycle will help remove excess detergent.

2. **Add a color catcher, dye magnet, or dye grabber to the washer.**

   Although you can test and prewash fabrics before using them in a quilt, a color catcher, dye magnet, or dye grabber can trap dyes and prevent them from transferring in the wash.

3. **Tumble dry on low heat until almost dry, then air-dry the rest of the way.**

   Lay the quilt on a sheet to finish air-drying; layer the quilt between two sheets if you air-dry outside. If the quilt is hand-quilted or you used a batting that requires special care, skip the dryer and air-dry only.

4. **Store the quilt in a fabric bag and out of sunlight.**

   Refold the quilt every season or roll it to prevent fold lines that weaken the fabric. Don't store a quilt on an unpainted wooden shelf (even in bags), in a cardboard box, or in a plastic bag or box. Don't use tissue to wrap a quilt unless the tissue is acid free. You can also layer a quilt on a guest bed to store it.

chapter # 11

Gallery of Projects

"Strawberry Preserves" Lap Quilt

Pink and brown quilts are classics that warm the heart. The colors and pattern of this quilt remind me of making strawberry preserves with my mother and sisters. Although it's fine to make this quilt using only a few fabrics, in this version, the more the merrier.

FINISHED SIZES

- **Overall:** 60 × 68 inches
- **Blocks:** 8 inches

MATERIALS LIST

- **Various light pinks:** ⅞ yard total from Fat Quarters and Fat Eighths (blocks)
- **Various medium to dark pinks:** 1⅜ yards total from Fat Quarters and Fat Eighths (blocks, Border #2)
- **Various light browns:** ¾ yard total from Fat Quarters and Fat Eighths (blocks)
- **Various medium browns:** ¼ yard total from Fat Eighths (Border #2)
- **Various dark browns:** 1 yard total from Fat Quarters and Fat Eighths (blocks, Border #2); 1¼ yards (Border #1, Border #3); ½ yard (binding)
- **Backing:** 3⅔ yards
- **Batting:** At least 66 × 74 inches (twin or full sized)

CUTTING DIRECTIONS

Various light pinks:
• For each Block Z, cut one square (A), 5¼ × 5¼ inches, for a total of 21 (A) squares
• For each Block Z, cut four squares (C), 2½ × 2½ inches, for a total of 84 (C) squares

Various medium pinks:
• For each Block Y, cut two squares (F), 3 × 3 inches, for a total of 42 (F) squares
• 28 squares (C), 2½ × 2½ inches (Border #2)

Various dark pinks:
• For each Block Z, cut four squares (B), 2⅞ × 2⅞ inches, for a total of 84 (B) squares
• For each Block Y, cut two rectangles (G), 1½ × 2½ inches, for a total of 42 (G) rectangles
• For each Block Y, cut two rectangles (H), 1½ × 4½ inches, for a total of 42 (H) rectangles
• 30 squares (C), 2½ × 2½ inches (Border #2)

Various light browns:
• For each Block Y, cut four rectangles (E), 2½ × 4½ inches, for a total of 84 (E) rectangles

Various medium browns:
• 28 squares (C), 2½ × 2½ inches (Border #2)

Dark brown yardage:
• 8 strips, 2½ × 42 inches (Border #1)
• 8 strips, 2½ × 42 inches (Border #3)
• 7 strips, 2 × 42 or 2¼ × 42 inches or as you prefer (binding)

Note: *Cut the border strips before cutting anything else. Trim the border strips to the right size after sewing the quilt center.*

Various dark browns:
• For each Block Z, cut one square (D), 4½ × 4½ inches, for a total of 21 (D) squares

• For each Block Y, cut one square (C), 2½ × 2½ inches, for a total of 21 (C) squares
• 30 squares (C), 2½ × 2½ inches for Border #2
• For each Block Y, cut two squares (F), 3 × 3 inches, for a total of 42 (F) squares

Backing:
• 2 strips, 66 × 42 inches

Assembling the Block Units

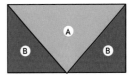

Unit 1 (make 84)

1. Using Method 2 for piecing flying geese units, make 84 flying geese (Unit 1). Use one A square and four B squares to make four matching flying geese units. Measure and trim each Unit 1 to 2½ × 4½ inches. Press away from the "geese" and toward the "sky" triangles.

Unit 2 (make 84)

2. Using Method 1 for piecing half-square triangles (HSTs), make 84 HSTs (Unit 2). Use one F square of each color to make two matching Unit 2s at one time. Measure and trim each Unit 2 to 2½ inches square. Press toward the dark.

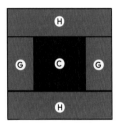

Unit 3 (make 21)

3. To make the center unit (Unit 3) of Block Y, sew two G rectangles to opposite sides of the C square. Press to G rectangles. Sew one H rectangle to each long side and press to the H rectangles. Make 21 Unit 3s. Unit 3 should measure 4½ inches square.

Assembling the Quilt Blocks

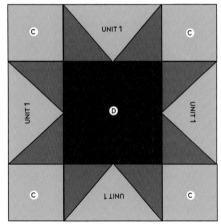

Block Z (make 21)

1. Join four Unit 1s, four light C squares, and one D square to create Block Z. Lay out the block first, being careful to arrange the Unit 1s with star points facing out.

2. Assemble each row of the block, pressing away from the Unit 1s. Sew rows together, pinning intersections so they'll match. Pin the flying geese carefully so you don't crop the points. If the points of your flying geese aren't exactly ¼ inch from the edge of the unit, mark your sewing line on the wrong side so it runs right through the point.

3. Press rows 1 and 3 away from row 2. Make 21 Block Zs. Block Z should measure 8½ × 8½ inches.

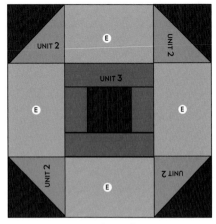

Block Y (make 21)

4. Join four Unit 2s, one Unit 3, and four E rectangles to create Block Y. Lay out the block first, being careful to arrange the Unit 2s correctly. (The dark triangles should be in the outside corners.) Make sure Unit 3 is oriented as shown, with the short borders on the sides.

5. Start by sewing E rectangles to each side of Unit 3. Press toward the E rectangles. Sew Unit 2s to the two remaining E rectangles, pressing toward the E rectangles. Sew these to the top and bottom of the center, pressing away from Unit 3. Make 21 Block Ys. Block Y should measure 8½ × 8½ inches.

Assembling the Quilt Center

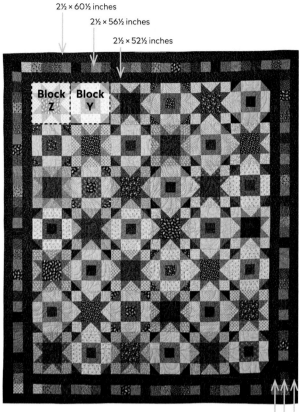

2½ × 60½ inches
2½ × 56½ inches
2½ × 52½ inches

Block Z   Block Y

2½ × 56½ inches
2½ × 60½ inches
2½ × 64½ inches

Quilt Assembly Diagram

1. Using the Quilt Assembly diagram, arrange the blocks in rows on your design wall. Pay attention to the placement of Block Zs and Block Ys, as they alternate within each row. Pin carefully at every intersection. If needed, mark the sewing line on the back of blocks so it goes through points. Sew the blocks together into rows. Press the seams in odd rows to the right and the seams in even rows to the left to aid in assembly of the rows.

2. Sew the rows together. Press row seams in the same direction. The center should measure 48½ × 56½ inches.

Adding the Borders

1. Sew two 2½ × 42-inch Border #1 strips together to create a 2½ × 83½-inch strip. Repeat to create 4 Border #1 strips.

2. Measure down the quilt center and cut two Border #1 strips that length. Sew these strips to the sides of the quilt center. If you sew one strip from the top of the quilt down and the other from the bottom of the quilt up, you'll avoid placing the border seam in the side borders in the same position on each side. Press toward Border #1.

3. Measure across the quilt center and cut the other two Border #1 strips that length. Sew these strips to the top and bottom of the quilt center, once again switching directions from which you sew the borders in order to stagger where the border seams are located. Press toward Border #1. The quilt should now measure 52½ × 60½ inches.

4. Lay out 30 C squares of various colors in a pleasing arrangement and sew them together to create one side of Border #2. Repeat to create a second side of Border #2. Press the seams in the same direction and then measure the borders. Measure down the center of the quilt. If your pieced borders don't equal this measurement, make adjustments to a few seams in the middle of each pieced border so the two measurements are the same. Sew the side borders to the quilt center. Press toward Border #1.

For example, if your quilt measures 60¼ inches down the center and your pieced borders are 60½ inches, then your border is ¼ inch too long. If you make two seams somewhere in the middle of each pieced border ⅜ inch deep (⅛ inch bigger than normal), you'll make your borders exactly 60¼ inches long.

5. Measure across the quilt center. The quilt should measure 56½ inches wide. Sew 28 C squares together to create the top Border #2, pressing the seams in the same direction. Repeat to create the bottom Border #2. Measure the borders and the width of the quilt, then make adjustments to the middle seams of the borders as needed. Sew the borders to the top and bottom of the quilt center. Press toward the Border #1 strips. The quilt should measure 56½ × 64½ inches.

6. Sew two 2½ × 42-inch strips together to create a 2½ × 83½-inch strip for Border #3. Repeat to create four Border #3 strips.

7. Measure down the quilt center and trim two Border #3 strips to that length. Sew these strips to the sides of the quilt center, sewing in opposite directions so the border seams area isn't in the same position on each side. Press toward the Border #3 strips.

8. Measure across the quilt center and trim the remaining two Border #3 strips that length. Sew these strips to the top and bottom of the quilt center, once again switching directions to stagger where the border seams are located. Press toward the Border #3 strips. The quilt should measure 60½ × 68½ inches.

Quilting and Finishing

1. Piece the backing by sewing the two 66 × 42-inch strips together to create a 66 × 83-inch rectangle. (Make sure the selvages have been removed.) Use a ½-inch seam allowance and backstitch at the beginning and end of the seam. Press open the seam.

2. Quilt as desired. The sample quilt was quilted with swirls and feathers.

3. Square up the quilted quilt and bind it. Add a label.

This quilt is easy to make scrappy by selecting a fabric and cutting what is needed for a single block. For example, select one light pink fabric and cut one A square and four C squares for each Block Z. Store the fabrics for each block in the same bag for ease in construction.

1930s fabrics are as traditional in quiltmaking as pink and brown. For a light and airy look, make this version, "Marmalade," using 1930s fabrics.

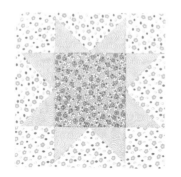 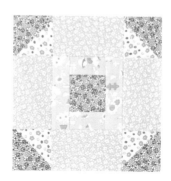

	Crib	**Toddler**	**Full**	**Queen**
Size	36 × 44 inches	44 × 60 inches	76 × 84 inches	84 × 92 inches
Block setting	3 × 4	4 × 6	8 × 9	9 × 10
Block Z	6	12	36	45
Block Y	6	12	36	45
Light pinks	⅜ yard	⅝ yard	1½ yards	1¾ yards
Medium to dark pinks	¾ yard	1 yard	2¼ yards	2¾ yards
Light browns	¼ yard	½ yard	1⅛ yards	1½ yards
Medium browns	½ yard	½ yard	½ yard	½ yard
Dark browns	1¼ yards	1⅝ yards	2¾ yards	3 yards
Binding	⅜ yard	½ yard	⅝ yard	⅝ yard
Backing	1½ yards	2¾ yards	5 yards	7½ yards
Batting	42 × 50 inches	50 × 66 inches	82 × 90 inches	90 × 98 inches

"Princess Charlotte" Crib Quilt

This charming crib quilt is named for my great-niece, Charlotte. Chevron quilts are popular in nurseries, but this chevron quilt is different: The chevrons are foundation paper pieced so you can mix the fabrics in each chevron.

FINISHED SIZES

- **Overall:** 35 × 42 inches
- **Blocks:** 7 inches

MATERIALS LIST

- **"Princess Charlotte" foundation paper-piecing templates**
- **Foundation paper:** 30 sheets
- **Various yellows:** ⅞ yard total from Fat Quarters and Fat Eighths (blocks)
- **Various teals:** ⅞ yard total from Fat Quarters and Fat Eighths (blocks)
- **Teal and yellow stripe:** ⅝ yard for bias binding as shown or ¼ yard for straight binding
- **Light gray:** 1⅜ yards (blocks)
- **Backing:** 1⅓ yards
- **Batting:** Crib size, at least 41 × 48 inches

CUTTING DIRECTIONS

Various yellows:
• 90 rectangles (A1, A2, A3, B1, B2, B3), 2¼ × 6 inches (blocks)

Various teals:
• 90 rectangles (A1, A2, A3, B1, B2, B3), 2¼ × 6 inches (blocks)

Light gray:
• 60 squares (A4, A5, B4, B5), 5½ inches, cut in half diagonally (blocks)

Teal and yellow stripe:
• 4 strips, 2 × 42 or 2¼ × 42 inches or as you prefer (straight binding)

• For bias binding, cut enough strips from a 23-inch square to equal 164 inches plus 2 inches for every two strips cut (for joining)

Backing:
• 1 rectangle, 41 × 48 inches

Making the Foundation Blocks

In foundation-piecing, you sew with the printed side of the foundation pattern facing up and the fabrics underneath. The resulting block is a mirror image of the printed foundation pattern.

1. Prepare the foundations by copying the pattern onto foundation paper. Prepare 30 foundations. Each foundation has two parts: the A side and the B side. You'll sew the two sides together after foundation-piecing each side. To help in placing the fabrics for the chevron, trim each foundation, leaving a ¼-inch seam allowance on all sides (¼ inch outside the solid outline).

2. Foundation-piece the A side of a Block Z (A1 to A5). Trim this section to 4 × 7½ inches, which includes the necessary seam allowances. Repeat to complete the A side of 15 Block Zs and 15 Block Ys.

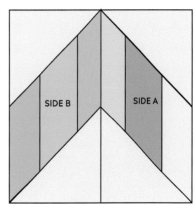

Block Z (make 15)

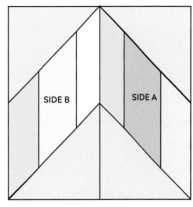

Block Y (make 15)

3. Foundation-piece the B side of a Block Z (B1 to B5). Trim this section to 4 × 7½ inches, which includes the necessary seam allowances. Repeat to complete the B side of 15 Block Zs and 15 Block Ys.

4. Carefully match the lines of the chevron and pin the A and B sides of a Block Z together (right sides together). Sew with a short stitch length to pierce the foundation paper. Press open the center seam between the A and B sides of the block. Repeat to complete 15 Block Zs and 15 Block Ys.

5. Trim each finished block to 7½ inches square, which includes the necessary seam allowances. Remove the foundation papers.

Assembling the Quilt Center

Quilt Assembly Diagram

1. Using the Quilt Assembly diagram, arrange the blocks in rows on your design wall. Pay attention to the placement of the blocks as they alternate colors in each row. Press the seams between blocks in odd rows to the left and even rows to the right to aid in the assembly of the rows.

2. Sew the rows together, taking care not to catch the tip (point) of each chevron. Press open the row seams. The quilt should measure 35½ × 42½ inches.

Quilting and Finishing

1. Remove the selvages from the backing before basting the quilt. Quilt as desired. The sample quilt was quilted with straight lines in the chevrons ¼ inch from the seams and with straight lines in the gray areas ½ inch from the seams.

2. Square up the quilt and bind it. Add a label.

For a fresh take on a modern chevron quilt, use 1930s reproduction fabrics and crisp white. The 1930s reproductions add a touch of whimsy with their charming motifs—perfect for a baby's room.

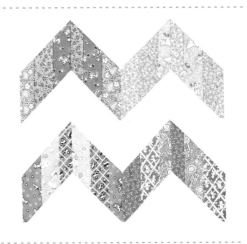

	Toddler	Lap	Full
Size	49 × 63 inches	63 × 70 inches	84 × 91 inches
Block setting	7 × 9	9 × 10	12 × 13
Block Z	35	45	84
Block Y	28	45	72
Various yellows	1½ yards	2⅔ yards	3⅞ yards
Various teals	2 yards	2⅔ yards	4½ yards
Light gray	2¾ yards	4½ yards	6⅞ yards
Binding	⅜ yard	½ yard	⅝ yard
Bias Binding	27-inch square, ¾ yard	28-inch square, ⅞ yard	32-inch square, 1 yard
Backing	3⅛ yards	3⅞ yards	5 yards
Batting	55 × 69 inches	69 × 76 inches	82 × 90 inches

"Elephants on Parade" Crib Quilt

This playful crib quilt features big, dimensional elephant ears that a baby can flip back and forth. The light prints provide a restful and modern look, while bolder, coordinating graphic prints add something bright and interesting for baby to look at.

FINISHED SIZES

- **Overall:** 40 × 40 inches
- **Blocks:** 32 inches

MATERIALS LIST

- "Elephants on Parade" appliqué templates
- **4 buttons:** 1 inch
- **Light lime:** ½ yard (block, Border #1)
- **Light teal:** ½ yard (block, Border #1)
- **Light salmon:** ½ yard (block, Border #1)
- **Light magenta:** ½ yard (block, Border #1)
- **Bright lime:** ⅜ yard (appliqué); ⅜ yard (binding)
- **Bright teal:** ⅜ yard (appliqué)
- **Bright salmon:** ⅜ yard (appliqué)
- **Bright magenta:** ⅜ yard (appliqué)
- **Backing:** 1⅔ yards
- **Batting:** Crib size, at least 46 × 46 inches
- **Elephant ears:** 4 scraps, 14 × 14 inches

CUTTING DIRECTIONS

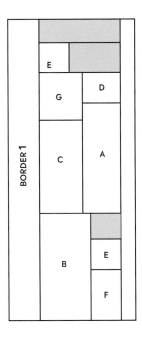

Light lime:
• 1 strip, 4½ × 42 inches (Border #1)
• 1 rectangle (A), 4½ × 14½ inches
• 1 rectangle (B), 8½ × 14½ inches
• 1 rectangle (C), 6½ × 12½ inches
• 1 square (D), 4½ × 4½ inches
• 2 squares (E), 2½ × 2½ inches
• 1 rectangle (F), 2½ × 6½ inches
• 1 square (G), 6½ × 6½ inches

Light teal:
• 1 strip, 4½ × 42 inches (Border #1)
• 1 rectangle (A), 4½ × 14½ inches
• 1 rectangle (B), 8½ × 14½ inches
• 1 rectangle (C), 6½ × 12½ inches
• 1 square (D), 4½ × 4½ inches
• 2 squares (E), 2½ × 2½ inches
• 1 rectangle (F), 2½ × 6½ inches
• 1 square (G), 6½ × 6½ inches

Light salmon:
• 1 strip 4½ × 42 inches (Border #1)
• 1 rectangle (A), 4½ × 14½ inches
• 1 rectangle (B), 8½ × 14½ inches
• 1 rectangle (C), 6½ × 12½ inches
• 1 square (D), 4½ × 4½ inches
• 2 squares (E), 2½ × 2½ inches
• 1 rectangle (F), 2½ × 6½ inches
• 1 square (G), 6½ × 6½ inches

Light magenta:
• 1 strip, 4½ × 42 inches (Border #1)
• 1 rectangle (A), 4½ × 14½ inches
• 1 rectangle (B), 8½ × 14½ inches
• 1 rectangle (C), 6½ × 12½ inches
• 1 square (D), 4½ × 4½ inches
• 2 squares (E), 2½ × 2½ inches
• 1 rectangle (F), 2½ × 6½ inches
• 1 square (G), 6½ × 6½ inches

Bright lime:
• 5 strips, 2 × 42 or 2¼ × 42 inches or as you prefer (binding)
• 1 pattern A (ear)
• 1 pattern A1 (ear)

Bright teal:
• 1 pattern A (ear)
• 1 pattern A1 (ear)

Bright salmon:
• 1 pattern A (ear)
• 1 pattern A1 (ear)

Bright magenta:
• 1 pattern A (ear)
• 1 pattern A1 (ear)

Backing:
• 1 rectangle, 46 × 42 inches
• 2 strips, 5 × 42 inches

Note: *Cut the border strips before cutting anything else. Trim them to the right size after sewing the quilt center. See the Cutting Diagram for help cutting the light fabrics.*

Assembling the Units

Unit 1 (make 1)

1. Lay out one E square of each color in a four-patch. Using Method 1 for piecing four-patch units, sew the four squares together to create Unit 1. Unit 1 should measure 4½ inches square. Press to the dark as you construct the four-patch and then press open or fan out the center seam.

Unit 2 (make 4)

2. Draw a diagonal line on the back of the four other E squares. Place the teal E square on the right end of a magenta F rectangle, right sides together. Sew on the diagonal line, flip the E square back, and press to make Unit 2. Trim the excess triangle fabric underneath the E triangle without trimming the F rectangle. Unit 2 should measure 2½ × 6½ inches.

3. Repeat step 2 to create three more Unit 2s in different colors.

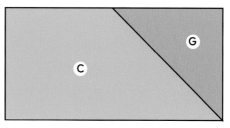

Unit 3 (make 4)

4. Draw a diagonal line on the back of the G squares. Place the magenta G square on the right end of the teal C rectangle, right sides together. Sew on the diagonal line, flip the G square back, and press to make Unit 3. Trim the excess triangle fabric underneath the G triangle without trimming the C rectangle. Unit 3 should measure 6½ × 12½ inches.

5. Repeat step 4 to create three more Unit 3s in different colors.

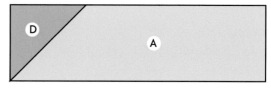

Unit 4 (make 4)

6. Draw a diagonal line on the back of the D squares. Place the magenta D square on the left end of the lime A rectangle, right sides together. Sew on the diagonal line, flip the D square back, and press to make Unit 4. Trim the excess triangle fabric underneath the triangle without trimming the A rectangle. Unit 4 should measure 4½ × 14½ inches.

7. Repeat step 6 to create three more Unit 4s in different colors. Sew a lime D square on a salmon A rectangle, a salmon D square on a teal A rectangle, and a teal D square on a magenta A rectangle to create the Unit 4s.

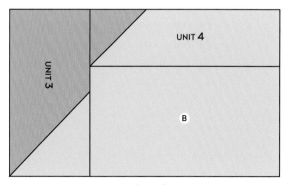

Unit 5 (make 4)

8. Sew the magenta–lime Unit 4 to the lime B rectangle. Press to the B rectangle. Sew the magenta–lime Unit 3 to the left end of this newly completed unit to create Unit 5. Unit 5 should measure 12½ × 20½ inches.

9. Repeat the previous step to make three more Unit 5s in different colors, as shown in the Quilt Assembly Diagram.

Assembling the Quilt Block

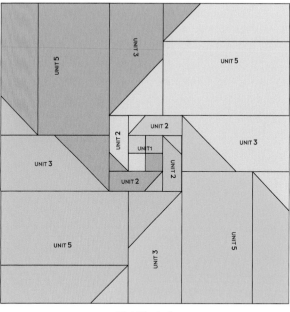

Block Z (make 1)

1. This quilt has only one block (Block Z). Join units to create Block Z. Lay out the block first, being careful to place each unit in the right place based on color.

2. Start by sewing the Unit 2s to the four-patch Unit 1. Sew the first Unit 2 onto Unit 1 using a partial seam and then add each Unit 2 in turn, returning to the first Unit 2 and sewing to complete the seam. Press to Unit 2.

3. Sew the Unit 5s to the central unit. Sew the first Unit 5 onto the central unit using a partial seam and then add each Unit 5 in turn, returning to the first Unit 5 and sewing to complete the seam. Press to Unit 5.

4. Block Z should measure 32½ × 32½ inches.

Assembling the Elephant Ears

1. To make floppy ears, trace ear patterns A and A1 on the back of each ear fabric and cut out. Trace four ear A1 patterns on the quilt batting and cut out.

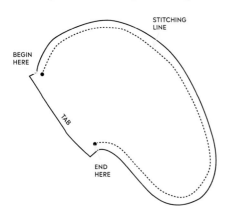

2. Place an A ear on top of a similarly colored A1 ear, right sides together. Place the quilt batting on top. Sew the shapes together, beginning and ending where marked and leaving the tab opening unsewn. Backstitch at the beginning and end of the seam. Clip curves and turn the shape right side out. Press all along the sewn edge. Repeat to sew the other ears.

3. Turn under the tabbed edges of one ear, leaving roughly a ½-inch tab. Sew close to the edge to close the opening. Be sure to backstitch at the beginning and end of the seam. Repeat for the other ears.

4. Quilt the ears with a simple pattern, such as diagonal lines, or use a unique pattern for each ear.

Adding the Borders

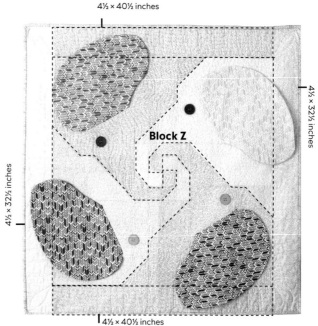

Quilt Assembly Diagram

1. Using the Quilt Assembly Diagram, arrange borders on the proper sides based on color.

2. Measure down the quilt center and cut the side Border #1 strips that length. Sew these to the sides of the quilt center. Press toward the strips.

3. Measure across the quilt center and cut the top and bottom Border #1 strips that length. Sew these strips to the top and bottom of the quilt center. Press toward the strips. The quilt should measure 40½ × 40½ inches.

If you prefer nonfloppy ears, you can appliqué them to the quilt instead. For hand-appliqué, use the ear pattern A1 (nonreversed) so you can trace it on the front of the fabric. For machine-appliqué, use the ear pattern A (reversed). Remove the ¼-inch seam allowance marked on the pattern if applicable to the appliqué method you're using.

Quilting and Finishing

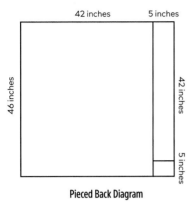

42 inches   5 inches

46 inches

42 inches

5 inches

Pieced Back Diagram
Diagram shows cut sizes

1. Remove the selvages and then piece the backing by sewing the two 5 × 42-inch strips together. Use a ½-inch seam to create a 5 × 83-inch strip. Backstitch at the beginning and end of the seam. Press open the seam.

2. Using the Pieced Back Diagram, sew the 5-inch strip you just made to the 46 × 42-inch strip along the 46-inch side, using a ½-inch seam allowance. Trim the excess section of the 5-inch strip even with the other strip.

3. Quilt as desired. The sample quilt was quilted with a different pattern for each elephant. The same patterns were used to quilt the ears.

4. Square up the quilted quilt and bind it. If this is to be a wall hanging, add a sleeve as well. Add a label.

Adding the Elephant Ears and Eyes

Adding the ears and eyes after the quilt is quilted eliminates the problem of keeping them out of the way while quilting.

1. Using the Quilt Assembly Diagram, arrange the ears on the quilt.

2. Without shifting the placement of the first ear, gently flip it over the tab end and pin in place. Sew the tab to the quilt along the marked line, backstitching at the beginning and end of the seam. Flip the ear back over the right way and press along the tab seam to flatten it in place. Stitch along the top edge of the tab, about ¼ inch from the edge.

3. To prevent the ears from flopping too much, tack them in place by hand-sewing with short stitches at a few points along the top edges of the ear, leaving the lower part of the ear floppy and playful. Use a matching thread, make a small quilter's knot and take a few appliqué (blind) stitches to hold each ear in place.

4. Using the Quilt Assembly Diagram, sew the four button eyes in place. If you prefer to appliqué the eyes instead, cut a 1-inch circular template and trace it on eye fabric. Add a ¼-inch seam allowance if applicable to the appliqué method you're using and then appliqué the eyes in place.

Babies are attracted to high-contrast patterns, so for a different look, make "Elephants on Parade" in bright fabrics.

"Life in the Tide Pool" Lap Quilt

Only the toughest organisms can survive life in a tide pool because of the strong currents and sun exposure. Making a quilt is also sometimes tough because of all the choices you need to make. This quilt has a secret to help you survive your quilting tide pool: It's made from precuts that not only save you time in construction but also guarantee you success when selecting fabrics because the precut fabrics are designed to go together.

FINISHED SIZES

- **Overall:** 60 × 72 inches
- **Blocks:** 8½ inches

MATERIALS LIST

- **1 batik Jelly Roll,** or 2⅞ yards from a variety of batiks (blocks, setting triangles, Border #2)
- **1 batik Charm Pack plus ⅝ yard** from a variety of batiks (blocks, setting triangles)
- If not using a Charm Pack, then 1¼ total yards from a variety of batiks
- **Dark batik:** ⅞ yard (Border #1 and #3); ½ yard (binding)
- **Backing:** 3⅞ yards
- **Batting:** At least 66 × 78 inches

CUTTING DIRECTIONS

From one Jelly Roll or a variety of batiks:
- 64 rectangles (A), 2½ × 9 inches (blocks)
- 64 rectangles (B), 2½ × 5 inches (blocks)
- 14 rectangles (E), 2½ × 7½ inches (setting triangles)
- 14 rectangles (F), 2½ × 9½ inches (setting triangles)
- 4 rectangles (H), 2½ × 9½ inches (setting triangles)
- 60 rectangles (I), 2½ × 4½ inches (Border #2)

To use the Jelly Roll:
- From all 40 strips, cut one A rectangle and one B rectangle.
- Select 24 of the 40 strips and cut one more A rectangle and one B rectangle from each for a total of 64 A rectangles and 64 B rectangles.
- Cut two I rectangles from each of the 24 strips for a total of 48 I rectangles. Set the 24 strips aside.
- Select 12 of the 16 remaining strips and cut one I rectangle from each. You should now have 60 I rectangles.
- Select two strips from the set of 16 strips and cut two H rectangles from each for a total of four H rectangles.
- From the remaining 14 strips, cut one E rectangle and one F rectangle for a total of 14 E and 14 F rectangles.

From one Charm Pack:
- 32 squares (C), 5 × 5 inches (blocks)

From a variety of batiks:
- 4 squares (D), 7⅞ × 7⅞ inches, cut diagonally in both directions (setting triangles) (Put two triangles aside for use in another project.)
- 2 squares (G), 4⅛ × 4⅛ inches, cut diagonally once (setting triangles)

Dark batik:
Note: *Cut the border strips before cutting anything else. Trim the border strips to the right size after sewing the quilt center.*
- 6 strips, 2½ × 42 inches (Border #1)
- 8 strips, 2½ × 42 inches (Border #3)
- 7 strips, 2 × 42 inches or 2¼ × 42 inches or as you prefer (binding)

Backing:
- 2 strips, at least 66 × 42 inches

Assembling the Quilt Blocks

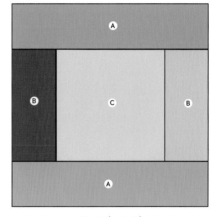

Block Z (make 32)

1. Sew one B rectangle to either side of one C square. Press to the B rectangles. Sew one A rectangle to the top and bottom of this unit to make Block Z. Make 32 Block Zs. Press half the blocks to the A rectangles and the other half to the C square. This will help you assemble your rows. Block Z should measure 9 × 9 inches.

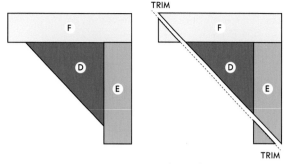

Side Setting Triangle Y (make 14)

4. For the pieced corner setting triangles, you'll partially piece a block and then trim it. Fold a G triangle in half to find its center. Also fold the H rectangle in half. Matching these centers, sew one G triangle to one H rectangle to make a corner setting Triangle X. Use a slightly shorter stitch length and backstitch at the beginning and end of the seam. Be careful not to stretch the bias edge of the triangle. Press to the H rectangle. Make four Triangle Xs.

5. Align a ruler to the edge of G triangle and trim. Trim all four Triangle Xs.

2. For the pieced side setting triangles, you'll partially piece a block and then trim it. Sew one D triangle to one E rectangle. Use a slightly shorter stitch length and backstitch at the beginning and end of the seam. Be careful not to stretch the bias edge of the triangle when adding the E rectangle. Press to the E rectangle. Sew the F rectangle to this unit to make the side setting Triangle Y, pressing to the F rectangle. Again, be careful of the bias edge on the triangle. Make 14 Triangle Ys.

3. Align a ruler to the edge of the D triangle and trim. Trim all 14 Triangle Ys.

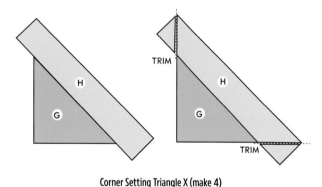

Corner Setting Triangle X (make 4)

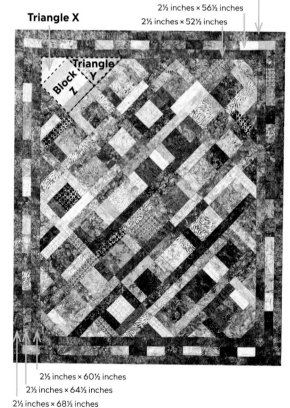

Triangle X

Block Z

Triangle Y

2½ inches × 60½ inches
2½ inches × 56½ inches
2½ inches × 52½ inches

2½ inches × 60½ inches
2½ inches × 64½ inches
2½ inches × 68½ inches

Quilt Assembly Diagram

Assembling the Quilt Center

1. Using the Quilt Assembly Diagram, arrange Block Zs in diagonal rows on your design wall. To make assembly easier, you might want to place Block Zs pressed to the A rectangles next to Block Zs pressed to the C squares. Add Triangle Xs and Triangle Ys where shown.

2. Start by sewing the blocks together to make each diagonal row. Add the side and/or corner setting triangles after joining the blocks in each row, then press toward the setting triangles. Press the blocks in odd rows to the left and blocks in even rows to the right to help when assembling rows.

3. Sew the rows together. Press the row seams in one direction. The quilt center should measure 48½ × 60½ inches.

Adding the Borders

1. Cut two 2½ × 42-inch Border #1 strips in half. Sew each half to the remaining four 2½ × 42-inch Border #1 strips to create four 2½ × 63-inch Border #1 strips.

2. Measure down the quilt center and cut two Border #1 strips that length. Sew these strips to the sides of the quilt center. If you sew one strip from the top of the quilt down and the other from the bottom of the quilt up, you'll avoid placing the border seam in the side borders in the same position on each side. Press toward Border #1.

3. Measure across the quilt center and cut the other two Border #1 strips that length. Sew these strips to the top and bottom of the quilt center, once again switching directions from which you sew the borders to stagger where the border seams are located. Press toward Border #1. The quilt should measure 52½ × 60½ inches.

4. Lay out 16 I rectangles of various colors in a pleasing arrangement and sew them together to create one side of Border #2. Repeat to create a second side of Border #2. Press the seams in the same direction and then measure the borders. Measure down the center of the quilt. If your pieced borders don't equal this measurement, make adjustments to a few seams in the middle of each pieced border so the two measurements are the same. Sew the side borders to the quilt center. Press toward Border #1.

5. Sew 14 I rectangles together to create a top Border #2 2½ × 56½ inches. Repeat to create the bottom Border #2. Press the seams in the same direction. Measure the borders and the width of the quilt, and make adjustments to the middle seams of the borders as needed. Sew the borders to the top and bottom of the quilt center. Press toward Border #1. The quilt should measure 56½ × 64½ inches.

6. Sew two of the 2½ × 42-inch Border #3 strips together. Repeat to create four 2½ × 83½-inch Border #3 strips.

7. Measure down the quilt center and cut two Border #3 strips that length. Sew these strips to the sides of the quilt center. Sew the strips in opposite directions so the seam isn't in the same position on each side. Press toward Border #3.

8. Measure across the quilt center and cut the other 2 Border #3 strips that length. Sew these strips to the top and bottom of the quilt center, once again switching directions to stagger where the seams are located. Press toward Border #3. The quilt should measure 60½ × 68½ inches.

Quilting and Finishing

1. Make sure you remove the selvages from the backing. Piece the backing by sewing the two 66 × 42-inch strips together with a ½-inch seam allowance, creating a 66 × 83-inch rectangle. Backstitch at the beginning and end of the seam. Press open the seam.

2. Quilt as desired. The sample quilt was quilted with curvy feathers in the squares and wavy lines that run diagonally down the strips.

3. Square up the quilted quilt and bind it. Add a label.

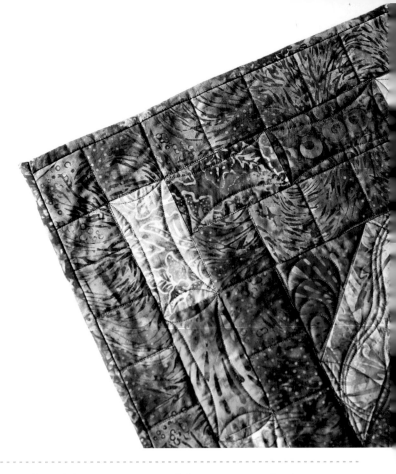

Bright fabrics with lots of white make this summer table runner sizzle. It uses four blocks, solid setting triangles, a skinny 1-inch inner border, and a wider 2½-inch outer border that's perfect for showcasing the beautiful quilting.

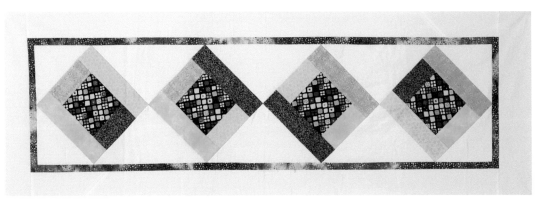

	Crib	**Toddler**	**Full**	**Queen**
Size	30 × 42 inches	43 × 55 inches	84 × 84 inches	96 × 96 inches
Block setting	2 × 3	3 × 4	6 × 6	7 × 7
Charm Packs	½ yard*	¾ yard*	2 packs plus ⅓ yard or 1½ yards total	2 packs plus ¾ yard or 2⅛ yards total
Jelly Rolls	¾ yard*	1¼ yards*	2 rolls or 4⅝ yards	2 rolls plus ½ yard or 6 yards total
Border #1	⅛ yard**	¼ yard**	⅝ yard	⅝ yard
Border #3	⅓ yard**	½ yard**	⅝ yard	⅝ yard
Backing	1⅓ yards	3 yards	7½ yards	8½ yards
Batting	36 × 48 inches	49 × 61 inches	90 × 90 inches	102 × 102 inches
Binding	⅓ yard	⅜ yard	⅝ yard	¾ yard

* Smaller quilts don't require a full Charm Pack or Jelly Roll; buy yardage instead.

** Three borders will overwhelm smaller quilts. For a toddler quilt, use two plain borders: the inner one 1-inch finished (cut at 1½ inches wide) and the outer one 2½ inches (cut at 3 inches wide). For a crib quilt, use a 1-inch inner border (cut at 1½ inches wide) and a 2-inch outer border (cut at 2½ wide).

"Conga Line" Lap Quilt

Like a conga line, the colors in this quilt weave in and out in an endless dance and are perfect for showcasing your favorite fabrics. Here, the look is clean and modern, while the alternate version, in Asian fabrics, is calm and restful.

FINISHED SIZES

- **Overall:** 55½ × 6½ inches
- **Blocks:** 13½ inches

MATERIALS LIST

- **Turquoise:** 1⅛ yards (blocks, binding)
- **Lime:** 1 yard (blocks)
- **White:** 1¾ yards (blocks, sashing, Border #1)
- **Backing:** 3½ yards
- **Batting:** Lap size, at least 61½ × 67½ inches

CUTTING DIRECTIONS

Turquoise:
• 6 strips, 2 × 42 or 2¼ × 42 inches or as you prefer (binding)
• Cut 10 strips, 3½ × 42, and then subcut for blocks:
  • 8 rectangles (A), 3½ × 12½ inches
  • 8 rectangles (F), 3½ × 11 inches
  • 6 rectangles (D), 3½ × 9½ inches
  • 2 rectangles (H), 3½ × 8 inches
  • 16 rectangles (G), 3½ × 6½ inches

Lime:
• Cut 10 strips, 3½ × 42 inches, and then subcut for blocks:
  • 8 rectangles (A), 3½ × 12½ inches
  • 8 rectangles (F), 3½ × 11 inches
  • 6 rectangles (D), 3½ × 9½ inches
  • 2 rectangles (H), 3½ × 8 inches
  • 16 rectangles (G), 3½ × 6½ inches

White:
• Fold the fabric with the selvages on the sides and then cut five strips, 2 × 63 inches (sashing)
• Refold the fabric with the selvages together and cut two strips, 2 × 32 inches (Border #1)
• Cut 20 strips, 2 × 32 inches, and then subcut the blocks:
  • 16 rectangles (E), 2 × 11 inches
  • 32 rectangles (C), 2 × 8 inches
  • 52 rectangles (B), 2 × 3½ inches

Note: *Cut the border and sashing strips first. Trim the border and sashing strips to the right size after sewing the quilt center.*

Backing:
• 1 strip, 63 × 42 inches
• 1 strip, 63 × 27 inches

Assembling the Units

Unit 1 (make 8)

Unit 1A (make 8)

1. Sew one B rectangle to the right side of a turquoise A rectangle to create Unit 1. Press to the A rectangle. Make eight Unit 1s. Sew a B rectangle to the right side of a lime A rectangle to make Unit 1A. Press to the A rectangle. Make eight Unit 1As. Unit 1 and Unit 1A should measure 3½ × 14 inches.

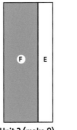

Unit 2 (make 8)

Unit 2A (make 8)

2. Sew an E rectangle to the right side of a turquoise F rectangle to create Unit 2. Press to the F rectangle. Make eight Unit 2s. Sew an E rectangle to the right side of a lime F rectangle to make Unit 2A. Press to the F rectangle. Make eight Unit 2As. Unit 2 and Unit 2A should measure 5 × 11 inches.

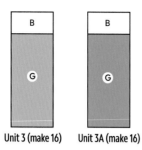

Unit 3 (make 16)   Unit 3A (make 16)

3. Sew a B rectangle to the top of a lime G rectangle. Press to the G rectangle to make Unit 3. Make 16 Unit 3s. Sew one B rectangle to the top of a turquoise G rectangle and press to the G rectangle to make Unit 3A. Make 16 Unit 3As. Unit 3 and Unit 3A should measure 8 × 3½ inches.

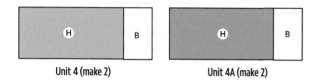

Unit 4 (make 2)   Unit 4A (make 2)

4. Sew a B rectangle to the right side of a lime H rectangle to make Unit 4. Press to the H rectangle. Make two Unit 4s. Sew a B rectangle to the right side of a turquoise H rectangle to make Unit 4A. Make two Unit 4As. Unit 4 and Unit 4A should measure 3½ × 9½ inches.

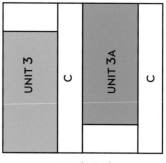

Unit 5 (make 8)

5. Sew a C rectangle to the right side of a Unit 3. Press to the C rectangle. Sew a Unit 3A to the right side of this subunit. Press to Unit 3A. Sew a C rectangle to the right side of this subunit to make Unit 5. Press to the C rectangle. Make eight Unit 5s. Unit 5 should measure 8 × 9½ inches.

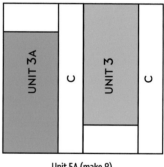

Unit 5A (make 8)

6. Sew a C rectangle to the right side of a Unit 3A. Press to the C rectangle. Sew a Unit 3 to the right side of this subunit. Press to Unit 3. Sew a C rectangle to the right side of this subunit to make Unit 5A. Press to the C rectangle. Make eight Unit 5As. Unit 5A should measure 8 × 9½ inches.

Assembling the Quilt Blocks

Four different blocks are required for this quilt. Blocks Z and Z1 are similar, as are Block Y and Y1.

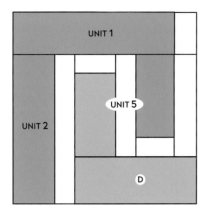

Block Z (make 6)

1. Lay out the pieces for Block Z, being careful to place each unit in the right place based on color. Sew a lime D rectangle to the bottom of one Unit 5. Press to the D rectangle. Sew Unit 2 to the left of this subunit, pressing to Unit 2. Sew Unit 1 to the top of this subunit, pressing to Unit 1. Make six Block Zs. Block Z should measure 14 × 14 inches.

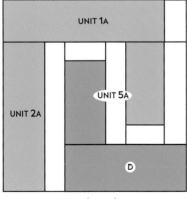

Block Y (make 6)

2. Follow a similar process to create Block Y. Lay out the block pieces first, being careful to place each unit in the right place. Sew a turquoise D rectangle to the bottom of a Unit 5A. Press to the D rectangle. Sew Unit 2A to the left of this subunit. Press to Unit 2A. Sew Unit 1A to the top of this subunit, pressing to Unit 1A. Make six Block Ys. Block Y should measure 14 × 14 inches.

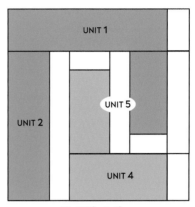

Block Z1 (make 2)

3. Lay out the pieces for Block Z1. Start by sewing a Unit 4 to the bottom of a Unit 5. Press to Unit 4. Sew Unit 2 to the left of this subunit, pressing to Unit 2. Sew Unit 1 to the top of this subunit, pressing to Unit 1. Make two Block Z1s. Block Z1 should measure 14 × 14 inches.

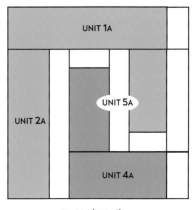

Block Y1 (make 2)

4. Lay out the pieces for Block Y1. Sew a Unit 4A to the bottom of a Unit 5A. Press to Unit 4A. Sew Unit 2A to the left of this subunit, pressing to Unit 2A. Sew Unit 1A to the top of this subunit, pressing to Unit 1A. Make two Block Y1s. Block Y1 should measure 14 × 14 inches.

Assembling the Quilt Center

2 inches × 54 inches

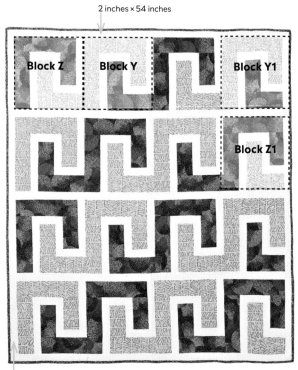

2 inches × 61½ inches

Quilt Assembly Diagram

1. Using the Quilt Assembly Diagram, arrange the blocks in rows on your design wall. Pay attention to the placement of Block Zs and Block Ys, as they alternate within each row. Place either a Block Z1 or a Block Y1 at the right side of each row.

2. Sew the rows together. Press the blocks in each row in the same direction. Rows should measure 14 × 54 inches.

Adding the Sashing and the Border

1. Measure your rows and cut the five sashing strips the average length of the rows.

2. Using the Quilt Assembly Diagram, arrange the sashing strips and block rows. Add sashing to the top of each row. Press to the sashing. Sew the last sashing strip to the bottom of Row 4.

3. Sew the sashed rows together to make the quilt top. Continue to press toward the sashing strips. The quilt should measure 54 × 61½ inches.

4. Sew the two Border #1 strips together. Measure down the quilt center and cut the Border #1 strip that length. Sew the strip to the left side of the quilt center. (Notice that there's only one border—on the left side of the quilt.) Press toward the strip. The quilt should measure 55½ × 61½ inches.

Quilting and Finishing

1. Remove the selvages from the backing fabric. Piece the backing by sewing the 63 × 42-inch rectangle to the 63 × 27-inch rectangle using a ½-inch seam along the 63-inch side to create a 63 × 68-inch rectangle. Backstitch at the beginning and end of the seam. Press the seam to one side.

2. Quilt as desired. The sample quilt was quilted with a large curvy meander in the turquoise patches, triangles in the lime patches, and a back-and-forth swirl in the white sashing.

3. Square up the quilted quilt and bind it. Add a label.

	Crib	**Twin**	**Queen**
Size	42 × 46½ inches	69 × 76½ inches	96 × 91½ inches
Block setting	3 × 3	5 × 5	7 × 6
Block Z	3	10	18
Block Y	3	10	18
Block Z1	2	3	3
Block Y1	1	2	3
Turquoise	⅝ yard plus ⅜ yard binding	1⅝ yards plus ½ yard binding	2¾ yards plus ⅝ yard binding
Lime	⅝ yard	1⅝ yards	2¾ yards
White	1⅛ yards	2⅛ yards	4⅛ yards
Backing	2⅔ yards	4¼ yards	8½ yards
Batting	48 × 52½ inches	75 × 82½ inches	102 × 97½ inches

For a less vivid look, try using Asian-inspired fabrics, which can lend tranquility to this design.

"Star-Crossed" Wall Hanging

Some of the most moving and memorable love stories involve star-crossed lovers. Their love seems doomed, but we can't help hoping they can somehow find a happy ending. Inspired by such love stories, this wall hanging combines pieced blocks with foundation-pieced sashing to create a secondary star-crossed pattern. The blocks come together quickly using strip sets.

FINISHED SIZES

- **Overall:** 42 × 42 inches
- **Blocks:** 8 inches

MATERIALS LIST

- **"Star-Crossed" foundation paper-piecing templates**
- **Foundation paper:** 16 sheets
- **Cream stripe:** ⅜ yard (blocks)
- **Cream with berries:** 1 yard (blocks, sashing)
- **Navy blue ribbons:** ⅜ yard (blocks)
- **Light blue feathers:** ⅜ yard (sashing, cornerstones)
- **Dark red plumes:** ⅝ yard (blocks, sashing, binding)
- **Dark blue plumes:** ⅜ yard (blocks, sashing)
- **Blue check:** ½ yard (Border #1, cornerstones)
- **Backing:** 1¾ yards
- **Batting:** Crib size, at least 48 × 48 inches

Cream stripe:
• 4 strips, 2½ × 42 inches (strip sets for blocks)

Cream with berries:
• 16 squares (A), 5 × 5 inches (blocks)
• 16 rectangles (A1), 3 × 6½ inches (sashing foundations)
• 8 rectangles, 2½ × 8½ inches (sashing)

Navy blue ribbons:
• 16 squares (A), 5 × 5 inches (blocks)

Light blue feathers:
• 16 rectangles (A2), 3 × 3¾ inches (sashing foundations)
• 4 squares, 2½ × 2½ inches (cornerstones)

Dark red plumes:
• 5 strips, 2 × 42 to 2¼ × 42 inches or as you prefer (binding)
• 2 strips, 2½ × 42 inches (strip sets for blocks)
• 8 rectangles (A3), 3 × 4½ inches (sashing foundations)

Dark blue plumes:
• 2 strips, 2½ × 42 inches (strip sets for blocks)
• 8 rectangles (A3), 3 × 4½ inches (sashing foundations)

Blue check:
• 5 strips, 2½ × 42 inches (Border #1)
• 5 squares, 2½ × 2½ inches (cornerstones)

Backing:
• 1 rectangle, 48 × 42 inches
• 1 rectangle, 7 × 42 inches
• 1 square, 7 × 7 inches

Note: *Cut the border strips before cutting anything else. Trim the border strips to the right size after sewing the quilt center.*

Making the Block Units

1. Using Method 2 for piecing four-patch units, make 16 dark red-and-cream striped four-patches. Use one cream stripe strip and one dark red strip to create one strip set. Press to the dark red. Repeat to create a second strip set.

Unit 1 (make 16)

2. Subcut the strip sets every 2½ inches to create 32 two-square units. Sew two of these units together to create a four-patch (Unit 1). Press the center seam open or fan it to reduce bulk. Make 16 Unit 1s. Unit 1 should measure 4½ × 4½ inches.

Unit 1A (make 16)

3. Repeat steps 1 and 2 to create 16 dark blue and cream striped four-patches (Unit 1As). Unit 1A should measure 4½ × 4½ inches.

4. Using Method 1 for piecing half-square triangles (HSTs), make 32 HSTs. Use one navy blue A square and one cream A square to make two HSTs. Press to the dark. Measure and trim each HST to 4½ × 4½ inches.

Assembling the Quilt Blocks

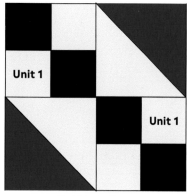

Block Z (make 8)

1. Join Unit 1s and HSTs to create Block Z. Assemble each row, paying particular attention to the arrangement of the dark red squares in the four-patches and the navy blue triangle in the HST. Pin the HST carefully to avoid cropping its point. Sew the two rows together and press open the seam. Make eight Block Zs. Block Z should measure 8½ inches square.

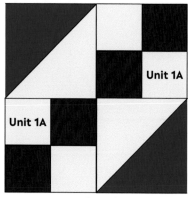

Block Y (make 8)

2. Join the Unit 1As and HSTs to create Block Y. Assemble each row, paying particular attention to the arrangement of the dark blue squares in the four-patches and the navy blue triangle in the HST. Pin the HST carefully to avoid cropping its point. Sew the two rows together and press open the seam. Make eight Block Ys. Block Y should measure 8½ inches square.

Assembling the Sashing

1. Prepare the foundations by copying the pattern onto foundation paper. Make 16 foundations.

Unit 2 (make 8)

2. Piece a foundation for the sashing to create Unit 2. Place the cream with berries fabric in the A1 spot, light blue in the A2 spot, and dark blue in the A3 spot. Repeat to make eight Unit 2s.

Unit 2A (make 8)

3. Piece another foundation for the sashing, placing the cream with berries fabric in the A1 spot, light blue in the A2 spot, and dark red in the A3 spot to create Unit 2A. Repeat to make eight Unit 2As.

4. Trim all foundations, leaving a ¼-inch seam allowance on all sides. Unit 2s and Unit 2As should measure 2½ × 8½ inches.

Assembling the Quilt Center

Quilt Assembly Diagram

1. Using the Quilt Assembly Diagram, join the Block Zs, Block Ys, Unit 2s, Unit 2As, and cornerstones to form the quilt center.

2. Sew the appropriate sashing (foundation-pieced or plain) to the right side of every block in columns 1, 2, and 3. When adding foundation-pieced sashing, pay particular attention to the orientation of the dark red or dark blue triangle. Press to the sashing.

3. Sew the appropriate sashing (foundation-pieced or plain) to the bottom of every block in rows 1, 2, and 3. Again, pay attention to the orientation of the triangles in the pieced sashing. Before you sew on the sashing, add a cornerstone to the right side of the sashing. Press to the sashing to aid in row assembly later. Then sew the appropriate sashing to the bottom of the blocks.

4. Lay out all the blocks and then sew them together in rows. Pin at every intersection. Press to the sashing. Sew rows together. Press the row seams in the same direction. The quilt center should measure 38½ × 38½ inches.

Adding the Borders

1. Measure down the quilt center and cut the side borders that length. Sew these strips to the sides of the quilt center. Press toward the strips.

2. Cut one of the remaining Border #1 strips in half and sew each half to the top and bottom Border #1 strips. Measure across the quilt center and cut the top and bottom borders that length. Sew these strips to the top and bottom of the quilt center and press toward the strips. The quilt should measure 42½ × 42½ inches.

Quilting and Finishing

The size of this quilt requires a pieced backing.

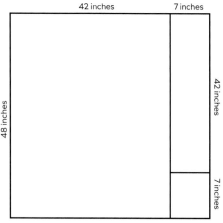

42 inches   7 inches

48 inches

42 inches

7 inches

Pieced Back Diagram
Diagram shows cut sizes

1. After removing the selvages from the backing fabric, piece the back as shown in the Pieced Back Diagram. Start by sewing the 7 × 42-inch rectangle to the 7-inch square along the 7-inch edge using a ½-inch seam allowance. Lock your stitches at the beginning and end of the seam by backstitching. Press the seam to one side.

2. Sew the just-stitched 7 × 48-inch rectangle to the 42 × 48-inch rectangle you cut earlier, again with a ½-inch seam allowance. Lock your stitches at the beginning and end of the seam by backstitching. Press the seam to one side.

3. Prepare the quilt for quilting and quilt as desired. The sample quilt was quilted with feathers and soft curves in the blocks as well as swirls in the sashing and borders.

4. Square up the quilted quilt and bind it. Add a label and a sleeve for hanging.

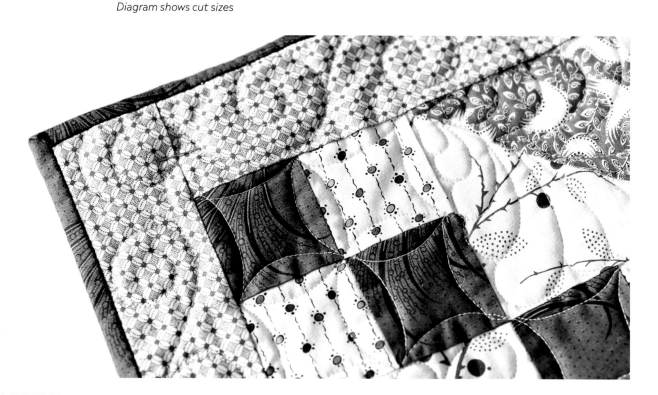

	Lap	Twin	Queen
Size	62 × 72 inches	72 × 82 inches	92 × 102 inches
Block setting	6 × 7	7 × 8	9 × 10
Block Z	21	28	45
Block Y	21	28	45
Cream stripe	¾ yard	1¼ yards	½ yard
Cream with berries	2⅛ yards	2¾ yards	4½ yards
Navy blue ribbons	1 yard	1¼ yards	2¼ yards
Light blue	⅝ yard	1 yard	1½ yards
Dark red	¾ yard	⅞ yard	1¼ yards
	½ yard (binding)	⅝ yard (binding)	¾ yard (binding)
Dark blue	¾ yard	⅞ yard	1¼ yards
Blue check	⅝ yard	⅞ yard	1 yard
Backing	2⅚ yards	5 yards	9 yards
Batting	68 × 78 inches	78 × 88 inches	98 × 108 inches

Instead of a wall hanging, make a table topper in bright, modern prints. In this version, the HSTs are arranged so the dark side is pointed inward toward the center of the block. Also, one of the four-patches in each block uses the same fabric used in the HST instead of white. Finally, the sashing foundation in this version is simpler, using only two colors instead of three.

"Swimming in the Gene Pool" Wall Hanging

This quilt uses three different block patterns—each with several color variations. The result looks a little like a double helix, which makes sense because you might say quilting is in my DNA. Take a swim through your fabric stash and create your own version of "Swimming in the Gene Pool."

FINISHED SIZES

- **Overall:** 32 × 36 inches
- **Blocks:** 3 × 9 inches

MATERIALS LIST

- **Moon multicolored:** ¼ yard (vertical sashing)
- **Chevron:** ⅜ yard (side borders)
- **White:** ½ yard (blocks)
- **Black dot:** ⅛ yard (blocks); ⅓ yard (binding)
- **Dark gray:** ¼ yard (blocks)
- **Light gray:** ⅛ yard (blocks)
- **Yellow:** ⅛ yard (blocks)
- **Medium gray:** ⅛ yard (blocks)
- **Stripe:** ⅛ yard (blocks)
- **Backing:** 1¼ yards
- **Batting:** Crib size, at least 38 × 42 inches

CUTTING DIRECTIONS

Moon multicolored:
• 1 rectangle, 6½ × 36½ inches (vertical sashing)

Chevron:
• 2 rectangles, 4½ × 36½ inches (side borders)

White:
• 9 rectangles (B), 3½ × 5¾ inches (blocks)
• 11 rectangles (F), 3½ × 4 inches (blocks)
• 4 rectangles (I), 2¾ × 3½ inches (blocks)
• 4 rectangles (J), 2¼ × 3½ inches (blocks)
• 11 rectangles (E), 2 × 3½ inches (blocks)
• 9 rectangles (A), 1¼ × 3½ inches (blocks)

Black dot:
• 4 strips, 2 × 42 or 2¼ × 42 inches or as you prefer (binding)
• 2 rectangles (L), 1¼ × 5½ inches (blocks)
• 4 rectangles (H), 1¼ × 4½ inches (blocks)
• 12 rectangles (A), 1¼ × 3½ inches (blocks)
• 18 rectangles (C), 1¼ × 2 inches (blocks)

Dark gray:
• 6 rectangles (L), 1¼ × 5½ inches (blocks)
• 14 rectangles (H), 1¼ × 4½ inches (blocks)
• 6 rectangles (A), 1¼ × 3½ inches (blocks)
• 26 rectangles (C), 1¼ × 2 inches (blocks)

Light gray:
• 2 rectangles (G), 2 × 3 inches (blocks)
• 3 squares (D), 2 × 2 inches (blocks)

Yellow:
• 1 rectangle (K), 2 × 4 inches (blocks)
• 2 squares (D), 2 × 2 inches (blocks)
• 4 rectangles (H), 1¼ × 4½ inches (blocks)
• 4 rectangles (C), 1¼ × 2 inches (blocks)

Medium gray:
• 2 rectangles (K), 2 × 4 inches (blocks)
• 5 rectangles (G), 2 × 3 inches (blocks)
• 3 squares (D), 2 × 2 inches (blocks)

Stripe:
• 1 rectangle (K), 2 × 4 inches (blocks)
• 4 rectangles (G), 2 × 3 inches (blocks)
• 1 square (D), 2 × 2 inches (blocks)

Backing:
• 1 rectangle, 38 × 42 inches

Note: *Trim the vertical sashing and border strips to the right size after sewing the quilt center.*

Assembling the Z Blocks

There are three different blocks (Block Z, Block Y, and Block X) in this quilt, with color variations within each block. All blocks should measure 3½ × 9½ inches.

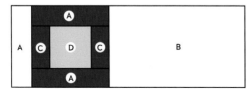

Block Z1 (make 3)

1. Sew a dark gray C rectangle to either side of one light gray D square. Press to the C rectangles. Sew a dark gray A rectangle to the top and bottom of this unit and press to the A rectangles.

2. Sew one white A rectangle to the left of the square unit, pressing to the A rectangle. Sew one white B rectangle to the right of the framed unit and press to the B rectangle. Make three Block Z1s.

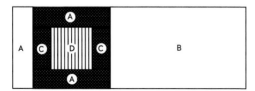

Block Z2 (make 1)

3. Block Z2 is the same as Block Z1, but it uses different colors. Sew two black dot A and C rectangles to a stripe D square. Add the white A and B rectangles and press as before. Make one Block Z2.

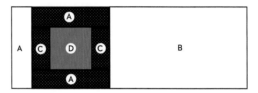

Block Z3 (make 3)

4. Block Z3 is the same as Block Z1, except sew two black dot A and C rectangles to a medium gray D square. Add the white A and B rectangles and press as before. Make three Block Z3s.

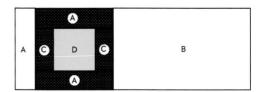

Block Z4 (make 2)

5. Block Z4 is the same as Block Z1, except sew two black dot A and C rectangles to a yellow D square. Add the white A and B rectangles and press as before. Make two Block Z4s.

Assembling the Y Blocks

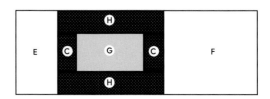

Block Y1 (make 2)

1. Sew one black dot C rectangle to each side of one light gray G rectangle. Press to the C rectangles. Sew one black dot H rectangle to the top and bottom of this unit and press to the H rectangles.

2. Sew one white E rectangle to the left of the framed unit, pressing to the E rectangle. Sew one white F rectangle to the right of the framed unit and press to the F rectangle. Make two Block Y1s.

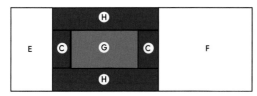

Block Y2 (make 5)

3. Block Y2 is the same as Block Y1, but it uses different colors. Sew two dark gray H and C rectangles to a medium gray G rectangle. Add the white E and F rectangles and press as before. Make five Y2s.

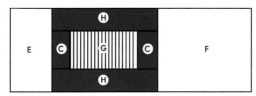

Block Y3 (make 2)

4. Block Y3 is the same as Block Y1, except sew two dark gray H and C rectangles to a stripe G rectangle. Add the white E and F rectangles and press as before. Make two Block Y3s.

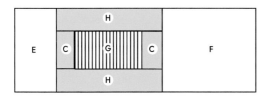

Block Y4 (make 2)

5. Block Y4 is the same as Block Y1, except sew two yellow H and C rectangles to a stripe G rectangle. Add the white E and F rectangles and press as before. Make two Block Y4s.

Assembling the X Blocks

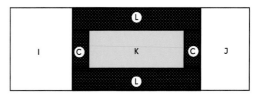

Block X1 (make 1)

1. Sew one black dot C rectangle to each side of one yellow K rectangle. Press to the C rectangles. Sew one black dot L rectangle to the top and bottom of this unit and press to the L rectangles.

2. Sew one white I rectangle to the left of the framed unit, pressing to the I rectangle. Sew one white J rectangle to the right of the framed unit and press to the J rectangle. Make one Block X1.

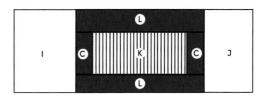

Block X2 (make 1)

3. Block X2 is the same as Block X1, but it uses different colors. Sew two dark gray L and C rectangles to a stripe K rectangle. Add the white I and J rectangles and press as before. Make one Block X2.

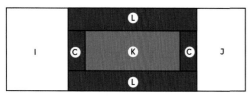

Block X3 (make 2)

4. Block X3 is the same as Block X1, except sew two dark gray L and C rectangles to a medium gray K rectangle. Add the white I and J rectangles and press as before. Make two Block X3s.

Assembling the Quilt Center

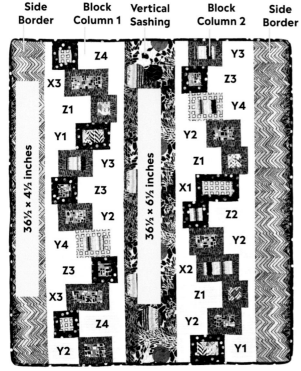

Quilt Assembly Diagram

1. Using the Quilt Assembly Diagram, join the Block Zs, Block Ys, Block Xs, and vertical sashing to form the quilt center.

2. Lay out the blocks in Block Column 1, being careful to note the position of the framed square in each block. You might need to rotate a block 180° to get the right orientation of the framed square.

3. Sew the blocks together. Press the seams in the same direction. The Block Column 1 should measure 9½ × 36½ inches.

4. Repeat steps 2 and 3 to sew the blocks in Block Column 2. The Block Column 2 should measure 9½ × 36½ inches.

5. Measure down the center of the two block columns and cut the vertical sashing this length. Sew the sashing to the right side of Block Column 1. Press to the sashing.

6. Sew Block Column 2 to the right side of the vertical sashing. Press to the sashing. The quilt center should measure 24½ × 36½ inches.

Adding the Borders

1. Measure down the quilt center and cut the two chevron side border rectangles that length. Sew these strips to the sides of the quilt center. Press toward the strips. The quilt should measure 32½ × 36½ inches.

Quilting and Finishing

1. Remove the selvages from the backing fabric before basting the quilt. Prepare the quilt for quilting and quilt as desired. The sample quilt was quilted with narrowly spaced straight lines in the white areas. The framed units were quilted with a triangle design, moving from one framed area to the next without stopping. The vertical sashing was quilted with a simple circular meander and the side borders were quilted with zigzag rows from top to bottom that echoed the chevron pattern in the fabric.

2. Square up the quilted quilt and bind it. Add a label and a sleeve for hanging.

	Lap	Twin	Queen
Size	62 × 72 inches	77 × 87 inches	92 × 93 inches
Block columns/ vertical sashing	4 with 24 blocks each, 3 sashings	5 with 29 blocks each, 4 sashings	6 with 31 blocks each, 5 sashings
Block Zs	36	56	72
Block Ys	44	66	84
Block Xs	16	23	30
Moon multicolored	1½ yards	1⅞ yards	2¼ yards
Chevron	¾ yard	¾ yard	¾ yard
White	1⅝ yards	2⅜ yards	2⅞ yards
Black dot	½ yard	⅝ yard	⅞ yard
	½ yard (binding)	⅝ yard (binding)	¾ yard (binding)
Dark gray	⅝ yard	1 yard	1¼ yards
Light gray	⅛ yard	⅛ yard	¼ yard
Yellow	¼ yard	¼ yard	⅜ yard
Medium gray	¼ yard	⅜ yard	⅜ yard
Stripe	⅛ yard	¼ yard	¼ yard
Backing	4⅜ yards	5¼ yards	8¼ yards
Batting	68 × 78 inches	83 × 93 inches	98 × 99 inches

For a quick project, try this table runner in bright modern prints. The gray shown here makes the colors pop, while the white lends an air of lightness.

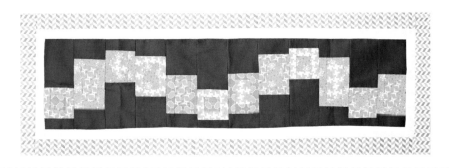

"Snake Eyes" Lap Quilt

Like a roll of the dice, the colors in this quilt appear to be chosen almost at random. However, if you look carefully, you'll see it's not luck but careful planning that determines the placement of the colors. The fabrics in this quilt are from a fabric collection, so they come together with just the right blend of light, medium, and dark fabrics. Why not roll the dice and see how your favorite collection of fabrics looks in this lap quilt?

FINISHED SIZES

- **Overall:** 58 × 66 inches
- **Blocks:** 8 inches

MATERIALS LIST

- **Medium gray solid:** 2¾ yards (blocks)
- **Medium gray print:** ¼ yard (border)
- **Various darks:** 1⅞ yards (blocks)
- **Various mediums:** 1⅞ yards (blocks); ½ yard (binding)
- **Various lights:** 1¼ yards (blocks)
- **Backing:** 3⅝ yards
- **Batting:** Lap size, at least 64 × 72 inches

CUTTING DIRECTIONS

Medium gray solid:

• 118 rectangles (F), 3 × 6½ inches (blocks)

• 118 rectangles (G), 3 × 11½ inches (blocks)

Various darks:

• 7 rectangles, 1½ × 21 inches (border)

• 26 squares (A), 3 × 3 inches (blocks)

• 66 rectangles (D), 1½ × 4½ inches (blocks)

• 66 rectangles (E), 1½ × 6½ inches (blocks)

Various mediums:

• 7 strips, 2 × 42 or 2¼ × 42 inches or as you prefer (binding)

• 7 rectangles, 1½ × 21 inches (border)

• 17 squares (A), 3 × 3 inches (blocks)

• 52 rectangles (D), 1½ × 4½ inches (blocks)

• 52 rectangles (E), 1½ × 6½ inches (blocks)

• 32 rectangles (B), 1¼ × 3 inches (blocks)

• 32 rectangles (C), 1¼ × 4½ inches (blocks)

Various lights:

• 16 squares (A), 3 × 3 inches (blocks)

• 86 rectangles (B), 1¼ × 3 inches (blocks)

• 86 rectangles (C), 1¼ × 4½ inches (blocks)

Backing:

• 2 rectangles, 64 × 42 inches

Note: *You'll sew the border rectangles together and trim the borders to the right size after sewing the quilt center.*

Assembling the Z Blocks

There are three similar blocks (Block Z, Block Y, and Block X) in this quilt; the only difference between the blocks is the placement of the light, medium, and dark fabrics. All blocks should initially measure 11½ × 11½ inches.

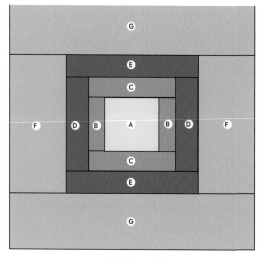

Block Z (make 16)

1. Sew one medium B rectangle to either side of one light A square. Press to the B rectangles. Sew the same color medium C rectangle to the top and bottom of the unit and press to the C rectangles.

2. Sew one dark D rectangle to either side of the square unit, pressing to the D rectangles. Sew the same color dark E rectangle to the top and bottom of the unit and press to the E rectangles.

3. Sew one F rectangle to either side of the square unit, pressing to the F rectangles. Sew one G rectangle to the top and bottom of the unit and press to the G rectangles. Make 16 Block Zs.

Assembling the Y Blocks

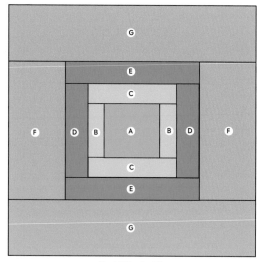

Block Y (make 17)

1. Sew one light B rectangle to either side of one medium A square. Press to the B rectangles. Sew the same color medium C rectangle to the top and bottom of the unit and press to the C rectangles.

2. Sew one dark D rectangle to either side of the square unit, pressing to the D rectangles. Sew the same color dark E rectangle to the top and bottom of the unit and press to the E rectangles.

3. Sew one F rectangle to either side of the square unit, pressing to the F rectangles. Sew one G rectangle to the top and bottom of the unit and press to the G rectangles. Make 17 Block Ys.

Assembling the X Blocks

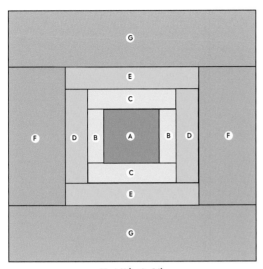

Block X (make 26)

1. Sew one light B rectangle to either side of one dark A square. Press to the B rectangles. Sew the same color light C rectangle to the top and bottom of the unit and press to the C rectangles.

2. Sew one medium D rectangle to either side of the square unit, pressing to the D rectangles. Sew the same color medium E rectangle to the top and bottom of the unit and press to the E rectangles.

3. Sew one F rectangle to either side of the square unit, pressing to the F rectangles. Sew one G rectangle to the top and bottom of the unit and press to the G rectangles. Make 26 Block Xs.

Tilting the Blocks

1. Create a template by drawing an 8½-inch square and marking the ¼-inch seam allowances on all sides. Cut out the template.

2. Lay a block on your cutting mat. Position the template on top, lining up the marked inner square on the template with the square within the gray borders of the block. Be careful to ensure you leave a ¼-inch seam allowance beyond every seam.

3. Trace around the template with a marking pen or pencil and then cut out the block on the marked lines. Tilt all Block Zs to the left, all but three Block Xs to the right, nine Block Ys to the left, and eight Block Ys to the right. After tilting and trimming, all blocks should be 8½ × 8½ inches.

Assembling the Quilt Center

66½ × 1½ inches

56½ × 1½ inches

Quilt Assembly Diagram

1. Using the Quilt Assembly diagram, join Block Zs, Block Ys, and Block Xs to form the quilt center.

2. Lay out the blocks in the first column, being careful to note the angle of the tilt for each block.

3. Sew the blocks together. Press the seams in the same direction. The column should measure 8½ × 64½ inches.

4. Repeat steps 2 and 3 to sew the blocks together in each column.

5. Sew the columns together, lining up the seams between the blocks in column 1 with the center of the blocks in column 2. Repeat this process to sew all the columns together, offsetting the blocks in the even-numbered columns with the ones in the odd-numbered columns.

6. Press the column seams in the same direction.

7. Trim the top and bottom of the quilt by aligning the ½-inch mark on a long ruler with the block corners in rows 1, 3, 5, and 7. The quilt center should measure 56½ × 64½ inches.

Adding the Borders

1. Sew three border rectangles together to create a side border strip that measures 1½ × 62 inches. Repeat to create another side border strip.

2. Measure down the quilt center and cut the side border strips that length. Sew these strips to the sides of the quilt center. Press toward the borders.

3. Sew four border rectangles together to create a top border strip that measures 1½ × 82½ inches. Repeat to create a bottom border strip.

4. Measure across the quilt center and cut the top and bottom border rectangles that length. Sew these strips to the top and bottom of the quilt center. Press toward the strips. The quilt should now measure 58½ × 66½ inches.

Quilting and Finishing

1. Make sure you've removed the selvages from the backing fabric. Sew the two backing rectangles together along the 64-inch sides. Backstitch at the beginning and end of the seam and press open the seam.

2. Prepare the quilt for quilting and quilt as desired. The sample quilt was quilted with an all-over circular spiral pattern.

3. Square up the quilted quilt and bind it. Add a label.

This three-block table runner has a simple monochromatic color scheme that makes the tilted blocks stand out. Choose a light, medium, and dark fabric in your favorite colors to make your own version.

"Mirage" Wall Hanging

This wall hanging features a variation of the New York Beauty block. The classic New York Beauty block echoes the points and round curves of the Statue of Liberty's crown and typically employs curved piecing in its construction. However, this variation uses straight lines, making this block easy to create using the foundation-piecing method. You can lay out the blocks in a variety of interesting ways, such as the five-medallion layout featured here.

FINISHED SIZES

- **Overall:** 28 × 28 inches
- **Blocks:** 7 inches

MATERIALS LIST

- **"Mirage" foundation paper-piecing templates**
- **Foundation paper:** 16 sheets
- **Tan:** ½ yard (blocks)
- **Turquoise:** ½ yard (blocks)
- **Dark turquoise:** ⅜ yard (blocks)
- **Dark red:** ¾ yard (blocks, binding)
- **Light brick red:** ⅜ yard (blocks)
- **Brown:** ½ yard (blocks)
- **Backing:** 1⅛ yards
- **Batting:** Crib size, at least 38 × 38 inches

CUTTING DIRECTIONS

Tan:
• 8 squares (B8), 8½ × 8½ inches, cut in half diagonally (foundations)

Turquoise:
• 48 rectangles (B2, B4, B6), 3¼ × 3¾ inches (foundations)

Dark turquoise:
• 96 rectangles (A1, A3, A5, A7, A10, A12), 2 × 2½ inches (foundations)

Dark red:
• 4 strips, 2 × 42 or 2¼ × 42 inches wide or as you prefer (binding)

• 16 rectangles (A9), 2¾ × 3¾ inches (foundations)

• 16 rectangles (A13), 2 × 7 inches (foundations)

Light brick red:
• 80 rectangles (A2, A4, A6, A8, A11), 2 × 2½ inches (foundations)

Brown:
• 64 rectangles (B1, B3, B5, B7), 3¼ × 3½ inches (foundations)

Backing:
• 1 square, 38 × 38 inches

Making the Foundation Blocks

1. Prepare the foundations by copying the pattern onto foundation paper. Prepare 16 foundations.

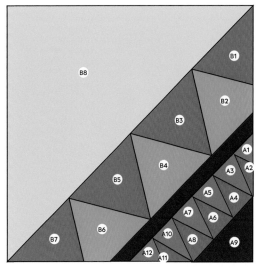

Block Z with colors in finished positions (make 16)

2. To create Block Z, foundation-piece the corner section of the block (A1 to A13). Trim this section, being careful to retain the necessary seam allowances. Repeat to complete the corner section of all 16 Block Zs.

3. Foundation-piece the main section of Block Z (B1 to B8). Trim this section, retaining the necessary seam allowances. Repeat to complete the main section of 16 Block Zs.

4. Pinning carefully to match the seam allowance lines on the foundations, pin the corner and main sections of a block together (right sides together). Sew with a short stitch length. Repeat to complete 16 Block Zs.

5. Trim each finished block to 7½ inches square, which includes the necessary seam allowances.

Assembling the Quilt Center

Quilt Assembly Diagram

1. Using the Quilt Assembly Diagram, arrange the blocks in rows on your design wall. Pay attention to the orientation of the blocks in order to create the pattern shown. Sew the blocks in each row together. Press open the seams between blocks.

2. Sew the rows together. Press the row seams in one direction. The quilt center should measure 28½ × 28½ inches.

3. Remove the foundation papers.

Quilting and Finishing

1. Remove the selvages from the backing fabric before basting the quilt. Prepare the quilt for quilting and quilt as desired. The sample quilt was quilted with sharp feathers in the tan triangles and outline-quilted in the New York Beauty areas.

2. Square up the quilted quilt and bind it. Add a label and a sleeve for hanging.

The blocks in this pattern can be laid out in a variety of settings, so use your design wall and have fun laying them out! This table runner, which features Asian fabrics, uses an alternate setting to create a lazy zigzag.

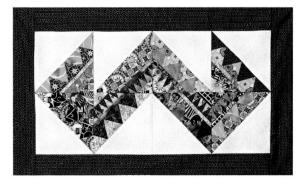

"Interwoven" Twin Quilt

I love how the blocks in this quilt seem to weave in and out of each other, like woven ribbons. The blocks in this quilt are made up of large pieces that are great for featuring your favorite fabrics.

FINISHED SIZES

- **Overall:** 58 × 75 inches
- **Blocks:** 12 inches

MATERIALS LIST

- **White:** 3 yards (blocks, Border 1)
- **Purple:** 1 yard (blocks); ½ yard (binding)
- **Blue:** ½ yard (blocks)
- **Yellow:** ½ yard (blocks)
- **Green:** ⅔ yard (Border 2)
- **Backing:** 3⅝ yards
- **Batting:** Twin size, at least 64 × 81 inches

CUTTING DIRECTIONS

White:

• 8 strips, 2 × 42 inches (Border 1)

• 10 strips, 5½ × 42 inches (for strip sets)

• 6 strips, 3½ × 42 inches (for strip sets)

• 4 strips, 1½ × 42 inches (for strip sets)

• 8 rectangles (B), 6½ × 7 inches (blocks)

Purple:

• 3 strips, 2½ × 42 inches (for strip sets)

• 24 rectangles, (A) 2½ × 12½ inches (blocks)

• 7 strips, 2 × 42 or 2¼ × 42 inches or as you prefer (binding)

Blue:

• 2 strips, 6½ × 42 inches (for strip sets)

• 16 rectangles (A), 2½ × 12½ inches (blocks)

• 2 rectangles (C), 1½ × 7 inches (blocks)

Yellow:

• 5 strips, 2½ × 42 inches (for strip sets)

• 2 rectangles (C), 1½ × 7 inches (blocks)

Green:

• 8 strips, 2½ × 42 inches (Border 2)

Backing:

• 2 rectangles, 64 × 42 inches

Note: *Cut the border strips first. Trim the border strips to the right size after sewing the quilt center.*

Assembling the Block Units

1. Make several strip sets. Piece the first strip sets by sewing one white 1½-inch strip to one blue 6½-inch strip and press to the dark. Sew one white 1½-inch strip to the blue strip in this strip set and press to the dark. The set should measure 8½ inches wide. Repeat to make two white-blue-white strip sets.

Unit 1 (make 24)

2. Subcut the white-blue-white strip sets every 2½ inches into rectangles 2½ × 8½ inches (Unit 1) for a total of 24.

3. Piece the next strip sets by sewing one white 3½-inch strip to one purple 2½-inch strip and press to the dark. Sew one white 3½-inch strip to the purple strip in this strip set and press to the dark. The set should measure 8½ inches wide. Repeat to make three white-purple-white strip sets.

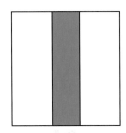

Unit 2 (make 12)

4. Subcut the white-purple-white strip sets every 8½ inches into squares 8½ × 8½ inches (Unit 2) for a total of 12.

5. Piece the last strip sets by sewing one white 5½-inch strip to one yellow 2½-inch strip and press to the dark. Sew one white 5½-inch strip to the yellow strip in this strip set and press to the dark. The set should measure 12½ inches wide. Repeat to make five white-yellow-white strip sets.

Unit 3 (make 32)

6. Subcut the white-yellow-white strip sets every 5½ inches into rectangles 12½ × 5½ inches (Unit 3) for a total of 32.

Assembling the Blocks

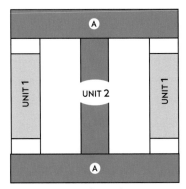

Block Z (make 12)

1. Sew one Unit 1 to either side of one Unit 2. Press to Unit 2.

2. Sew one purple A rectangle to the top and bottom of this unit, pressing to the A rectangles. Make 12 Block Zs. Block Zs should measure 12½ inches square.

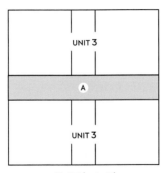

Block Y (make 16)

3. Sew one Unit 3 to the top and bottom of one blue A rectangle, pressing to the A rectangle. Make 16 Block Ys. Block Ys should measure 12½ inches square.

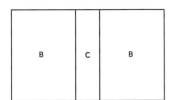

Block X1 (make 2)

4. Sew one white B rectangle to either side of one yellow C rectangle. Press to the C rectangle. Make two Block X1s. Block X1s should measure 12½ × 7 inches.

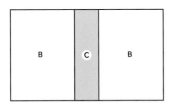

Block X2 (make 2)

5. Sew one white B rectangle to either side of one blue C rectangle. Press to the C rectangle. Make two Block X2s. Block X2s should measure 12½ × 7 inches.

Assembling the Quilt Center

Quilt Assembly Diagram

1. Using the Quilt Assembly Diagram, arrange the blocks in diagonal rows on your design wall. Pay attention to the placement of Block Zs and Block Ys. Add side setting triangles (Block Ys) at the ends of the appropriate rows. You'll trim the Block Ys after assembling the quilt center. Add corner setting triangles (Block X1s and X2s) where shown in the Quilt Assembly diagram. Again, you'll trim these later.

2. Start by sewing the blocks together to make each diagonal row. Press toward the Block Ys. Add the side setting blocks (Block Ys) with each row; press toward the setting blocks.

3. Sew the rows together. Press the seams in the same direction.

4. Add the corner setting blocks (Block X1s and X2s) last. Press to the setting blocks.

5. Trim the sides of the quilt by aligning the ¼-inch mark on a long ruler with the corners of the Block Zs. The quilt center should measure roughly 51½ × 68½ inches.

Adding the Borders

1. Sew two white Border 1 strips together. Repeat to create four strips 2 × 83½ inches.

2. Measure down the quilt center and cut the side Border 1 rectangles that length. Sew these strips to the sides of the center. Press toward the strips.

3. Measure across the quilt center and cut the top and bottom Border 1 rectangles that length. Sew these strips to the top and bottom of the quilt center. Press toward the strips. The quilt should now measure 54½ × 71½ inches.

4. Sew two green Border 2 strips together. Repeat to create four strips 2½ × 83½ inches.

5. Measure down the quilt center and cut the side Border 2 rectangles that length. Sew these strips to the sides of the center. Press toward the strips.

6. Measure across the quilt center and cut the top and bottom Border 2 rectangles that length. Sew these strips to the top and bottom of the quilt center. Press toward the strips. The quilt should now measure 58½ × 75½ inches.

Quilting and Finishing

1. Make sure you've removed the selvages from the backing fabric. Sew the two backing rectangles together along the 64-inch sides using a ½-inch seam. Backstitch at the beginning and end of the seam and press open the seam.

2. Prepare the quilt for quilting and quilt as desired. The sample quilt was quilted with straight lines back and forth across the woven ribbons, feathers in the setting triangles and border, and a variety of modern quilting patterns in the white areas between the ribbons.

3. Square up the quilted quilt and bind it. Add a label.

	Toddler	Lap	Queen
Size	41 × 58 inches	58 × 75 inches	92 × 92 inches
Block setting	2 × 3	3 × 4	5 × 5
Block Z	6	12	25
Block Y	8	16	32
Block X1	2	2	2
Block X2	2	2	2
White	1¾ yards	2¾ yards	5½ yards
Purple	¾ yard plus ⅜ yard (binding)	⅞ yard plus ½ yard (binding)	1⅔ yards plus ¾ yard (binding)
Blue	⅓ yard	⅞ yard	1⅝ yards
Yellow	½ yard	¾ yard	¾ yard
Green	⅜ yard	¾ yard	¾ yard
Backing	2⅝ yards	4½ yards	8¼ yards
Batting	47 × 64 inches	64 × 81 inches	98 × 98 inches

For a dramatically different look, use modern prints instead of 1930s reproduction fabrics.

"Fall Romance" Table Runner

Autumn is all about colors that range from vivid red to bright gold. Even if you live in an area that doesn't experience changes in color, you can make this table runner come alive with the colors you do see. This pattern uses the same fabrics in each leaf block, but you can use your scraps and vary the colors from block to block.

FINISHED SIZES

- **Overall:** 40 × 12 inches
- **Blocks:** 7 inches

MATERIALS LIST

- **"Fall Romance" foundation paper-piecing templates**
- **Foundation paper:** 5 sheets
- **Gold 1:** ⅛ yard (foundations)
- **Gold 2:** ⅛ yard (Border 1)
- **Orange 1:** ⅛ yard (foundations)
- **Orange 2:** ⅛ yard (foundations)
- **Red 1:** ⅛ yard (foundations)
- **Red 2:** ½ yard (foundations, Border 2); ¼ yard (binding)
- **Brown:** ¼ yard (foundations, Border 2)
- **Green 1:** ⅛ yard (foundations)
- **Green 2:** ⅛ yard (foundations)
- **Green 3:** ⅛ yard (foundations)
- **Green 4:** ⅛ yard (foundations)
- **Green 5:** ⅛ yard (foundations)
- **Green 6:** ⅛ yard (foundations)
- **Green 7:** ⅛ yard (foundations)
- **Backing:** ⅔ yard
- **Batting:** Scrap, at least 46 × 18 inches

CUTTING DIRECTIONS

Gold 1:
• 5 squares (A6), 2¾ × 2¾ inches (foundations)

Gold 2:
• 3 strips, 1 × 42 inches (Border 1)

Orange 1:
• 5 rectangles (A5), 3 × 4½ inches (foundations)

Orange 2:
• 5 rectangles (B4), 2 × 2½ inches (foundations)

Red 1:
• 5 rectangles (A4), 3 × 4¾ inches (foundations)

Red 2:
• 3 strips, 2 × 42 or 2¼ × 42 inches or as you prefer (binding)
• 3 strips, 1½ × 42 inches (Border 2)
• 5 rectangles (B2), 3¼ × 4 inches (foundations)

Brown:
• 3 strips 1½ × 42 inches (Border 2)
• 5 rectangles (B3) 3¼ × 4¼ inches (foundations)
• 5 rectangles (A1) 2¼ × 1½ inches (foundations)

Green 1:
• 5 rectangles (A2) 3¾ × 4 inches (foundations)

Green 2:
• 5 rectangles (A3) 2½ × 2¾ inches (foundations)

Green 3:
• 5 rectangles (A7) 2¾ × 4½ inches (foundations)

Green 4:
• 5 rectangles (A8) 3 × 8¼ inches (foundations)

Green 5:
• 5 rectangles (B6) 3½ × 7¼ inches (foundations)

Green 6:
• 5 rectangles (B5) 2½ × 4¾ inches (foundations)

Green 7:
• 5 squares (B1) 3½ × 3½ inches (foundations)

Backing:
• 1 strip 18 × 42 inches
• 1 rectangle 5 × 18 inches

Note: *Trim the border strips to the right size after sewing the quilt center.*

For a fresh look, make a table runner with spring pastels instead.

Making the Foundation Blocks

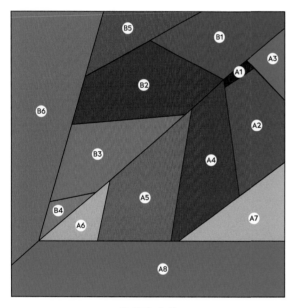

Block Z (make 5)

Block shown with colors in finished positions

1. Prepare the foundations by copying the pattern onto foundation paper. Prepare five foundations.

2. To create Block Z, foundation-piece the first section of one block (A1 to A8). Trim this section, being careful to retain the ¼-inch seam allowances. Repeat to complete the first half of all five Block Zs.

3. Foundation-piece the second section of Block Z (B1 to B6). Trim this section, retaining the necessary seam allowances. Repeat to complete the second half of five Block Zs.

4. Pinning carefully to match the seam allowance lines on the foundations, pin the A and B sections of a block together, right sides together. Sew with a short stitch length. Repeat to complete five Block Zs.

5. Trim each finished block to 7½ inches square, which includes the necessary seam allowances.

Assembling the Quilt Center

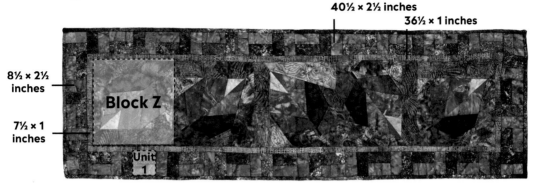

40½ × 2½ inches

36½ × 1 inches

8½ × 2½ inches

7½ × 1 inches

Block Z

Unit 1

Quilt Assembly Diagram

1. Using the Quilt Assembly Diagram, arrange the blocks in a row on your design wall. Pay attention to the orientation of the blocks in order to create the pattern shown. Sew the blocks together and press open the seams between blocks. The quilt center should measure 35½ × 7½ inches.

Adding the Borders

1. Measure down the quilt center and cut two rectangles from one of the Border 1 strips that length. Sew these strips to the sides of the quilt center. Press toward the strips.

2. Measure across the quilt center and cut the top and bottom Border 1 strips that length. Sew these strips to the top and bottom of the quilt center. Press toward the strips. The quilt should now measure 36½ × 8½ inches.

3. Remove the foundation papers.

4. Using the method given for piecing strip sets, sew one brown Border 2 strip to one red Border 2 strip and press to the dark. The set should measure 2½ inches wide. Repeat to make three strip sets.

5. Subcut the strip sets every 2½ inches into squares 2½ × 2½ inches (Unit 1) for a total of 48 Unit 1s.

Unit 1 (make 48)

6. Using the Quilt Assembly Diagram, piece four Unit 1s together to make a side border. Pay particular attention to the orientation of the squares to form the pattern shown. Press the seams in the same direction. Repeat to make a second side border.

7. Sew the side borders to the short sides of the quilt. Press to Border 1.

8. Using the Quilt Assembly Diagram, piece 20 Unit 1s together to make a top border. Pay particular attention to the orientation of the squares to form the pattern shown. Press the seams in the same direction. Repeat to make the bottom border.

9. Sew the top and bottom borders to the long sides of the quilt. Press to Border 1. The quilt should measure 40½ × 12½ inches.

Quilting and Finishing

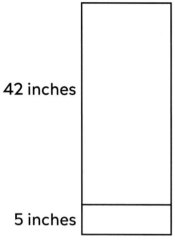

18 inches

42 inches

5 inches

Pieced Back Diagram

Diagram shows size of cut pieces

1. Remove the selvages from the backing fabric and
    piece the back as shown in the Pieced Back
    Diagram. Sew the two backing rectangles together
    using a ½-inch seam allowance, along the 18-inch
    edge. The result is a rectangle 18 × 46 inches.

2. Prepare the quilt for quilting and quilt as desired.
    The sample quilt was quilted in the ditch between
    the leaf sections in each block and in the borders.
    The background behind the leaves was quilted
    with a continuous line curvy meander.

3. Square up the quilted quilt and bind it. Add a label.

Glossary

Add-A-Quarter Ruler   A special ruler designed to mark an exact ¼-inch seam allowance.

appliqué   A small shape, such as a flower or a heart, that's stitched to background fabric to create a quilt block or border.

background fabric   A neutral fabric used throughout a set of pieced blocks or behind appliqué pieces in a set of appliquéd blocks.

backing   The bottom layer of a quilt, below the quilt top and batting. A quilt backing can be pieced or a single piece of fabric.

baste   The process of pinning or loosely stitching the layers of a quilt together in preparation for quilting.

batting   The middle layer of a quilt, placed between the quilt top and the backing. Also known as "wadding" or simply "batt," batting can be made of cotton, polyester, wool, silk, bamboo, or other fibers.

bearding   Tiny bits of batting that creep through a quilt top after quilting. Some batt types are more prone to bearding than others.

bias   The diagonal grain of fabric. Bias is very stretchy, so you must be careful when sewing along it.

binding   A small strip of fabric that's folded over the edge of a quilt and sewn down to finish it.

block   A quilt is composed of separate quilt blocks—appliquéd or pieced—that are sewn together to create a quilt center.

bobbin fill   A type of bobbin thread specially made for use with difficult-to-use top threads, such as monofilament, metallics, and heavy weight threads.

border   Fabric that frames the quilt center. Borders can be pieced or appliquéd and mitered at the corners or butted (straight).

butted seams   *See* nested seams.

chain-piecing   A method of sewing similar sets of block units together, in which each set is sewn one after the other without stopping.

cornerstones   Fabric squares placed where sashing strips should meet.

crosswise grain   The grain of fabric that runs perpendicular to the selvage edge. Crosswise grain is slightly more stretchy than lengthwise grain but not as stretchy as bias.

cross-wound thread   Thread that's wound in a crossing X pattern on the spool. Load cross-wound threads horizontally.

custom quilting   Quilting in which different patterns are chosen for the borders, sashing, and blocks. *See also* pantograph.

design wall   Batting- or flannel-covered panel on which quilt blocks can be arranged (laid out) prior to sewing them together.

dog ears   Small triangles that appear at either end of a seam when triangles, diamonds, and similar shapes are aligned correctly with other block pieces prior to sewing.

echo quilting   A type of quilting that follows the edges of appliqué or block shapes.

English paper piecing Method of piecing shapes together. The edges of each shape are turned under using paper templates, the shapes are whipstitched together, and the papers are removed.

feed dogs Part of a sewing machine that grabs the fabric and feeds it under the needle at an even pace. If you lower the feed dogs, you can move the fabric in any direction for free-motion quilting.

flange Special edge treatment for a quilt that uses a strip of fabric folded in half.

flying geese unit A block unit composed of a single rectangle, overlaid on both sides by triangles. The corner triangles are called the "sky," while the triangle in the center is known as the "goose."

foundation paper piecing See paper piecing.

four-patch unit A block unit of four squares.

free-motion quilting Quilting in any direction with the feed dogs down using an appliqué, darning, or open-toe foot. See also straight-line quilting.

fusible A web of glue used to iron (fuse) appliqué shapes to background fabric. Fusibles come in various types; choose the one that works best for your machine-appliqué method.

fussy cutting Isolating a specific motif in fabric for use in a quilt block.

half-square triangles 1. A right triangle created by cutting a square in half diagonally. 2. A block unit composed of two right triangles that form a square. Also known as "HSTs" and "triangle squares."

hera marker A tool used to create temporary creases on a quilt top that can then be followed by hand-quilting.

hourglass unit A block unit composed of triangles that form two perpendicular hourglass shapes.

HST See half-square triangles.

hue A pure color, such as pure blue. See tint; tone; shade.

in the ditch A quilting method in which you quilt in the seam between blocks or units.

lengthwise grain The grain of the fabric that runs parallel to the selvage. Lengthwise grain is the least stretchy grain and is preferred for use in quilt borders.

longarmer Professional quilter who quilts a quilt using an industrial sewing machine with a long sewing arm on a frame on which the quilt is rolled so a large section of it can be quilted at one time.

miter A method of joining two edges (such as a quilt's binding or border) so they form a perfect 45° angle, like a picture frame.

monofilament thread Invisible thread used in machine-appliqué or machine-quilting to create a hand-appliquéd or hand-quilted look.

nested seams A method of joining block units in which seam allowances are pressed in opposite directions so they can be nested (butted) together.

opposing seams See nested seams.

pantograph An all-over pattern that's quilted back and forth across a quilt top, without obvious breaks. See also custom quilting.

paper piecing Method of constructing a block in which fabrics are sewn to a paper foundation printed with the block pattern. Also known as "foundation paper piecing."

partial seam A block seam that's sewn only partway initially, allowing the rest of the units in a block to be sewn to a central unit. After that, the partial seam is sewn the rest of the way, completing the seam.

piece To stitch together fabric pieces by hand or by machine.

pillowcase finish A method for finishing the edge of a quilt without binding.

prairie points Folded fabric triangles used to create a decorative edge to a quilt or border.

precuts Similar cuts from each of the fabrics in a collection sold as a set. Because they're already cut and the fabrics coordinate, precuts make it easy to create a quilt. Common precuts include Fat Quarters, 2½-inch strips, 5-inch squares, and 10-inch squares.

quarter-square triangles Also known as a "QST," a quarter-square triangle is created by cutting a square in both directions diagonally. *See also* half-square triangles.

quilt A quilt consists of three layers—quilt top, batting, and backing—stitched (quilted) through all the layers.

quilt center Composed of quilt blocks and sashing but not borders (which are added after the center is constructed).

quilter's knot A special way of forming a knot at the end of a piece of thread, which involves twisting the thread around the needle.

quilting The process of stitching the layers of a quilt (top, batting, backing) together. *See also* free-motion quilting; straight-line quilting.

raw edge An unfinished (unsewn) fabric edge.

right side of fabric The printed side of fabric. You sew block pieces with the right sides together (rst). Some fabrics, such as batiks, don't have a right or wrong side. *See also* wrong side of fabric.

rotary cutter Fitted with a sharp circular blade, a rotary cutter looks like a pizza cutter and is used to cut fabric by simply rolling over it. Use a rotary cutter only with special acrylic rulers designed for rotary cutting and a self-healing cutting mat.

rst Short for "right sides together." Block pieces are sewn together after placing the right sides of the two pieces together.

sashing Small strips of fabric placed between blocks in a horizontal or diagonal setting to set them apart. In a vertical setting, the sashing is wider and sets block columns apart.

saturation The amount of color in a print. Fully saturated prints are bright and impactful. Undersaturated prints are grayed and peaceful.

seam allowance Measured from the edge of the fabric to the sewing line. In quilting, the standard seam allowance is ¼ inch; unfinished units or blocks are ½ inch bigger than when finished.

selvage The tightly woven edges of fabric yardage, often printed with the manufacturer's name, fabric line, and the colors used in the fabric.

setting The arrangement of blocks that form the quilt center. Common settings include horizontal, vertical, on point, and medallion.

setting triangles In an on-point (diagonal) setting, side setting and corner setting triangles are used at the ends of each row of blocks to form a straight edge to the quilt top.

shade A hue to which black has been added.

square-in-square   A block unit composed of a square surrounded by triangles in each corner. Also known as a "diamond-in-a-square unit".

stabilizer   Used to stabilize fabric and prevent puckering when machine-appliquéing. Stabilizers come in cutaway, tearaway, and washaway forms.

stacked thread   Thread that's wound around the spool in a parallel fashion so it's stacked on top of the previous round. Load stacked threads vertically.

staystitch   Stitching close to the edge of a stitch to keep the seams from opening up during quilting and to keep the quilt from stretching out of shape.

stencil   A pattern used to mark a quilt top for quilting.

stippling   Type of free-motion quilting in which the quilting line simply meanders around, filling the space. A larger version of stippling is called "meandering."

straight-line quilting   Quilting in straight lines or soft curves by using a walking foot. *See also* free-motion quilting.

straight-wound thread *See* stacked thread.

strip set   Multiple fabric strips sewn together and then subcut into smaller block units, such as two-bar or three-bar units.

subcutting   Cutting a fabric strip or strip set into smaller block units, such as squares, rectangles, and triangles.

template   A traceable pattern for block or appliqué pieces made from template plastic or freezer paper.

throat plate   A sewing machine part through which the feed dogs and needle move. A zigzag (standard) throat plate has a horizontal hole and is used in machine-appliqué. A straight-stitch (single hole) throat plate has a single hole and is used in machine-piecing.

tint   A hue to which white has been added.

tone   A hue to which gray has been added.

triangle square   *See* half-square triangles.

two-bar unit   A block unit composed of two rectangles sewn together to form a square. A similar unit is a three-bar unit, which is composed of three rectangles.

tying a quilt   A method of quilting a quilt in which the layers are tied with crochet thread, pearl cotton, yarn, or embroidery floss in a grid approximately 4 inches apart. *See also* pillowcase finish.

unit   A common part of a quilt block, such as a four-patch, two-bar, three-bar, flying geese, half-square triangle, square-in-square, or hourglass unit. You create these common units first, then sew them together to create a quilt block.

walking foot   A sewing machine foot that helps feed fabric layers under the needle evenly. Use a walking foot when straight-line quilting.

wof   Width of fabric; typically 42 or 44 inches.

wrong side of fabric   The unprinted side of fabric. *See also* right side of fabric.

wst   Short for "wrong sides together." This is when the unprinted sides of a fabric face each other.

Y-seam   A Y-seam joins three block pieces with intersecting seams that together form a "Y" shape.

Index

Credits

The quilts used as examples in this book are made from copyrighted patterns. Many of the fabrics used are also under copyright. Every effort has been made to include the names of the pattern makers and fabric manufacturers for the quilts and fabrics shown in this book.

Chapter 1

Fabric: Freespirit, Judie Rothermel for Marcus Brothers, Caryl Bryer Fallert for Benartex, Williams Inn by Nancy Halverson for Benartex **Patterns:** "Simply Delicious!," Piece O' Cake Designs

Chapter 2

Fabric: Heritage Studio Collection by Fabric Traditions, Fabrice de Villeneuve for Springs Creative Products Group, Riley Blake Designs, Simply Style by Vanessa Christenson of V and Co., Sonnet Collection by April Connell for Moda, Poetry Collection by April Connell for Moda, Spirit by Lila Tueller for Moda, Odds and Ends by Julie Comstock of Cosmo Cricket, Don't Be Afraid by Deborah Edwards for Northcott Studio, Joel Dewberry Fabrics

Chapter 3

Fabric: New Basics by P&B Textiles, Marie Antoinette by Deborah Edwards for Northcott Fabrics, Impressions by Patricia B. Campbell and Michelle L. Jack for Benartex, Finger Paints by Stephanie Brandenburg for Camelot Cottons, Riley Blake Designs, West by Timeless Treasures, Fifi & Fido Collection by Anna Griffin, Shadow Flower by Jackie Shapiro of French Bull for Windham Fabrics, Amy Butler for Westminster Fibers, Josephine Kimberling for Blend Fabrics Global Bazaar, The Sweetest Thing by Zoe Pearn for Riley Blake Designs

Chapter 4

Fabric: Sunnyside by Katie Spain for Moda, P&B Textiles Sara Moe for Blank Quilting, Mama Said Sew by Sweetwater for Moda, Fruit A La Carte by Hoodie for Timeless Treasures, Illustrations by O&B Fabrics, Phoebe by Wendy Slotboom for In the Beginning Fabrics, Picnic Parade Jenean Morrison for Freespirit, Riley Blake Designs, Bliss by Bonnie & Camille for Moda, The Best of Mary Lou by Mary Lou Weidman for Benartex, The Sweetest Thing by Zoe Pearn for Riley Blake Designs, Novella by Valori Wells for Free Spirit, Garden Party by Yolanda Fundora for Blank Quilting

Chapter 5

Fabric: Phoebe by Wendy Slotboom for In the Beginning Fabrics, Picnic Parade by Jenean Morrison for Freespirit, Riley Blake Designs, Heaven Can Wait by Ro Gregg for Northcott, Bliss by Bonnie & Camille for Moda, The Best of Mary Lou by Mary Lou Weidman for Benartex, Kona Cotton by Robert Kaufman

Chapter 6

Fabric: Building Blocks by Nancy Murty for Andover Fabrics, Sunnyside by Katie Spain for Moda, Simply Style by Vanessa Christenson of V and Co., Habitat by Michele D'Amore for Benartex, Cuzco by Kate Spain for Moda, Shadow Flower by Jackie Shapiro of French Bull Windham Fabrics, Simply Style by Venessa Christenson of V and Co., Henry Glass & Co., Seattle Bay Fabrics, Finger Paints by Stephanie Brandenburg for Camelot Cottons, Marble Mate by Moda, Krystal Michael Miller, Pieces From My Heart by Sandy Gowais for Moda

Chapter 7

Fabric: Sidewalks by October Afternoon for Riley Blake Designs, Riley Blake Designs, Fruit A La Carte by Hoodie for Timeless Treasures, Grace by 3 Sisters for Moda, Mama Said Sew by Sweetwater for Moda, Jinny Beyer for RJR Fashion Fabrics, Cherry Berry Chickens by In the Beginning Fabrics, Illustrations by O&B Fabrics, Kensington Studio for Quilting Treasures, Lily by Timeless Treasures Fabrics, Kiwi by Alice Kennedy for Timeless Treasures Fabric, Winter Wonderland by Hoffman Fabrics, Screen Prints by Robert Kaufman, P&B Textiles, Kona Bay Fabrics **Patterns:** "Spring," Suzie Wetzel Designs; "Simply Delicious!," Piece O' Cake Designs; "Captivating Cone Flower," Wendy Butler Berns

Chapter 8

Fabric: Simply Style by Vanessa Christenson of V and Co., Marcus Fabrics, Katie by Jennifer Young for Benartex, It's Christmas by Jennifer Heynen for In the Beginning Fabrics, Robert Allen Group, Paris Cats by Broadway Studios for Benartex, Elementals by Lunn Studios for Robert Kaufman

Chapter 9

Fabric: Sonnet Collection by April Comell for Moda, Modern Love by Kelly Panacci for Northcott, Button Button Designs by Cheri for SSI, Fresh Flowers by Deb Strain for Moda, Simply Style by Vanessa Christenson of V and Co., Marcus Fabrics, Katie by Jennifer Young for Benartex, It's Christmas by Jennifer Heynen for In the Beginning Fabrics, Robert Allen Group, Tuscan Wildflower II by Peggy Toole for Robert Kaufman **Patterns:** "Little Blue Baskets," pattern by Suzie Wetzel, based on an antique quilt in the Indianapolis Museum of Art's quilt collection

Chapter 10

Fabric: Marble Mate by Moda, Krystal Michael Miller, Pieces From My Heart by Sandy Gowais for Moda, Seattle Bay Fabrics, Finger Paints by Stephanie Brandenburg for Camelot Cottons

Chapter 11

"Strawberry Preserves" fabric: Woodlands by Erin McAllister for Benartex's American Folk Art Studio, Mary's Favorite Blue by Windham Fabrics, Chelsea Market RJR Fabrics, Laurel by Sentimental Studios for Moda, Windham Fabrics, Cabin Clothprints by Carol Endres for Fabrics by Spectrix, Colonies Brown II by Windham Fabrics, Morning Garden by Alex Anderson for P&B Textiles, Charleston IV 1850-1865 by Judie Rothermel for Marcus Brothers, English Cottage by Ro Gregg for Northcott, The Art of Broderie Perse by RJR Fabrics, Past and Present by Fons & Porter for Benartex, Rocky Mountain Quilt Museum by Marcus Fabrics, Amalie Collection by Darlene Zimmerman for Robert Kaufman, Faye Burgos for Marcus Brothers, Williams Inn by Benartex, Floursack by Whistler Studios for Windham Fabrics, Once Upon a Storybook by Whistler Studios for Windham Fabrics

"Princess Charlotte" fabric: Fort Firefly by Teagan White for Birch Fabrics, Sweethearts by Benartex, Avignon by Emily Taylor Design for Riley Blake Designs, Cuzco by Kate Spain for Moda, Cold Spring Dreams by Mary McGuire for RJR Fabrics, Birds & Berries by Lauren & Jessi Jung for Moda, Acacia by Tula Pink for Freespirit, Mind's Eye by Anna Maria Horner for Freespirit, Patchworks by Diana Leone for Northcott, Little Things Organic by Arrin Turnmire for Moda, Once Upon a Storybook by Whistler Studios for Windham Fabrics, Aunt Grace Scrapbag by Judie Rothermel for Marcus Brothers, Just Makin' Conversation by Maywood Studio, Granny's Twelve by Darlene Zimmerman from Chanteclaire, Sewing Circles of the 30s & 40s by Brackman & Thompson for Moda

"Elephants on Parade" fabric: Sun Print by Allison Glass for Andover Fabrics, Tiny Hearts by Timeless Treasures Fabrics, Timeless Treasures Fabrics of SoHo, Let's Play Dolls by Andover Fabrics, Extreme Color by Paula Nadlestern for Benartex, Moda Marbles by Moda Fabrics, Chevron by Riley Blake Designs, Solitaire Whites by Maywood Studios

"Life in the Tide Pool" fabric: Tidepool Batiks by Moda, Kona Cotton by Robert Kaufmann, Starbursts by Marie Keizer for Westminster Fabrics, Screenprints by Hoffman International Fabrics, Suede by P&B Textiles, Phoebe by Wendy Slotboom for In the Beginning Fabrics

"Conga Line" fabric: Kona Cotton by Robert Kaufmann, Ecco by Greta Lynn for Kanvas and Benartex, Simple Marks by Malka Dubrawsky for Moda, Best Friends by Granola Girl Debbie Field for Troy Corporation

"Star-Crossed" fabric: Downton Abbey®: Lady Mary Collection by Andover Fabrics, Downton Abbey®: Lady Sybil Collection by Andover Fabrics, Downton Abbey®: The Women's Collection by Andover Fabrics, The Sweetest Thing by Zoe Pearn for Riley Blake Designs, Sun Print by Allison Glass for Andover Fabrics, Solitaire Whites by Maywood Studios, Silent Cinema by Jenean Morrison for Freespirit, Timeless Treasures Fabrics

"Swimming in the Gene Pool" fabric: Eclipse by Timeless Treasures Fabrics, Whimsy Windows by Swirly Girls Design for Michael Miller Clubhouse, Cosmopolitan by Michele D'Amore Designs for Benartex, Mellow Yellow by Red Rooster Studio for Red Rooster Fabrics, Gracie Girl by Lori Hall of Bee in My Bonnet for Riley Blake Designs

"Snake Eyes" fabric: Palette by Marcia Derse for Windham Fabrics, Architectures by Carolyn Friedlander for Robert Kaufman, Botanics by Carolyn Friedlander for Robert Kaufman, Jazz City by Art of Possibility Studios for FreeSpirit Fabrics, Daydreams by Deb Strain for Moda

"Mirage" fabric: West by Timeless Treasures, Artifacts by John Flynn for Benartex, Sayomi by Hoffman of California, Lux by Timeless Treasures, Bohemian Rhapsody by Greta Lynn for Kanvas and Benartex

"Interwoven" fabric: Once Upon a Storybook by Whistler Studios for Windham Fabrics, Scrumptious by Bonnie & Camille for Moda, Toy Box III by Sara Morgan for Blue Hill Fabrics, Grandma's Garden by Darlene Zimmerman for Robert Kaufman, Kona Cotton by Robert Kaufman, Floursack by Whistler Studios for Windham Fabrics, Déjà Vu by Paula Nadelstern for Benartex, Kathy Schmitz Studio for Moda

"Fall Romance" fabric: Prismaglass by Paula Nadelstern for Benartex, Michael Miller Fabrics, V.I.P. Prints by Cranston Print Works, Juliette by Moda, Picnic Parade by Jenna Morrison for Free Spirit, Maywood Studio, Blank Quilting, Scent-i-ments by Hoffman of California International Fabrics